Walkin
Sydney

3214

£1.99

SYDNEY

Pennant Hills Rd

LANE COVE RD

EPPING RD

PARRAMATTA

VICTORIA RD

Bicentennial Park

PARRAMATTA RD

HUME HWY

To Cronulla and

Walking
Sydney

JEFF TOGHILL

NEW
HOLLAND

First published in Australia in 2000 by
New Holland Publishers (Australia) Pty Ltd
Sydney • Auckland • London • Cape Town

14 Aquatic Drive Frenchs Forest NSW 2086 Australia
218 Lake Road Northcote Auckland New Zealand
24 Nutford Place London W1H 6DQ United Kingdom
80 McKenzie Street Cape Town 8001 South Africa

National Library of Australia
    Cataloguing-in-Publication Data:
    Toghill, Jeff 1932-.
    Walking Sydney.
    Includes index.

    ISBN   1 86436 510 2

Walking – New South Wales – Sydney – Guidebooks.
Hiking – New South Wales – Sydney – Guidebooks.
Sydney (N.S.W.) – Guidebooks. Vane, Mitch. II. Title.
919.4410466

Commissioning Editor: Anouska Good
Editors: Jan Hutchinson and Jennifer Lane
Project Coordinator: Jennifer Lane
Designer: Peta Nugent
Layout: Melbourne Media Services
Printer: Times Offset, Malaysia

The authors and publishers have made every effort to ensure the information in this book was correct
at the time of going to press and accept no responsibility for any errors that may have occurred.
Prices, opening times, facilities, locations or amenities can change over time so it is recommended
that the reader call the operator or service and confirm any information that might be required.

Contents

Acknowledgements | viii • Introduction | 1 • Sydney's History | 3
Walks in Order of Length & Key to Maps | 7

city walks

1. Circular Quay to Woolloomooloo | 8
2. The Rocks | 18
3. Sydney Harbour Bridge | 28
4. Central City | 38

harbour walks

5. Cremorne to Mosman | 48
6. Mosman Bay to Clifton Gardens | 56
7. The Fortifications of South Head | 64
8. North Head | 70
9. Middle Head | 78
10. Rose Bay and Neilsen Park | 84
11. Spit Bridge to Manly | 92

suburban walks

12. Blackwattle and Rozelle bays | 100
13. Potts Point and Kings Cross | 108
14. Paddington | 116
15. Birchgrove and Balmain | 122
16. Bicentennial Park | 130
17. Historic Parramatta | 138
18. Elegant Hunters Hill| 148

coastal walks

19. Royal National Park | 156
20. La Perouse | 162
21. The Cape Baily Track | 168
22. Palm Beach to Barrenjoey Head | 176
23. Bondi to Coogee | 184

Bibliography | 192 • Index | 192

Acknowledgements

In the course of their work as librarians, historians, tourist information officers, guides and the like, so many people helped with this book in some way or another that it would be impossible to mention them all individually, although my old seafaring buddy John Milne is deserving of particular thanks for his company and valuable assistance on some of the more difficult walks.

The one person who warrants my very special thanks for her total dedication to the book is my wife, Diana. By tramping the untold kilometres of the walks with me, often twice or more, she made the whole thing an enjoyable exercise rather than a wearisome chore. She also handled much of the background work, taking notes, chasing up information and helping with the proofing; assistance which was invaluable and without which the book would probably never have been completed, let alone met its deadline.

Introduction

It is hard to imagine a city with a greater choice of walks than Sydney.

To start with, it has one of the finest harbours in the world and the foreshores of the harbour alone contain enough walks to fill a book. Much of these foreshores consist of national park, so encounters with bush animals, birds and native vegetation are all part of the walks, to say nothing of the superb water views and the tranquil atmosphere. Signs of early Aboriginal presence are often in evidence, with middens, rock art and shelters providing an insight into the lifestyle of the early residents. And all this within a few minutes of the CBD.

Away from the foreshores, through the streets and parks of the metropolitan region, are buildings that add variety and historical interest to walks. Early residences such as Vaucluse House and Elizabeth Farm tell of how the first white settlers carved their own lifestyle from their isolated and primitive new land, while soaring city skyscrapers and the unique world-acclaimed Opera House reveal just how far Sydney has come in two centuries.

Sydney may be young in comparison with cities around the world, but therein lies its charm – because it is so new, you can virtually re-live its history just walking around the city. What could be more real than standing on the very rock that Captain Cook stepped onto when he first set foot in Botany Bay? Or feel the fear and tension in the dark, narrow alleys of The Rocks where 'The Push' gangs robbed straggling pedestrians and press-ganged drunken sailors to a life of slavery on the whaling ships. Or stand on a rock platform on Dobroyd Head, from the heights above the harbour entrance, and visualise the local Aboriginal clans engaging in serious tribal business on that very rock platform and recording it in engraved pictures and signs that exist to this day. No meeting house or parliament or congress anywhere in the world had such a magnificent setting.

All the walks are within the metropolitan area and all are accessible by public transport from the city. Where a bus, ferry or train ride is necessary to reach the starting point of the walk, the journey is never longer than one hour from its departure point in the city. Transport to the starting point of each walk is from the central city area, with Circular Quay the main departure point for buses and ferries and Central Railway Station for buses and trains. Any other departure points in the CBD are noted.

The walks in this book are fairly evenly divided between city, harbour, suburban and coastal walks. Sydney is built on ridges and valleys so most walks are across undulating terrain, but all are suitable for walkers of an average level of fitness. In those that are a little long, exit points are indicated along the way and the walk can be broken and handled in sections.

Many walks include features such as historic buildings, museums, lookouts, secluded bays and maritime attractions that need a diversion for closer inspection or some time to examine them in detail. Obviously such diversions will add time to the walk so the times and distances given in this book are approximate and must be varied according to personal requirements. Gardeners, for example, are unlikely to walk through the Royal Botanic Gardens in less than half a day, while non-gardeners might zoom through in half an hour but later spend several hours in a museum or historic building. For this reason the times given are based on the average walker moving at a steady pace and do not include digressions.

The walks in suburban areas are best done during the week since walking is a popular recreation in Sydney, and some areas become crowded on a fine weekend. Similarly, the best time to do the city walks is on the weekend when the streets are far less crowded and travelling is easier as there is no 'peak-hour' traffic. Some of the city features, such as museums, libraries and galleries, may become crowded on the weekend, but they can also be busy during the week.

Early morning is the best time for all walks. Apart from avoiding the heat of mid-summer days and the crowds that go with them, there is something acutely refreshing, crisp and clean about the early mornings, which adds another dimension to the walk. The foreshore bush walks, in particular, have an ambience in the mornings that is as atmospheric as a Heysen painting; the pungent smell of the eucalypts, the clear warbling call of the magpies and the buzz of insect life stirring to the command of the rising sun.

Enjoy your walks.

Sydney's History

Although the capital cities of other states would undoubtedly disagree, Sydney ranks as the most important city in Australia, if only because it was here, in 1788, that the nation was established. For the next 15 years, until a second outpost was begun in Tasmania, Sydney, and its penal colony of Norfolk Island, was the only European settlement on the continent. It was in Sydney that the growth of the nation was focused and the tentacles of exploration and colonisation spread outwards to establish other settlements, which eventually became new cities in new states.

Sydney's early history is something of a mixed bag. Following Captain Cook's discovery, the British Government decided on Botany Bay as the ideal location for a new convict settlement. But within days of the First Fleet's arrival, Governor Phillip began looking for a more suitable area.

Sydney Cove was chosen because of its sheltered, deep water anchorage and freshwater stream. However, this also was far from perfect, as the surrounding rocky terrain failed to produce sufficient crops to sustain the new colony.

After a three-month search upstream, Rose Hill (now Parramatta) was discovered as having the best potential for farming, and since farming would be a prime factor in the self-sufficiency of the colony, the first agricultural settlement was established there in November, 1788. Farming proved so successful it seemed that the capital of New South Wales might be 24 kilometres upstream from the original landing site and Sydney would merely act as its port. But the narrow and winding river, and the long haul upstream against fluky winds and tides, made shipping difficult and slow. Equally difficult was the journey on land.

Roads were primitive, making transport slow, and few horses were available. Parramatta slipped into the secondary role of rural centre for the new colony, although remaining the major farming district, while Sydney Cove regained its status as the capital and port for the new colony.

Governor Macquarie, who arrived at the colony in 1809, proved to be innovative and energetic. He set about bringing a semblance of order to the settlement, which was developing by accident rather than design. Earlier governors, in particular Governor Phillip, who returned to England in 1792, had attempted to plan the streets along orderly lines. But the hilly nature of the terrain, combined with the formation of convenient tracks through the bush by settlers who ignored the government's plans, meant the town evolved in random fashion, much the way it is today. By the time Macquarie arrived in Sydney, it was too late to change the layout of the town, but in 1810 he issued a directive announcing his intention to 'enlarge the streets and avenues'. He immediately set about naming the streets and erected an obelisk in Macquarie Place to mark the starting point for all roads radiating outwards.

A public-spirited man, Macquarie was conscious of the physical and spiritual well-being of his people. He converted a large open space in the town centre (previously used as an exercise ground for soldiers) to a cricket pitch and racecourse. Although today somewhat smaller, this space, now known as Hyde Park, is still used for public recreation. Macquarie also set aside a permanent site for a market and today this, too, fulfils its original function, albeit in somewhat more salubrious surroundings – the old market site is now home to one of the most elegant of all shopping centres – the magnificent Queen Victoria Building.

Gradually, Governor Macquarie converted the shanty town into a prosperous trading centre and by the 1830s Sydney had its fair share of wealthy merchants and landowners. Exclusive residences began to appear in Glebe and Balmain, Potts Point and Elizabeth Bay, and a number of these mansions survive to this day, some as private homes, some preserved for future generations as part of the National Estate. Similarly, many public buildings which formed a part of Australia's early history are now retained under the protection of the Australian Heritage Commission. Sadly, records pertaining to history before white settlement are sparse since early Aborigines were not builders of permanent structures, nor did they write journals. However, a number of sites which contain important rock carvings or middens indicating Aboriginal occupation and use are located around the Sydney area and are jealously preserved as historic records of pre-white activities.

The styles of many buildings that formed the foundation of Sydney Town were difficult to classify, but later Edwardian and then Victorian influences, evident today, made an impact on the local scene. Elizabeth Bay House and Vaucluse House are fine examples of that era, as are many fine civic buildings huddled around Macquarie Street, the focal point of government and business in the early days.

One of the most important of the city's early merchants was Robert Campbell who arrived in 1798 and whose wool stores at Campbell's Wharf in The Rocks are still widely used, albeit not for the purpose he originally intended. Like many of the old buildings in The Rocks, the stores have been carefully converted into restaurants, offices and tourist attractions. Many of the wool stores in the Darling Harbour and Pyrmont area have been renovated as apartment blocks and hotels.

The gold rush of the 1850s brought huge changes to the fast-growing city. The town experienced a few years of stagnation as workers were swept up in the mass exodus, westward to the goldfields.

Then, as the precious metal was retrieved from the ground and shipped to the city, Sydney glowed with a new affluence. New buildings sprang up like morning mushrooms, and not just commercial buildings, for the new found wealth, whether through gold or industry, fostered a rash of magnificent new residences in wealthy suburbs such as Hunters Hill and Potts Point.

By 1854 Sydney Cove had been reclaimed with extensive wharf structures forming the basis of what is now Circular Quay. Around the wharves huge sailing ships discharged vital cargoes and passengers from England, then loaded even more important cargoes of wool and wheat for the European markets. Europe, particularly Britain, could not get enough of the prized Australian merino wool and the port of Sydney became the focal point of the wool export trade (as evidenced by the fine wool stores around the waterfront areas).

By the mid-19th century the waterside city was experiencing a mini-Industrial Revolution. Shipping was its lifeblood so it was natural that the foremost industries in those early years were related to maritime activities. Mort Dock in Balmain was typical of the rapid industrial growth, creating high-density workers' suburbs along the foreshores of Snails, Woolloomooloo and Mort bays. The terrace houses of that era, with their iron latticework derived from the ballast carried in the large windjammers, are a feature of those suburbs today.

Two world wars and the Great Depression in the first half of the 20th century did little to hinder or help the growth of the new colony and development was modest, although consistent. Federation at the turn of the century provided a new beginning and gave the continent a new maturity, but it was only after the Second World War that the country as a whole, and Sydney in particular, entered a huge boom period with the sudden avalanche of migrants.

This most significant period of growth in Sydney was epitomised by the fast-spreading suburbs, especially to the south and west of the city. Open plains, pastures and market gardens disappeared under a tide of red roofs, while motorways and railways snaked outwards in a frenetic attempt to keep up with the demand for transport to and from these areas. City buildings sprouted upwards like seedlings in some magic garden to accommodate the increasing workforce as Sydney raced towards a population of 3.5 million by 1986.

But happily, despite the upwards and outwards thrust, most of the significant old buildings were retained. There will always be a few victims in such rapid growth but, generally speaking, Sydney's record in saving and restoring the old for the benefit of the new, has been both notable and worthy. The very first roots of the nation are still visible in the spot where they were planted, and much of what has grown since has been sympathetically restored and retained.

One facet of Sydney that has changed little in the two centuries of white settlement is its magnificent harbour. Once the domain of many different Aboriginal clans, traces of which can be seen in many places to this day, the ragged fringes of the foreshores are little changed in the lower reaches. While the areas above the bridge have been despoiled with commercial and residential development, the main harbour has for the most part survived. A fortuitous accident, in the form of a military presence, has preserved the headlands, the natural rocky foreshores, the indented bays and beaches and the tree-covered promontories in their natural state. In the paranoia of an invasion scare in the mid-19th century, all headlands, most islands and other strategic points of the lower harbour were commandeered by the military as sites for fortresses, gun batteries or other defence establishments. The scare receded but other imagined threats plus two world wars — one of which saw those defences tested — caused the structures to be retained although the hardware was removed. Since military bases are out of bounds to civilians, public access to some of the harbour's most delightful spots was denied and they remained in their natural state until now, when they are being placed under the protective care of the National Parks and Wildlife Service.

While history cannot be reversed in terms of the upper reaches, new projects such as the striking Bicentennial Park, the incredible Millennium Park and similar efforts to return industrial waterfront sites to public space are making amends.

Pollution is being brought under control and an increasing awareness of what our children nearly lost is ensuring that even the foreshores of the Parramatta River will one day resume at least some of the former natural glory that made them so appealing to the early settlers.

Sydney has little more than two hundred years of settlement history, yet there is much to enjoy in reliving the past, as well as walking through the more recent developments. This book is intended to offer a variety of ways in which to explore everything that has made Sydney a vibrant and exciting Olympic city. Enjoy.

Key to Maps

 Hospital

 Church

 Parks and gardens

 Information

 Parking

 Tram stop

 Bus stop

 Post office

 Gallery

 Public toilets

 Railway station

Route Marks

• • ▷ • • • route of walk

7 key numbers

S walk start

F walk finish

An easy-to-follow illustrative map accompanies each walk. The walk route is clearly marked in green; buildings and sites are dark blue; parks and gardens are green; and 'general' areas are shaded light blue.

On each map the walk route begins at the point **S** and finishes at **F**. Key numbers are located on the map as well as in the walk text. The Key to Maps, left, displays full details of symbols that appear on the maps in order to assist the walker.

Walks in Order of Length

Middle Head | 2km
Cremorne to Mosman | 2.5km
Paddington | 2.5km
Central City | 3km
Palm Beach to Barrenjoey Head | 3.5km
Potts Point and Kings Cross | 3.5km
The Cape Baily Track | 4km, 10km or 12.5km
The Rocks | 4km
Bondi to Coogee | 4.5km
Blackwattle and Rozelle bays | 4.5km
Rose Bay and Nielsen Park | 4.5km
Royal National Park | 4.5km
Sydney Harbour Bridge | 4.5km
Elegant Hunters Hill | 5km
North Head | 5km
The Fortifications of South Head | 5.5km
Circular Quay to Woolloomooloo | 6km
Mosman Bay to Clifton Gardens | 6km
Historic Parramatta | 6.5km
Bicentennial Park | 7km
La Perouse | 8km
Spit Bridge to Manly | 9km
Birchgrove and Balmain | 10.5km

Circular Quay to Woolloomooloo

Australia's first farm

Start

Circular Quay ferry wharves.

Finish

Circular Quay ferry wharves.

Length/Time

6 km/2.5 hours

Wheelchairs

Generally easy, but there are steps down from Mrs Maquarie Road to Woolloomooloo and Hills Stairs, Woolloomooloo.

In contrast to the western side of Circular Quay and the tightly packed buildings of The Rocks, the eastern side has always provided the 'lungs' of Sydney. Originally the location of the first ever farm in Australia, it now provides open spaces of city parklands and the green lushness of the Royal Botanic Gardens. This walk crosses time and cultural barriers, encompassing features of the earliest settlement as well as modern icons such as the Sydney Opera House.

Walk key

1. Sydney Cove | 2. Sydney Opera House | 3. The Domain | 4. Royal Botanic Gardens | 5. Queen Elizabeth II Gates | 6. Farm Cove | 7. Mrs Macquarie's Point | 8. Mrs Macquarie's Chair | 9. Andrew (Boy) Charlton Swimming Pool | 10. Woolloomooloo | 11. Garden Island Dockyard | 12. McElhone Stairs | 13. Butlers Stairs | 14. Forbes Street | 15. Conservatorium of Music | 16. Government House

Start at the ferry wharves on Circular Quay and walk around the eastern walkway towards the Opera House. This is called Writers Walk, for among the pseudo cobblestones of this walkway circular brass plaques honour some of the more notable writers of bygone years. High-rise apartment and office buildings that line the walk have replaced the wool stores which, until relatively recent years, were a reminder of the shipping activities that once buzzed along this quay. Those original three-and four-storey sandstone buildings with their barred, sightless windows are no more although smaller versions still exist in The Rocks (covered in walk 2) on the opposite side of **Sydney Cove |1|**. Few relics remain of those heady days when windjammers lined this foreshore, one of which is a flight of stone steps, squeezed between the buildings on the right about halfway along. These and a number of similar steps once provided access to the Quay from the higher level of Macquarie Street.

It is hard, now, to visualise the bustling activity of this side of Circular Quay in the days when it was the hub of the new city. A forest of masts and rigging overshadowed the wool stores while between them ant-like stevedores bustled back and forth wheeling large bales of wool and barrels of tallow which were quickly hoisted up and lowered into the gaping maws of the ships' holds. Those were the days when the Quay was a hive of busy waterfront industry; now it sees only the placid movement of tourists as they meander along the unhurried walkways towards Sydney's prime attraction — the Opera House.

And not only the activity along this side of the Quay has been replaced. The fine old sandstone wool stores are gone and on their foundations stand tall, inelegant apartment and office buildings. It seems that with the departure of the graceful old windjammers, Sydney's waterfront underwent a personality change; most noticeable here in the high-rise blocks, the shops and the restaurants. The building at the end of the row gained some notoriety in the mid-1990s when it became the focal point of considerable angst from city residents and visitors alike. Nicknamed 'the Toaster' because of its unimaginative design, the outcry was caused by its blocking the view of the Opera House from the central quay area. Despite attempts to buy it back and pull it down, the building survived and remains, with its immediate neighbours, as a striking contrast with the vintage buildings on the opposite side of Sydney Cove.

The Sydney Opera House

Continue on to the forecourt of **Sydney Opera House |2|** and marvel at this magnificent building, designed by Danish architect Joern Utzon and completed in 1973. Known throughout the world for its striking sail-like roof design, the Opera House had a rocky gestation when Utzon fell out with the state government over changes to his plans, and in 1966 he resigned from the project. It was completed by Australian architects who generally adhered faithfully to Utzon's original intentions. The white tiled roofs of the side-by-side Concert Halls and Theatres soar above a reconstituted red granite base giving the structure an exciting visual impact from almost any angle. A wide pedestrian promenade goes around the entire outside and a massive entrance forecourt gives the building an island-like appearance at the approaches to Circular Quay. The Concert Hall seats an audience of 2,690 and the Opera Theatre 1,547.

Bennelong Point, on which the Opera House stands, was once a small rocky islet, cut off from the mainland at high tide, and named after the Aboriginal boy befriended by Governor Phillip in 1792 and subsequently taken on a visit to Britain. The point was originally called Cattle Point as it was part of the first farm, but its strategic position at the entrance to the Sydney Cove settlement made it an ideal fortress on which two large cannons were mounted. Together with the battery on Dawes Point, on the other side of Sydney Cove, these gun emplacements offered perfect protection for the new settlers, at least from any water-borne threat. Fort Macquarie, as it was known, became redundant as the military threat receded. It had a chequered history culminating in its use as a tram depot during the early part of the 20th century. Bennelong Point now enjoys fame as the site of one of the world's finest buildings.

Sydney Opera House is open for conducted tours every day and of course performances and concerts are held continually throughout the year. A stroll around

Opening Times

Sydney Opera House:
Daily guided tours 9am–4pm.
Royal Botanic Gardens:
Daily from 7am to sunset.

Refreshments

Cafes, restaurants, bars and take-away food outlets are found at Circular Quay, the Opera House and in Woolloomooloo. There is a kiosk at the Andrew (Boy) Charlton Swimming Pool and a kiosk and restaurant in the Royal Botanic Gardens. Water bubblers can be found in the Domain and Royal Botanic Gardens.

the outside, however, offers a seductive introduction to be followed later by a tour or a performance which will allow you to enjoy the full fruits of this structure. From the walkway that leads into the forecourt walk down the left hand side of the main building and follow The Broadwalk which circumnavigates the base providing spectacular views of the harbour and the Sydney Harbour Bridge – another Sydney icon known across the world. Often there are performers offering street theatre or music along the open spaces of The Broadwalk while restaurants and cafes provide refreshments against a striking backdrop of the soaring white 'sails' of the building and the magnificent blue of the harbour all around.

Sydney Opera House

The Domain

The Broadwalk returns along the western side of the building to the Opera House steps and the first of many gateways into **The Domain |3|** and **Royal Botanic Gardens |4|**. These ornate sandstone and wrought iron gates are known as the **Queen Elizabeth II Gates |5|**. Walk through them and follow the sandstone wall around the perimeter of **Farm Cove |6|** across the site of Australia's first farm. When the first settlers landed in 1788 their immediate need was food, and it was on this eastern side of Sydney Cove behind Farm Cove that Australia's first crops were grown and stock grazed. It is not difficult, as you walk through the lush green parkland, to visualise the meagre herds of those first farmers enjoying the peaceful atmosphere after their harrowing

ocean pasage. The herds were so meagre, in fact, that he solitary bull, four cows, one calf, one stallion, three mares and three colts that arrived with the First Fleet, created the foundation for what was to become one of the world's major agricultural industries.

Continue around the foreshores of Farm Cove to the eastern promontory, known as **Mrs Macquarie's Point |7|**, a rocky outcrop at the tip of the headland that separates Farm Cove from Woolloomooloo Bay. So captivated was Governor Macquarie's wife by the harbour views from this point that she had a carriage road built from Government House and a seat specially carved in the sandstone rock, so she could drive out and sit contemplating the wide expanse of

Sydney Harbour. The carved seat, known appropriately as **Mrs Macquarie's Chair |8|**, remains to this day and bus loads of tourists daily follow this route onto the point to enjoy the enchanting view from the lookout. In particular the scene to the west, taking in Sydney Harbour Bridge and the Opera House, is popular with overseas tourists.

From Mrs Macquarie's Chair follow the footpath back along the western side of Woolloomooloo Bay to the **Andrew (Boy) Charlton Swimming Pool |9|**. This pool, originally known as the Domain Baths, was first built in 1908 on the site of two earlier structures. Male swimmers once swam nude here and used the local Moreton Bay Fig trees as diving platforms; but as women achieved the right to bathe with them, modesty took over and the men were required to wear trunks. At one stage an old ship's hulk was moored between two sections of the foreshore to ensure segregation of the swimming sexes! The new baths, built in 1966, were named after Andrew 'Boy' Charlton, one of Australia's great swimming champions.

Continue along the footpath past the pool towards **Woolloomooloo |10|** and on the left an old 'finger wharf' is visible sticking far out into the water from the head of the bay. Nowadays redeveloped into a modern complex of apartments and offices, the original historic wharf was one of a number of finger wharves in Sydney Harbour used to berth cargo and passenger ships from all over the world. The reno-

vation and development of this wharf was the centre of great controversy and the project changed hands many times before development finally took place in 1998/99. Heritage groups wanted the structure retained as a memento of Sydney's early maritime history, but cost factors, particularly the replacing of the hundreds of wood piles that supported it, resulted in it becoming a commercial enterprise.

Woolloomooloo

On the opposite side of the bay, with a little luck, will be the pride of Australia's naval fleet, for this is the western side of **Garden Island Dockyard |11|** and when the fleet is in, many of the ships are berthed down the eastern side of Woolloomooloo Bay. A walk along this side of the bay has some interesting features and is covered in walk 13, page 110. At this point the footpath leaves the foreshore and climbs up to Mrs Macquarie's Road, then a steep flight of steps leads down to Woolloomooloo roadway. Follow these down to the street level, and bear left along Cowper Wharf Road, with the famous Bells and Woolloomooloo Bay pubs on the opposite corner.

Walk across the head of the bay and facing you is a skyline of terraced apartment buildings perched high and somewhat precariously above the suburb of Woolloomooloo. These buildings are on the high ridge which once dominated the area from Darlinghurst to Garden Island. The ridge was quarried to provide stone for the construction of the naval dockyard and for years sheer sandstone cliffs were a feature of the landscape here. Now the top of the cliffs is dominated by the apartment complexes, while the sandstone cliff face is mostly concealed by an ugly multi-storey car park, happily screened by a fine stand of casuarina trees along Cowpers Wharf Road.

In the early days of settlement a number of windmills were located on top of this ridge in order to catch the wind coming off the sea which would turn the sails to grind corn. There was no direct road access to the Woolloomooloo Heights, as they were called, and the only way wheeled traffic from the city could reach the windmills was by a wide detour through what is now the Taylor Square area. It was possible to reach the top of the ridge from Woolloomooloo by foot but this involved climbing steep goat tracks. In the 1880s a series of stone steps were built to make the climb easier and some of these still exist. Cross the road at Brougham Street and the first flight can be seen climbing the cliff beneath a canopy of trees. This is a double flight of stone steps known as **McElhone Stairs |12|**, and there are others further along. The Potts Point and Darlinghurst areas which now cover the top of the ridge are described in walk 13, page 112.

From the foot of McElhone Stairs bear right into Brougham Street and walk up the hill beneath the towering apartment blocks perched high above the narrow road. At one stage a sheer section of the sandstone cliff overshadows the road with more apartment buildings sitting perilously near

the edge at the top. A second flight of stone steps – the Hordern Stairs – scales this cliff, but continue past these and the quaint old cottages on the right hand side until you reach a third set of steps. These are **Butlers Stairs |13|** and right opposite are Hills Stairs leading down to Sydney Place, thus making a complete pedestrian walkway from the top of the ridge down to the centre of Woolloomooloo. Follow this old path down the Hills Stairs to Sydney Place then turn left into McElhone Street. On either side of this street are rows of delightful terrace houses that were once home to the dock workers who laboured either in the naval dockyard or on the waterfront wharves.

Turn right into Reid Street and then right again into Dowling Street. On the next corner is another of the area's traditional pubs – the Old Fitzroy. Nowadays the railway rumbles behind these old buildings, but since they retain their old charm it is not difficult to imagine an era when, after a hard day on the docks, grimy wharfies climbed the hill to sit on the stoop or lean on the bar of fine old pubs like this.

Forbes Street

Turn the corner to the left around the Old Fitzroy and walk down Cathedral Street to **Forbes Street |14|** which is on the right of Cathedral Street where the overhead rail viaduct sweeps round towards The Domain. Forbes Street is one of the streets in this area that have been redeveloped. This is the heart of the Woolloomooloo community where time has brought immense changes. Being a disused dockland suburb, many of the streets were degenerating almost to slums, so a massive new project was undertaken to bring the standards of Woolloomooloo up to those of other Sydney suburbs, while retaining the charm and something of the original atmosphere. It was a very successful plan and now the area enjoys a delightful mix of the old and the new, with Forbes Street as a classical showplace.

The street is closed off so there is no traffic; instead the roadway is dotted with flower gardens and lawns and the entire street is planted with *Robinia,* or golden locust trees, which in spring and summer create a delightful canopy of yellow and give Forbes Street the ambience of suburban Paris rather than dockland Sydney. There are still many of the old terrace houses, some beautifully restored and renovated, as well as modern red brick terraces that retain the old atmosphere but offer better living for the residents. Walk around this area for a while and enjoy the benefits of a masterful piece of town planning that could well be copied in a number of other run-down Sydney suburbs.

Continue to follow Forbes Street down to the waterfront at Woolloomooloo Bay or digress among the quaint narrow streets with their terrace houses and corner shops that make up the body of the suburb. In the lower section of Forbes Street the golden locust trees are replaced with a grove of palms and the terrace houses by

the Tilbury Hotel. Take a break on the wide forecourt of the Tilbury or continue on to Cowper Wharf Road for the next leg of the walk. Cross over and veer left back across the waterfront into Lincoln Crescent and climb the steps leading up to Mrs Macquarie's Road. Turn left across Mrs Macquarie's Road to the Woolloomooloo Gates and enter the Royal Botanic Gardens.

The Royal Botanic Gardens

Originally, what are now the Royal Botanic Gardens were part of Governor Phillip's first 'nine acre' farm, established in 1788 to feed the settlers. The area was part of The Domain until 1816 when Governor Macquarie appointed Charles Fraser as the colonial botanist and placed in his care a section to be reserved as a botanic garden. The gardens today cover more than 30 hectares and provide a spectacular display of more than 7500 species of plants. Since it would take at least half a day – and possibly a full one – to cover the entire range of interesting exhibits in the gardens, this section of our walk will follow a track that takes in only the more prominent features.

Having entered through the Woolloomooloo Gate, turn right at the first fork and follow the path down the hill. On the right are the administration buildings and the Visitors Centre where detailed information about the gardens can be obtained. On the left is the Palm House just past which, on either side of the footpath, is the First Farm Exhibition. This unusual section contains numerous garden vegetables, some rarely seen in this part of the world. They represent the first vegetables grown in Australia on this very spot from seed brought out with the First Fleet from Britain, so it is not surprising that many familiar British vegetables are to be found here. Governor Phillip also collected seeds – but not necessarily vegetables – at Rio de Janeiro and Cape Town en route to Australia and some of these were subsequently germinated in the gardens.

Although the initial farming venture was considered a failure because of its barren soil and an epidemic of rust which destroyed the wheat, plants were gradually encouraged to grow and by 1825 almost 3000 specimens were thriving. The Colonial Office took an interest and requested half-yearly reports on the progress of the gardens. It also initiated a research program into useful plants from overseas that might be suited to the climate and conditions of New South Wales.

Continue on down the central path to Macquarie's Wall, an extensive stone capped and rubble wall and gateway built around 1812 to keep undesirables – both human and animal – out of the gardens. Sections of the original wall are still in place although the gardens have now stretched beyond the wall to become part of The Domain, so it no longer serves the purpose for which it was built.

Rather than rejoin the path from the Opera House across the foreshore of Farm Cove, take the first path left after passing through Macquarie's Wall and walk down

to the ponds, with the restaurant, kiosk and toilets behind. This is the central point of the gardens and an ideal spot to take a breather and enjoy a meal or a snack in the beautiful surroundings, dominated here by tall palms with bamboo and clivia growing in their dense shade. From here walk directly towards the harbour to the main pond where waterfowl of all kinds wait to be fed. In the Sydney Festival of 1999 this pond was used as the location of the Vietnamese Water Puppets performances, an unusual and intriguing display of fine eastern craft. Behind the main pond to the west the CBD office blocks rise, seemingly through the jungle of ferns and palms that fringe the pond.

Return to the kiosk and restaurant and continue past bearing right and taking the left fork towards the Sydney Tropical Centre, which consists of two large glasshouses with a huge variety of tropical exhibits. Continue along the path that follows this boundary towards the city and bear right into the Pioneer Garden and the Rose Garden, located between the Morshead Fountain gate and the Palace Garden gates, both on the south-west corner of the gardens. There is much for domestic garden lovers to enjoy here, including the herb garden just to the north and on the right of the Conservatorium of Music which intrudes into the gardens at this point. Bear left to the Rose Garden Gate which provides access to the **Conservatorium of Music |15|** from the south side and Government House Gate from the north.

The Conservatorium of Music was built by Francis Greenway as stables and servants quarters for **Government House** |16|. It was completed in 1821. The stuccoed brick structure was modelled along the lines of a castle with a central courtyard and keep, surrounded by high parapeted walls with octagonal towers at each corner and at the entrance. It was converted to its present use as the state's Conservatorium of Music between 1908 and 1915. In 1998 it was the scene of considerable excitement when, during renovations, a section of the original convict road built by Governor Macquarie was unearthed.

Leaving this important historic building, bear right at the Macquarie Street entrance and enter the Gardens once again through the Government House Gate. A service road leads directly to what was once the residence of the state governor but is now used for a variety of functions. It is a large Gothic Revival building with crenellated battlements and turrets supported by Gothic arches, built of sandstone with a slate roof and stone flagged verandah. Walk around the superbly kept grounds of Government House before inspecting the interior, then take any gate on the Macquarie Street side to re-enter the Gardens. Bear right across the grassy spaces and beneath the giant fig trees to join the footpath which runs down a gentle slope all the way to the steps and the forecourt of the Sydney Opera House. This terminates the walk effectively where it began after a long stroll through what were once the green pastures of Australia's first farm.

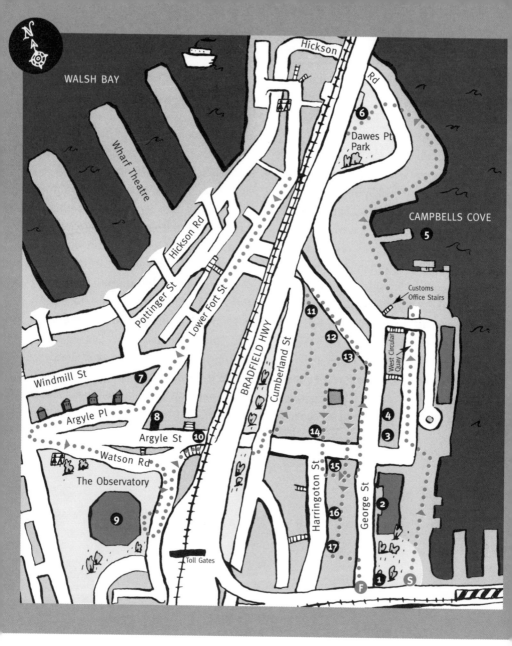

Walk key

1. First Fleet Park | 2. Museum of Contemporary Art | 3. Cadman's Cottage | 4. The Sailors' Home |
5. Campbells Cove | 6. Dawes Point Battery | 7. Hero of Waterloo Hotel | 8. Garrison Church |
9. Sydney Observatory | 10. Argyle Cut | 11. Bunker Hill | 12. The Merchants House | 13. The Rocks
Square | 14. Argyle Stores | 15. Reynold's Cottage | 16. Original hospital site | 17. Bakehouse Place

The Rocks

The village that became a nation

Start

First Fleet Park at Circular Quay.

Finish

Circular Quay.

Length/Time

4 km/1.5 hours

Wheelchairs

Fine on the footpaths, but difficult at the Argyle Stairs, Dawes Point Park and steps in some places.

Few places can have greater fascination for Sydneysiders than The Rocks. It was here, more than two centuries ago, that their city – indeed their country – was born. And it is here, among the cobbled lanes and sandstone houses, that they can wonder at the fortitude that built one of the world's most vibrant and modern cities out of a virtually abandoned colony of villains. It all began right here among a huddle of tents and shacks beneath the 40 metre high, frowning sandstone promontory that gave the place its name – The Rocks.

To walk around The Rocks is to walk through history in the very real sense of the word. Not history European style, where time is measured in millennia. Not history Aboriginal style, where events are recorded in legend. This is history that should never have been created. The history of a people cast out, yet who eventually contributed to one of the bravest and most colourful histories ever written. It is a history so recent you can relive it here in The Rocks.

Circular Quay

The logical place to commence a walk in The Rocks is Circular Quay, for it was the Tank Stream that determined the location of the first settlement, and the Tank Stream runs into Sydney Cove close to where **First Fleet Park |1|** is located on the western side of the Quay immediately adjacent to The Rocks. Governor Phillip chose to establish his party on the eastern side of the stream, with the main body of convicts and their guards camped on the western side. The stream ran back above Bridge Street, and was crossed by a wooden bridge which gave the road its name.

Walk across First Fleet Park towards the Overseas Passenger Terminal, past the buskers who are active along this walkway on weekends and past the Art Deco style **Museum of Contemporary Art |2|**. On the lawn in front of the museum is a stone tablet from the Commissariat Store Building, built by Governor Macquarie in 1812 on an adjacent site, and a bust of Governor Phillip. A pleasant grove of jacarandas and

palms lines the open pavement of the Quay and a large stand of Moreton Bay figs (described in walk 3, page 30) can be seen at the foot of Argyle Street.

Walk across West Circular Quay Road and veer right past a statue of Captain Bligh to **Cadman's Cottage |3|**, which faces out across the open waters of Circular Quay as it has for almost two centuries. This delightful cottage is one of the oldest surviving buildings in Australia, having been built in 1816 for the coxswain and crew of the governor's boats. John Cadman, who was the superintendent of boats between 1827 and 1846, lived in this cottage which now accommodates the National Parks and Wildlife Service information centre. If the cottage appears a little sunken it is because it was originally built on the foreshore and reclamation since that time has raised the level of the surrounding streets.

The cottage lies adjacent to **The Sailors' Home |4|**, a fine Romanesque Revival style building built in 1864 to keep sailors off the streets, or more correctly out of the pubs and brothels which thrived in this area. It performed this commendable task for over 100 years until, in the 1970s, it was refurbished as The Rocks Visitors Centre. The West Circular Quay road takes you behind the Sailors' Home and under the access ramp past the Overseas Passenger Terminal, built in 1964 to provide a more central berthing point for the giant liners which, in those days, were the principal means of travel to any part of the world. This building, located almost exactly where the First Fleet anchored, is remembered by thousands of post-war migrants as the first place onto which they set foot in Australia.

Phillip commented that his choice of Sydney Cove as a site for the settlement was partly due to the deep water right up to the shore, which would allow for easy berthing of ships. He would have been impressed with the Overseas Passenger Terminal which has more than 10 metres of water alongside and has berthed some of the world's largest liners. By way of diversion, a walk along the upper deck of the terminal offers superb views of the Opera House, the CBD and the historic waterfront of The Rocks. But continuing at ground level, on the left are a number of old warehouses with flights of steps at intervals between them. Originally Robert Campbell, one of Sydney's first merchants and a customs naval officer, built his house near the end of this block, just to the south of the last flight of steps, appropriately called Customs Officers Stairs.

Campbells Wharf

West Circular Quay Road and the Overseas Passenger Terminal end at a wide, paved waterfront square fronting a row of fine old warehouses which have now been restored and refurbished as restaurants in this magnificent setting overlooking **Campbells Cove** |5|. In 1800 Campbell purchased a waterfront site at The Rocks on which he built the first commercial wharf in Australia. Its warehouses stored the cargo he shipped in from all parts of the world, as well as the

Opening Times

The Rocks Visitors Centre (Sailors' Home): Daily 9am–6pm.
Museum of Contemporary Art: Daily 10am–6pm.
Argyle Stores: Daily 8am till late.
National Parks and Wildlife Information Centre (Cadman's Cottage): Daily 9am–5pm.
Sydney Observatory: Daily 10am–5pm (night viewing by appointment).
NSW State Archives: Mon–Fri 9am–5pm.
Rocks Markets: Sat and Sun early till late.

Refreshments

All manner of cafes, restaurants, kiosks, food shops, hotels, taverns and bars are at numerous points throughout the walk. Water bubblers can be found in Dawes Point Park and First Fleet Park.

sealskins and whale oil he exported. In 1839 he began building these sandstone warehouses which were extended at different times up until the turn of the century. Eleven of these storehouses survive to this day. The interiors have been carefully and sympathetically preserved, and eating in one of the restaurants inside these buildings is a memorable experience. Much of Campbell's wharf structure has gone, but a section of the original sea wall is still visible at the front of the forecourt.

From the fluttering flags of Campbells Cove follow the boardwalk around in front of the Park Hyatt Hotel to Dawes Point where, on Hickson Road, almost under the bridge, there is a Horse Ferry dock dating from 1880. Cross the road into Dawes Point and climb up the grassy slopes towards the towering structure of Sydney Harbour Bridge and the forbidding grey stone of the south-east pylon. This particular pylon has a lookout at the top which is described in walk 3, page 31 of this book. Curving up into the northern sky is the mighty fabricated steel arch of the bridge.

Wrought-iron lampost in George Street

Dawes Point

Immediately beneath the pylon are five cannons, neatly aligned on their wooden carriages so that their field of fire covers the entrance to Sydney Cove. These once formed part of **Dawes Point Battery |6|**, built in 1788 as the first line of defence for the new colony and the first fort built in Australia. It was enlarged from time to time with a notable expansion in 1836 and manned until 1916, but was demolished in the 1920s when work commenced on the Sydney Harbour Bridge.

Lieutenant Dawes arrived in the First Fleet as an astronomer rather than a military man, and was very influential in developing the cultural side of the settlement. He was a keen observer of the Aborigines and at one stage compiled a vocabulary of their language. He was also an explorer, gave piano lessons to the ladies of the colony, surveyed land distributions and generally encouraged the arts and culture in a place far removed from any semblance of European civilisation and culture.

Walk past the cannons, all of which are engraved with the Victorian royal crest, and a wire fence which encloses excavation operations currently taking place on the site of the old fort. Head along the grassy spaces under the bridge deck to reach George Street where it joins Lower Fort Street. On the right, on the other side of Lower Fort Street, is a row of fine three-storey terrace houses. Together with elegant Georgian and

Victorian houses that run along the west side of Lower Fort Street, these create a superb streetscape leading to Argyle Place. One notable building is at No. 43 – a fine Georgian mansion once known as Bligh House, first built in 1825 and thought to be the oldest residence in Sydney. It was bought and renovated by Robert Campbell's son in 1833 and renamed Blight House. Now called Clyde Bank, it has been faithfully restored to provide a home for a collection of early 19th century colonial paintings, furnishings and decorative art.

Millers Point

On the right hand side of George Street where it intersects with Lower Fort Street (under the bridge) is an interesting relic of Victorian times – a cast iron pissoir dated 1890. Follow Lower Fort Street and where it runs into Windmill Street stands one of the best known buildings in The Rocks – the **Hero of Waterloo Hotel |7|**. Traditionally this old sailors' pub has been the focal point for revellers in The Rocks since it was first built in 1843. A favourite watering hole for the soldiers of the Dawes Battery, it also catered for the sailors and whalers whose ships lay beneath the headland known as Millers Point.

A relic of those heady days still exists in the form of a tunnel burrowed through the sandstone from the cellar of the Hero of Waterloo to the harbour foreshore. The press gangs preyed on drunken sailors by hijacking them down the tunnel and whisking them off onto ships lying in the stream. A reverse trade of smuggling goods and spirits up the tunnel made the old pub a busy place for all kinds of illicit activity. Today the 'Hero', like a number of the Rocks' pubs, is a popular venue for young people.

The names Windmill Street and Millers Point are synonymous with grain milling activity and indeed, in order to catch the fresh sea breezes, windmills were located high on the hill above The Rocks. Windmill Street with Windmill Steps at the bottom provided the link between the ships landing grain on the foreshores and the windmills grinding it to flour on the ridge. The grain was not carried up the steep incline, but winched up by cable from the foreshore rock platforms where it had been landed.

Continue past the Hero of Waterloo along Lower Fort Street to where it enters the wide, tree-lined avenue of Argyle Place. On the left is one of Sydney's most loved places of worship – the **Garrison Church |8|**. The church obtained its name from the official military services, which were first held in the 1840s when it was built, and which are still held, together with other services, to this day. The inside of the fine sandstone building is lined with regimental flags and decorated with plaques commemorating men and events of past military history, both British and Australian.

From the Garrison Church cross to the north side of Argyle Place, where there is another fine display of terrace houses facing onto the park in the centre. At the end of this row of terraces, on the corner of Kent Street is Sydney's oldest hostelry – the Lord Nelson Hotel. This white sandstone building is quite unmistakable and makes a fine place to take a break in the walk. With the delightful outlook onto Argyle Green, the pub's home brew and a fine brasserie on the first floor, the temptation to linger and perhaps continue the walk another day can become very strong! But resist the temptation, leave Sydney's oldest pub behind and cross Argyle Place to head up Watson Road, or the steps opposite the Garrison Church, to Upper Fort Street and the **Sydney Observatory |9|** on Windmill Hill. This area was once known as 'The Quarries' since stone for the construction of local buildings was quarried here, as can be seen in the cliff that surrounds Observatory Hill.

On the grassy slopes beneath the observatory a relic of early 20th century Sydney dominates the scene – a band rotunda built in 1912, beneath which is a memorial to those who fought in the Boer War. But perhaps the most interesting feature here is the wall in front of the observatory which is the remaining structure of the original Fort Phillip. The fine defensive position of Windmill Hill convinced Governor King to erect a fort at the top as a better line of defence than the Dawes Point Battery below, but it was never fully completed. It was replaced in 1858 by the present observatory although two walls and some battlements from the original Fort Phillip still remain and it is these that are visible from the surrounding parkland.

Originally this spot was called Flagstaff Hill on account of a flagstaff erected in 1788 to communicate with the signal station on South Head (see walk 7, page 66), but it became known as Windmill Hill after Governor Hunter arrived in 1795 with a prefabricated wooden windmill which was erected on the present site of the observatory. The windmill was the first in Sydney and convicts climbed the many steps up the hill to have their rations of grain ground into meal. Nowadays the area is known as Observatory Hill and the present observatory tower was completed in 1857. From 1858 a time ball on the weathervane was dropped at 1pm each day and a cannon fired from Fort Macquarie (walk 1, page 11). Later the gun was fired from Dawes Point Battery and then from Fort Denison.

An interesting feature of the observatory building is the copper domes which still rotate on their original bearings – cannon balls! It is now used as a museum and tours are available, which are of particular interest when comets or other night sky phenomena can be seen. Fort Street School, which lies just to the south, was originally built in 1815 as a military hospital but became a school in the 1850s and remained as such until the late 1970s when it became the headquarters of the National Trust.

The Argyle Cut

Return back down the steps to Upper Fort Street, but don't turn left into Watson Road. Instead bear right down more steps into a pedestrian tunnel which runs beside the **Argyle Cut |10|**, itself a fascinating part of early Sydney history. The giant sandstone ridge which separated the settlement from the windmills, the maritime activity and the developing industries in Walsh and Cockle bays was an obvious impediment to commercial activity, and in 1843 convict labour was used to hand cut a pass through the rock. A ban on the use of convicts in 1845 threatened the completion of the cut, but it was deemed so important that eventually it was completed using commercial labour. Initially only the width of a cart, it was widened as time and traffic demanded to its present four-lane width.

Walk through the Argyle pedestrian tunnel and cross Cumberland Street, bearing left to where a set of stone steps leads down off the right, providing pedestrian access to Argyle Street. The original Argyle Stairs were cut into the sandstone by convicts in 1815 to provide a footpath over the rocky ridge before the Argyle Cut was made. But don't descend both flights to Argyle Street; at the bottom of the first flight walk straight ahead along a narrow paved walkway that runs across the back of the houses fronting Cumberland Street. This is Gloucester Walkway, and since it runs at rooftop height to the buildings on the right an interesting vista of the old sandstone wool stores and the narrow, almost claustrophobic back alleys behind the houses below is obtained as you proceed down a modest gradient to Bunker Hill |11|.

Bunker Hill and its adjacent Foundation Park have a number of relics from The Rocks of the mid-19th century. The remains of cottages built into the cliff face in the 1870s can still be seen precariously cling-ing to the sandstone face above steep steps leading down to the lower Rocks area. The cliff above was the site of Bunker Hill, considered in the 1820s to be the 'dress circle' of the settlement. Captain Bunker, after whom the area was named, was a whaling captain who subsequently became one of Sydney's wealthiest and most influ-ential figures. Continue along Gloucester Walk, through its pretty avenue of plane trees, and look down onto the busy activity in the courtyards and cafes below, until it joins George Street at the triangular Mercantile Hotel.

The Rocks Village

On Saturdays and Sundays George Street, from this point down to its junction with Hickson Road, is closed off to provide the location of The Rocks Markets, one of the most colourful and extensive displays of merchandise, arts and crafts to be seen anywhere in Sydney. Canvas market umbrel-las are erected down the length of the street to provide shelter from sun or rain and provide a soft light that heightens the colour of the offerings and enhances the market ambience. The Mercantile Hotel on the corner is a fine specimen of Sydney's turn of the century pubs, with an excellent example of Art Nouveau tiles on its exterior walls.

Keeping the pub on your right, walk down George Street. A series of typical Rocks terrace houses continues on from where the Mercantile Hotel ends; one of them, at No. 43, is a Georgian townhouse, built for Martyn and Combes for their business as 'painters, glaziers and plumbers' and named **The Merchants House |12|**. It is now the only building of this unique type left standing in The Rocks.

On the left the old commercial buildings have been converted into up-market galleries and restaurants, including the Mining Museum, once an electric power station, now known as the Earth Exchange, which contains one of the world's greatest mineral collections, including the largest gold nugget in Australia, as well as fossils and rocks dating back to 1875. At the corner of Hickson Road and George Street turn right into Playfair Street; straight ahead is picturesque Atherden Street, the shortest street in Sydney, with its beautifully restored facades and paved street ending in a sheer cliff face of sandstone. At one time this area was occupied by warehouses belonging to the early colonial trader Ben Boyd, who stored whale oil and seal skins here prior to shipping them overseas from the wharves below.

Follow Playfair Street as it bears left into **The Rocks Square |13|**. As its name suggests, this is the focal point of the village and where The Rocks really comes into its own. Walk past the pioneer monument and into the paved street which is lined with fascinating terrace cottages, most of which were workers' dwellings but have now been superbly restored. Many are restaurants or cafes; others are tourist shops full of bric-a-brac and other souvenirs. Take time out to walk through the narrow, almost claus-trophobic passageways and explore the delights of Argyle Place with its low doorways, tiny windows and cobbled footpaths.

After exploring this fascinating area, move on along Playfair Street to the well-known **Argyle Stores |14|**, several fine old warehouses that have been magnificently restored with the original large doorways, granite cobbled courtyards and massive sandstone walls, most of which were built in or around the early 19th century. Mary Reiby, arguably Australia's first successful business woman, once owned part of these stores; a significant achievement considering she was first transported as a convict at the age of 13 for joy-riding on a horse and cart!

Cross Argyle Street and bear right into Harrington Street where, on the left at No. 28 is **Reynold's Cottage |15|**, built in the 1820s for a local blacksmith who carried on his trade at the back. These and other adjacent cottages were originally only one room deep; cramped living was the order of the day in those harsh times. To the left as you walk along Harrington Street is a narrow lane with the unusual name of Suez Canal, once an open sewer, then a stormwater drain. The origin of the name is lost in time, but probably relates to the amount of water that rushed down it during heavy rainstorms. Its reputation, however, is far more sinister. This cramped alleyway, which narrows almost to one person width at the bottom, was the haunt of gangsters and hoodlums in the days of 'The Rocks Push', a period of lawlessness in the late 19th century when to walk through the narrow lanes of The Rocks was to invite certain mugging or robbery. But it is quite safe now to walk down the flagstoned Suez Canal and note the delightful backyard restaurants and bistros on either side.

Turn left into George Street from Suez Canal and walk back across Argyle Street. On the opposite corner stands the Georgian style Orient Hotel, which was built as a business house in 1843 but has operated as a licensed hotel since 1851. Like many of the pubs in The Rocks area, this is a popular social venue, especially for young people. All along this section of George Street there are some fine old buildings including Unwin's Stores, The Coachhouse and Samson's Cottage, all of which date back to the busy 1840s when Sydney Cove was a hive of maritime and commercial activity and these buildings were but a stone's throw from the waterfront. Here also were some of the infamous sailors' pubs, notably the Observer Tavern and the Waterman's Arms, both prominent features of the waterfront district in the 1840s.

Turn left into Mill Lane and left again into Kendall Lane for a final browse through a typical Rocks scene. This narrow lane with its small cobbled road surface runs behind the old buildings facing onto George Street. The use of the lane for delivery and loading of goods is evident from the first and second floor loading bays and the timber gantries reaching out across the street. Cross over Argyle Street yet again and enter an arched alleyway called Green-

way Lane, after the convict Francis Greenway who became one of the most notable early architects of 19th century Sydney. This confined alleyway leads under the buildings to courtyards behind, now housing delightful open air bistros. The cobbles in this alley, by contrast with those in Kendall Lane, are large, square flagstones.

From the courtyard bistros walk across Suez Canal and along Nurses' Walk, which runs close to the site of the original hospital |16|. The first hospital, established in 1788, consisted of rough buildings with even rougher facilities; herbs were grown in the hospital grounds as few drugs were available in the colony. The second hospital was a portable building which arrived with the Second Fleet in June 1790. So great was the demand that, one month after it was erected, there were 488 patients in the hospital proper and over 100 tents erected to provide for the overflow.

Mission Steps, on the right of Nurses' Walk relates to the establishment of a mission and school for abandoned girls, while opposite is **Bakehouse Place |17|**, where the first bakehouse was established in 1788.

Keep walking along Nurses' Walk – the origin of the name is obvious – and turn left into Globe Street, where the State Archives are housed, recording the early life and times of the colony. Walk down Globe Street and across George Street to return to First Fleet Park, thus completing our walk through the once infamous, now intriguing birthplace of the nation – The Rocks.

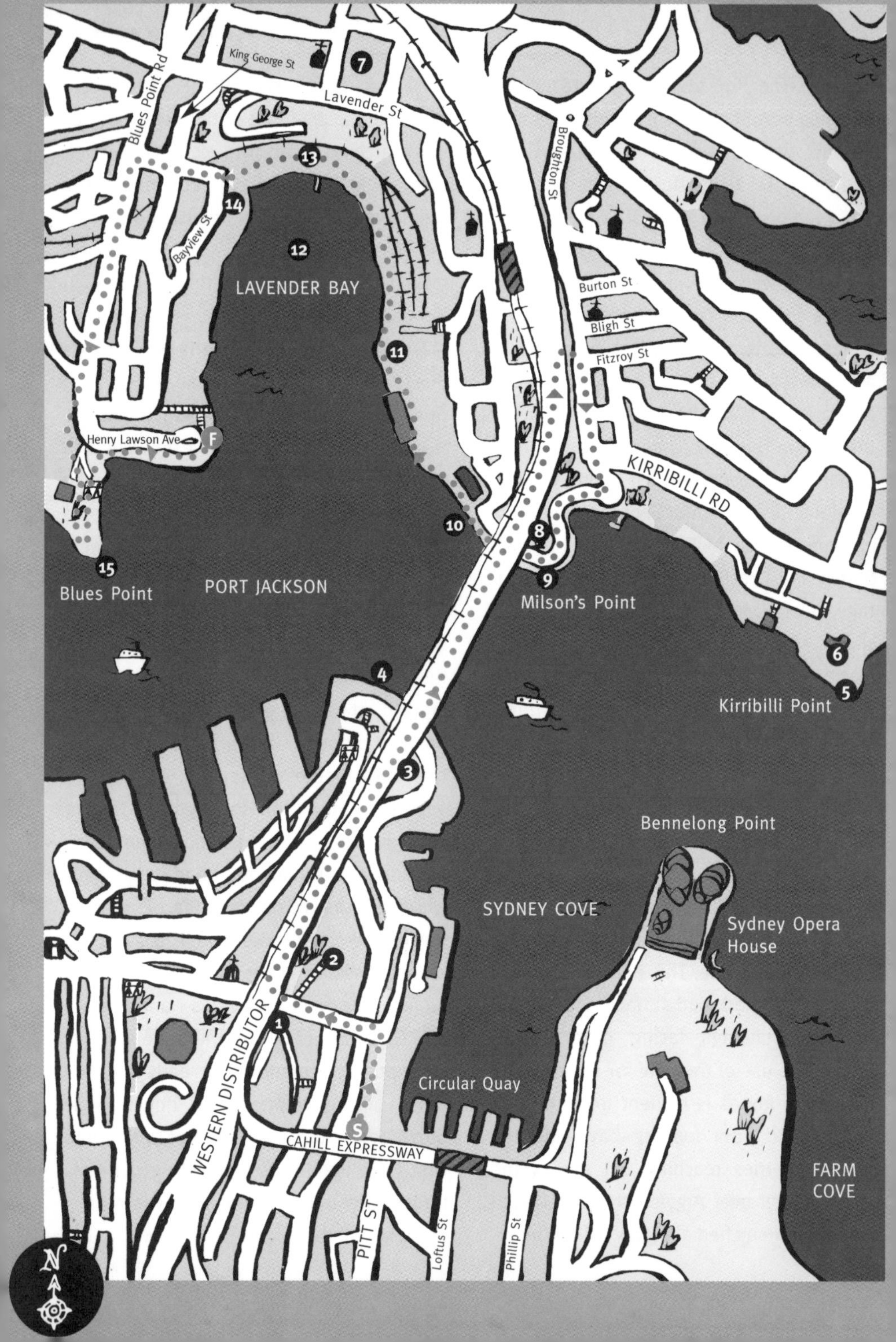
King George St
Lavender St
Blues Point Rd
Broughton St
Bayview St
LAVENDER BAY
Burton St
Bligh St
Fitzroy St
Henry Lawson Ave
KIRRIBILLI RD
Blues Point
PORT JACKSON
Milson's Point
Kirribilli Point
Bennelong Point
SYDNEY COVE
Sydney Opera House
Circular Quay
WESTERN DISTRIBUTOR
CAHILL EXPRESSWAY
PITT ST
Loftus St
Phillip St
FARM COVE
N

Sydney Harbour Bridge
Following the first ferryman

Start
Circular Quay West.

Finish
Blues Point. Catch a Hegarty's ferry or a State Transit ferry to Circular Quay.

Length/time
4.5 km/1.5 hours

Wheelchairs
No wheelchair access.

Walk key

1. Argyle Cut | 2. The Rocks | 3. Bridge pylon | 4. Dawes Point | 5. Kirribilli Point | 6. Admiralty House | 7. North Sydney | 8. Bradfield Park | 9. Milsons Point | 10. North Sydney Olympic Pool | 11. Luna Park | 12. Lavender Bay | 13. Watt Park | 14. Neptune Engineering Company site | 15. Blues Point

Crossing the Sydney Harbour Bridge is perhaps the most popular of all city walks. Other than from the air, there is no way the scenic beauty of the city and its magnificent harbour can be enjoyed so completely as when viewed from the bridge, either from the footpath, 60 metres above the water, or from the top of the arch, 130 metres high. Access to both these vantage points is described in this walk. The full panorama of the north and south shorelines, the islands, the CBD skyscrapers and the wide expanse of sparkling water leading away to the heads changes with every metre of the walk. Few walks in Sydney encompass so much and are so rewarding.

The starting point for this walk is Circular Quay. From the ferry wharves, walk around the west side along the paved open area in front of First Fleet Park towards the Overseas Passenger Terminal. Just before the terminal there is an unusual group of quite splendid Moreton Bay figs in the middle of the walkway with an interesting story attached to them. They were planted at this spot, together with a number of native trees, to create an 'authentic' Australian welcome for Her Majesty Queen Elizabeth II on her 1970 tour.

To add to the authenticity, koalas were placed in the trees although probably not in the fig trees since fig leaves do not form part of the koala diet! The native trees and koalas were removed later, but the Moreton Bay figs were left in place where they have flourished to this day.

The Sydney Harbour Bridge pylon

The Rocks

Turn left at this group of trees and head up Argyle Street towards **Argyle Cut** |1| (described in more detail in walk 2, page 24) and the overpass of Cumberland Street. Before entering the Cut, with its fascinating early settlement connections, on the immediate right is a flight of stone steps leading upwards to Cumberland Street. Climb these, cross Cumberland Street and climb another set of steps – this time concrete, not stone – which lead up to the bridge walkway, a footpath running across the Sydney Harbour Bridge on the eastern side of the roadway.

Taking in the whole historic area of West Circular Quay, the walk up Argyle and Cumberland streets through The Rocks is itself a delight, but this area is dealt with elsewhere in this book.

However, at this stage take time to look down from the stairway leading up to the bridge walkway as it not only offers an interesting perspective on the sandstone buildings and barred windows of the old wool stores below where Australia's commerce first began, but also reveals the tight, winding configuration of the narrow streets and alleys of **The Rocks** |2|. It is easy to visualise the shadowy 'Rocks Push', gangs of footpads and pickpockets of those early days, as they crept through the dark back lanes looking for unsuspecting victims to rob.

Sydney Harbour Bridge

There are four flights of steps up to the bridge deck but they are relatively easy and even unfit or elderly walkers should be able to handle them, while the landings offer a spot to take a spell, if needs be, as well as take in the sights. Once up on the bridge, the walking is level and has a very easy gradient as the approach span runs towards the first **bridge pylon |3|**. The aerial view of the lower Rocks area and **Dawes Point |4|** become more dramatic with the added height, and the bustling ferries with their white 'tail feathers' zoom in and out of Circular Quay like homing pigeons.

The first bridge pylon offers an interesting diversion as it has a lookout at the top. As the walkway passes through the arch of the huge granite tower, a stairway leads off to the right and climbs up inside the pylon. To reach the top is quite a demanding climb, with 200 narrow steps to the mezzanine level, where there is a fine display of photographs and drawings illustrating the building of the bridge and the way it affected the landscape on either side. It costs $2 to climb the extra steps to the 87 metre high parapet but is well worth the expense and effort since, like the climb to the top of the arch, it adds another dimension to the panorama of the harbour below.

It also provides views across the bridge structure of the inner harbour, which cannot be clearly seen from the eastern walkway. A notable Sydney icon that rears above the wharves and wool stores of the upper reaches is the graceful ANZAC Bridge which

Opening Times

The bridge pylon lookout:
Daily 10am–5pm.
North Sydney Olympic Pool:
During summer, open Mon–Fri 6am–9pm; Sat and Sun 7am–7pm. During winter, open daily 7am–7pm.
Luna Park: temporarily closed.

Refreshments

Numerous cafes, coffee shops, restaurants and bars are at Circular Quay and The Rocks, Kirribilli and Blues Point Road, North Sydney. There is a kiosk inside North Sydney Olympic Pool and water bubblers in Bradfield Park, Watt Park and Blues Point Reserve.

is etched against the western skyline when seen from the top of the pylon lookout. This sophisticated structure, one of the most recent additions to the Sydney skyline, is covered in walk 12, page 102 as part of the walk around Blackwattle and Rozelle bays.

But it is the view downstream from the pylon that really captures the imagination. On the right or southern shore is the most famous of all this city's buildings, the Sydney Opera House, while beyond the ferry wharves the green of the Domain and the proud structure of Government House stand clear to the left of the high rise office buildings in what are now canyon-like streets. Behind the Opera House lie the grey ships and historic buildings of the naval base at Garden Island and beyond that again the distant eastern suburbs of Point Piper and Rose Bay with the distinctive outline of Shark Island in front of them.

On the northern side the trees on **Kirribilli Point |5|** provide a green screen permitting only a glimpse of **Admiralty House |6|**, the Sydney residence of the Governor-General while behind it, totally obscured from this angle, is Kirribilli House, the Sydney residence of the Prime Minister. Protruding headlands at Cremorne and Bradleys Head divide the north side into a series of bays, while standing defiantly in the middle of the harbour is the round martello tower of Pinchgut, or Fort Denison.

From the pylon entrance turn right and continue along the walkway across the main part of the bridge deck, taking in the massive, complex steel structure overhead.

There may be walkers climbing one of the grey arches, enjoying one of Sydney's more adventurous tourist attractions – a walk across the arch – mentioned earlier. If you are lucky an ocean-going ship may be passing beneath your feet – another quite unique experience. Certainly there will be dozens of tiny 'toy' boats buzzing around on the water some 60 metres below. There is always lots of activity on Sydney Harbour, as is obvious during any walk around the foreshores, but nowhere is the sight of the harbour more enchanting than from the bridge where the elevation gives the whole scene an unreal atmosphere of clockwork toys on a working model.

Continue across the walkway, which now begins a downwards gradient, past the northern pylon and step out from under the massive steel bridge structure into the open air again. Now the views of the city of Sydney are replaced by views of **North Sydney |7|**. There are fewer impressive high rise buildings here, but the apartment buildings and office towers of North Sydney CBD create a fine sight as they line the western side of the Warringah Expressway like corn stalks growing beside the path in some giant's garden.

Kirribilli

Look to the right across the protective wall on the bridge walkway and the contrast is remarkable; where the buildings of the western side have reared skywards, on the eastern side there is architectural chaos! Clustered tightly together, the tree-lined streets and slate-roofed houses of Kirribilli nostalgically try to retain the village atmosphere it had long before the bridge was built, but this is somewhat spoiled by the unimaginative square apartment blocks which have sprouted up among them. The little waterfront suburb seems to be a throw back to the time when there was no such thing as town planning. Originally, this land was part of a grant to James Milson who, in the 1820s, grew vegetables and ran a dairy farm to supply visiting ships with fresh produce. In 1831 he excavated a stone quarry nearby to create a reservoir from which fresh water was also supplied to the ships.

The steps from the bridge walkway lead down to the ground opposite the small shopping centre of Kirribilli. There are 69 steps here, which seems rather a sad anachronism since these steps and those at the other end of the bridge walkway are the only things which inhibit wheelchairs from taking what is otherwise an easy and spectacular walk. The village shops of Kirribilli offer an excellent opportunity to take a break and enjoy coffee or a meal at the local street cafes or enjoy a beer in the pub.

With bodily needs catered for, it is time to move on. Continue the walk by heading down Broughton Street towards the water, following the road or walking down grassy **Bradfield Park |8|** to the foreshore. A footpath follows the roadway round the water's edge and under the bridge. While this is an attractive walk, the noise can be fairly horrendous as vehicles and trains thunder

overhead. On the right, the footings of the northern pylons reveal the mighty load-bearing steel pins which carry the weight of the bridge. These are clearly visible, one on each pylon – there are two identical pins on the south pylons – each 368mm in thickness and 4.2 metres long.

North Sydney

Before the harbour bridge established the necessary link between the city of Sydney and the north shore of the harbour, the only means across was by ferry. Although ferries of different types had been runinng to **Blues Point** for some time, the North Shore Ferry Company was established in 1861 to run a passenger service between Circular Quay and **Milsons iPont |9|** near the end of Alfred Street South. This service, together with services running to points around Lavender Bay, McMahons Point and Blues Point, catered for the bulk of the traffic crossing the harbour. Passengers at Milsons Point were met by trams which were hoisted by cable up the length of Miller Street.

Close to the spot where those busy ferries once discharged their passengers at the foot of Alfred Street South is the smiling face of **Luna Park |11|**, standing colourful and proud despite its changing fortunes in recent years. Like Coney Island in New York and Blackpool Pier in Britain, Luna Parks have been an Australian icon for years. Unfortunately an accident in 1979 in which some children were killed on a fun ride led to the demise of the original Luna Park in Sydney, and although it was restored

– and made bigger and better into the bargain – local residents fought a long and bitter but eventually successful court case to have it closed down. Although the cheerful clown's face has not lost its famous smile, it must be feeling desolate and unloved, not having heard the happy laughter of children enjoying its rides and sideshows for many years.

Walk along the paved walkway towards Luna Park and on the right is another well-known landmark – the **North Sydney Olympic Pool |10|**. In this popular pool many famous Australian swimmers have trained for Olympic and Commonwealth games from which they returned with medals and accolades, having established Australia as one of the world's leading swimming nations. The pool is getting old now although it is still used year round, often by recognised swimmers, and moves are afoot to restore it to its original condition. In winter the pool presents an unusual appearance as it is covered with its inflated dome to keep the air and water inside at a pleasant temperature. In summer, of course, the Australian sunshine takes care of that, so the pool loses its top and the surrounding terraces and patios become covered with family groups. Follow the walkway past the pool and onto the boardwalk around the fenced perimeter of ghostly Luna Park until it reaches the fringes of **Lavender Bay |12|**, where a footpath takes over and continues along the foreshore between gardens and small parks.

Originally called Quibree Bay, the Aboriginal term for fresh water, Lavender Bay is steeped in history as it is located directly opposite the site of the original Sydney Town settlement. Since access was solely by water, Lavender Bay became a busy centre of marine activity. The convict hulk *Phoenix* was moored here and gave the bay its first name of Hulk Bay. This was later changed to honour the boatswain of the *Phoenix* who settled ashore here. George Lavender later married the daughter of another notable waterman of those early days, Billy Blue, whose name is synonymous with many features on this side of the harbour, notably Blues Point, described later in this walk.

Follow the footpath around the foreshores of Lavender Bay to the point where a railway viaduct separates it from the parkland behind. Arches in the viaduct and wide flights of steps running up through the steep park provide access and bear witness to the many passengers who crossed from the city to this point when the ferry was the only harbour transport. **Watt Park |13|** was once the garden of an elegant residence noted for its fine English trees and island palms, many of which are still standing. It also had a good freshwater stream and in times of drought, barrels of water would be rowed over to Sydney Town and sold for five shillings each. A house at the head of this park, where the steps come down from Walker Street, was once the home of the late artist, Brett Whiteley. Another famous Australian artist, Norman Lindsay, also once lived nearby. Return to the waterfront and the ferry wharf at the head of Lavender Bay and continue on around the foreshore footpath. In the corner of the bay is a relic of the maritime industry that was dominant in this area in the early days. For over 100 years the **Neptune Engineering Company |14|** operated a major waterfront boat yard with its main base and slipway in this corner of Lavender Bay. The slipway is still in place and preserved as a memento of those bustling days. Walk out onto the sea wall to the left of the slipway and look to the right of the bridge across the kilometre-wide stretch of water to Walsh Bay where a panorama of old timber 'finger wharves' fringe the southern foreshores and evoke memories of the days when tall-stacked steamships – the lifeblood of the young colony – lined those wharves.

Return to the footpath and walk past the Neptune slipway, bearing right to a steep flight of stairs. The 57 steps are fairly demanding, although taken steadily can be handled by average walkers; they lead up to the corner of King George and Bay View streets. Follow King George Street up the moderate hill to Blues Point Road, turn left and walk into another era. Like Kirribilli, this area has escaped much of the high rise office development of the North Sydney CBD. The road itself is one of the few remaining original convict-made roads and is lined with fine old sandstone cottages, interesting street cafes and shops. Walk down Blues Point Road, noting the many and varied homes built in many and varied styles. Particularly

note number Nos. 89, 73 and 68 which somehow epitomise the character of this old suburb, while No. 45 is reputed to stand on the site of Billy Blue's old cottage.

Billy Blue was a prominent character in North Sydney's early history. Part West Indian, he arrived as a convict in 1801, but set himself up as a boatman, rowing passengers across the harbour in what was to become the first Sydney ferry service. His efforts were rewarded by Governor Macquarie in 1817 when he was granted 32 hectares of land on what is now known as **Blues Point |15|**. At one time his fleet consisted of seven boats plying between the point, then known as Murdering Point, and Millers Point at The Rocks. His eccentric behaviour earned him the nickname 'Commodore' which is carried on to this day in the Old Commodore hotel in Blues Point Road. The original hotel was built in 1848 by one of Billy's children and was managed by his son-in-law, George Lavender. Continue down the hill to the foreshore park where, on the east side of the point, a plaque marks the spot where the first cross-harbour steam ferry berthed in 1842.

Billy Blue's pioneering spirit has been carried through in more recent years by the Hegarty family, who have for years run a ferry service using old traditional wooden boats between Blues Point and Circular Quay. Walk around the waterfront towards the bridge where, from McMahons Point Wharf, either a Hegarty's or State Transit ferry will conclude the walk by returning you to Circular Quay.

The Bridge Climb

For those who are adventurous, enterprising and intrepid, unquestionably the most exciting of all Sydney walks is a climb over the arch of the bridge. In fact it is quite easy and well within the capabilities of the average person with an average fitness level.

The plans for the Sydney Harbour Bridge were first drawn up in 1921 and construction began in 1923. On 19 March 1932 the bridge was opened to pedestrian, road and rail traffic. The main span is 503 metres long and together with the approach span stretches 1149 metres. The deck at its centre is 59 metres above the sea level to allow the masts of large ocean going ships to pass under it, while the crown of the arch is 134 metres above sea level. The arch, which supports the bridge's massive 52,800 tonnes, rests on four steel pins at the base of the four 87 metre granite-faced pylons.

Because the bridge climb is different to the normal, ground level walk, there are some basic procedures to be followed before setting out. Behind the reception desk at No. 5 Cumberland Street is the briefing room where preparations for the walk are made. Each group is issued with a climb suit. This is rather like a pair of grey overalls, but made of lightweight showerproof and windproof material. It is important that walkers wear rubber soled shoes as PVC and leather-soled shoes are unsuitable.

It is obviously imperative that nothing is dropped from the heights above, so the only item that can be worn or carried on the walk is personal glasses — sunglasses or prescription glasses — which are secured by a lanyard. Hats are supplied, also with a lanyard, except in very windy conditions, as are gloves in cold conditions. All lanyards are secured to a ring on the zipper at the back of the suit; the whole process ensuring that nothing can be dropped while the walk is in progress. Cameras must be left behind although the exciting moments are captured by each team leader on digital camera and prints are available at the end of the walk.

The most important part of the equipment is the safety harness which is chosen to match the size and build of each climber. Each harness is made of strong webbing and secured by the team leader with a nylon tie cable which cannot be removed once in place, and has to be cut off at the end of the walk. To the safety harness is fitted the latch which secures each walker to the steel safety wire running the length of the walk and allows easy forward and backward movement and simple manipulation through corners and up and down ladders. This latch, once secured onto the safety wire, also cannot be undone and the only way of removing it from the harness is by cutting the strong lanyard which secures it in place.

In addition to all these personal safety factors, it goes without saying that the leaders of each team are highly skilled professionals, some of whom have spent time climbing in the Himalayas and other climbing epicentres. Permanent staff are positioned at key points on the bridge, to observe and report on any factors which might concern the climbers. Each team is limited to a maximum of 10 walkers plus one leader and leave at approximately ten minute intervals. The walk takes three hours and covers around 1500 metres.

The final stage of preparation involves the use of a simulator in which a section of the walkway is reproduced to scale complete with latches and ladders in order to create an authentic atmosphere for the team leader's briefing. A radio is secured on to each walker's harness so the leader can communicate with his team and provide a running commentary as the climb progresses. As part of the safety procedures, each walker is then breathalysed, at which point the instruction is completed and the walk begins.

First stage is very much at street level as the group walks through the office and down Cumberland Street from No. 5 to No. 1, where access to the bridge structure is provided. A number of security doors and staircases lead upwards to what is known as The Tunnel' — a walkway cut through the abutment wall of the southern approach span which leads out onto the eastern spar of the approach structure. This is where each walker's latch is clipped on to the static safety wire, and remains clipped on until the team returns to this point at the end of the walk. A single handrail provides support on the catwalk as the team walks along a spar beneath the roadway towards the southeast pylon then up stairs leading to the mezzanine floor of the pylon.

The vertical girder between the upper and lower arches of the bridge at each end is known as the King Post, and a near vertical ladder provides access through the road deck and upwards to the top of the King Post and the end of the upper arch girder — called the 'Chord' — at a point named Pitt Street East. At this point the team lines up for the main part of the walk.

Twin handrails and an easy gradient make the walk over the arch easy and no more demanding than a walk up a moderate hill, but the environment is totally unequalled by any walk at ground level. As the climb reaches the upper levels of the arch, the Pacific Ocean and The Heads are seen across the wooded promontory of Bradleys Head. To the south Botany Bay is clearly visible with its toy aircraft climbing from and descending into the toy airport, while to the west, seen over the spreading Sydney suburbs, is the hazy blue of the Blue Mountains as they encircle the Sydney Basin.

The girder that crosses between the two arch chords is called the Summit Transverse and reaches the epicentre of the bridge. The team make their way across the transverse and onto the mesh platform of the western arch and another pause to take in the unforgettable view. From here on it is all downhill as the procedures for the walk are reversed.

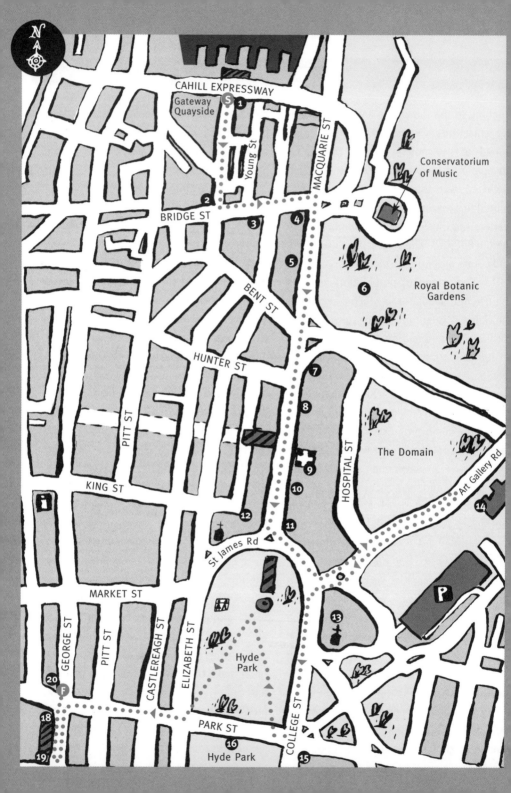

Central City
Historic buildings of the CBD

Start
Customs House, Circular Quay.

Finish
Queen Victoria Building,
Town Hall.

Length/Time
3 km/1.5 hours

Wheelchairs
Easy access along the
city streets but access to
some buildings may be
inhibited by steps.

There are few cities in the world with a history as recent as that of Sydney. It was little more than two hundred years ago that the First Fleet landed its cargo of convicts at what is now Circular Quay. For this reason it is easy to relate to those early days and relive the experiences of those first settlers. And where better to step back in time than in the buildings that marked their progress towards a new era. This walk takes in some of the early structures that were the foundations of what is now one of the world's prominent cities.

Walk key

1. Customs House | 2. Macquarie Place | 3. Museum of Sydney | 4. Chief Secretary's Building | 5. History House | 6. Domain and Royal Botanic Gardens | 7. Matthew Flinders statue | 8. NSW State Parliament | 9. Sydney Hospital | 10. Australian Mint Museum | 11. Hyde Park Barracks | 12. St James Square | 13. St Mary's Cathedral | 14. Art Gallery of NSW | 15. Australian Museum | 16. Hyde Park | 17. Sydney Town Hall | 18. St Andrew's Cathedral | 19. Queen Victoria Building

Start this walk at Circular Quay in front of the old **Customs House |1|**. When Captain Phillip landed the first white settlers here in 1788 there was nothing but bush and a good sized stream. The Tank Stream, as it was called, was one of the major reasons for selecting this spot for the new settlement as it provided water for the new colony and continued to do so until the 1830s when it was superseded by a bore in Hyde Park. The Tank Stream ran into Sydney Cove just a little to the west of Customs House and Governor Phillip raised the first flag on Australian soil close by. The head of the cove, including the Tank Stream, now lies at this spot beneath busy Circular Quay. The inhabitants of the cove in those early days were the Eora people.

Customs are a part of any port and the first customs service was commenced in Sydney in 1827. The original building on this site was a small, two-storey structure built in 1845 and additions were made in 1885 and again in 1930. The present Customs House stands out against other buildings on Circular Quay. Although dwarfed by massive skyscrapers, its Classical Revival style is eye-catching and the wide paved forecourt – depicting the original tidal zone – gives it an ambience of space and time. This fine old structure has now been refurbished to house a major cultural centre including an indigenous gallery.

From the Customs House walk up Loftus Street, to the right, and cross over to enter a small, open space. This park is dedicated to the women of Australia and includes plaques and memorials to the pioneer women and to those who served in the defence forces during times of war. The park, with neat grassy lawns and gardens, is named Jessie Street Gardens after one of Australia's foremost campaigners for women's rights. Jessie Street (1889–1970) was particularly noted for her involvement in the 1967 referendum to end discrimination against Aborigines. Cross over Reiby Place, also named after one of Australia's foremost women, to one of Sydney's most historic locations – **Macquarie Place |2|**.

Macquarie Place

This small, triangular square was once a sizeable park and was gazetted as public space by Governor Macquarie on land which once formed part of the gardens of the first Government House. Its importance lies in a number of features, principally the sandstone obelisk which can be seen near the southern corner.

As its inscription indicates, this obelisk was erected in 1818 by Macquarie to mark the point from which all public roads in the colony were to be measured. Also of great historic importance, and mounted on a pedestal on the opposite side of the square, is the anchor and cannon from the escort vessel *HMS Sirius*, arguably the most important vessel in the First Fleet. *HMS Sirius* was lost on the rugged shores of Norfolk Island in the early days of settlement, dealing a bitter blow to the struggling colony. The cannon had already been placed ashore in 1788 to serve as a signalling device; the anchor was recovered from the waters of Norfolk Island and placed on the pedestal in 1907. Of perhaps less significance, but still historically important is the domed gentlemen's lavatory built in 1908 and the statue to Thomas Sutcliffe Mort, one of the city's early industrialists. A small but delightful wrought iron drinking fountain dated 1857 adds a touch of Victoriana.

Bridge Street

The Tank Stream flowed along the depression just to the west of Macquarie Place and the bridge which joined east and west sides of the early settlement gave its name to the street which now displays some fine examples of Victorian civic architecture. Stand for a moment beside Mort's statue in Macquarie Place and take in the magnificent sandstone facade of the Lands Department building dominating this part of Bridge Street. Built of dressed sandstone between 1876 and 1888, it was previously the Judge Advocate's residence and the Surveyor General's Office. Walk up Bridge Street across Loftus Street and past a similar sandstone structure – the Department of Education building; both are fine examples of Victorian civic architecture. Now cross Young Street and a complete change of architectural styles can be seen on the right. Taking up the corner of Bridge and Phillip streets is a modern museum built on an historic site – the **Museum of Sydney |3|**.

This is one of Sydney's most important historical sites, for within the museum are

Opening Times

Customs House (Djamu Gallery):
Mon–Sun 9.30am–5.00pm. Closed
Christmas Day and Good Friday.
Museum of Sydney: Daily 10am–5pm.
State Library: Mon–Fri 9am–9pm.
Sat and Sun 11am–5pm.
State Parliament House:
Mon–Fri 9.30am–4pm.
Hyde Park Barracks: Daily 10am–5pm.
NSW Art Gallery: Daily 10am–5pm.
Australian Museum: Daily 9.30am–5pm.

Refreshments

As this walk is through the city streets there are numerous places where refreshments can be obtained, ranging from coffee and snacks to full restaurant meals. Water bubblers are located in Hyde Park and The Domain.

the original foundations of the first permanent Government House. Unearthed during excavations for a new office block, these valuable relics from the earliest years of white Australia's history are carefully preserved *in situ* in a museum dedicated to both the Aboriginal and white inhabitants of those early days. The initial Government House was a portable canvas structure that Captain Phillip brought with him in the First Fleet, but this leaked in the rain so in July 1788 he built the first permanent structure on the corner of Phillip and Bridge streets where the original foundations remain and can be inspected to this day.

Continue up Bridge Street across Phillip Street to two more fine examples of government building in the Victorian era. On the right is the **Chief Secretary's Building |4|** (formerly the Colonial Secretary's building) a Classical Revival structure, c.1878, designed by James Barnet and built in dressed sandstone. On the opposite side on the corner of Bridge and Macquarie streets is the façade of the former Treasury Building and Premier's Office, now part of the Intercontinental Hotel. Similar to the Chief Secretary's building in Classical Revival style and sandstone, the original building was designed by another well-known architect of the time – Mortimer Lewis. It was built c.1849 and added to in 1896. An imposing entrance with granite columns faces Macquarie Street.

Macquarie Street

From Bridge Street turn right into Macquarie Street and begin exploring a series of build-

Hyde Park Barracks, a gaol for nearly 30 years.

ings which trace Sydney's history back from colonial days to present times. Built in an extensive range of architecture styles, these have been designed by almost every Colonial Architect of New South Wales. The western side of Macquarie Street originally contained many elegant residential buildings, mostly three- or four-storey terrace houses which were used as city homes for wealthy families. Only a few remain and these have mostly been converted to upmarket club premises or retained as consulting rooms; the rest have been replaced by modern office blocks.

Walk up to No. 133 Macquarie Street to get a close look at one of these fine old residences, now called **History House |5|**. A fine example of a Victorian town house, this sandstone terrace with cast iron verandah and balustrades, characteristic of the mid- to late 1800s, was built in 1871. In the 1970s it was beautifully renovated by the Royal Australian Historical Society, the current occupiers. Next door, at No. 135, is a complete contrast in architectural styles. BMA House, built around 1929, is a 13-storey tower occupied mostly by doctors and surgeons; it is typical of a style of building popular in the 1920s. The tiled facade is decorated with Australian fauna and flora as well as medical symbols. Further along at No. 145 is another example of the elegant living of Sydney's wealthy in the mid-19th century. Now occupied by the Royal Australasian College of Physicians, the original Georgian structure was one of a group of five buildings built in 1848 and owned by John Fairfax, the newspaper magnate. It was two storeys high but was extended to four storeys in 1910.

The eastern side of Macquarie Street, from the harbour foreshores to Bridge Street, provides the 'lungs' of the city, as it has done since early days, with the delightful **Domain and Royal Botanic Gardens |6|**. These tracts of green space create an oasis against the tall towers of the CBD. Included in this verdant parkland is the Conservatorium of Music and Government House, both of which are covered in this walk. In the 19th century, when the Macquarie Street residences were occupied by private families, the lush vegetation of the Gardens and The Domain would have provided a magnificent 'front garden' and exotic foreground to the harbour vista seen from the terraces.

The Gardens end at Bent Street and now the east side of Macquarie Street takes on a different personality. Elegance and greenery give way to history, for many of the buildings along the next section were erected in the early days of settlement and the signs of convict labour are everywhere. Cross over Macquarie Street at the intersection with Bent Street and among the trees, a little to the right, is a statue of Australia's greatest navigator and the man who, between 1796 and 1803, literally put this continent on the map. The **statue of Matthew Flinders |7|** stands in front of the sandstone facade of what was once the State Library but is now the Mitchell Wing of the State Library. Look closely and behind Matthew Flinders on the windowsill of the library window is a bronze cat. This is Trim, faithful companion of the great navigator throughout his voyages, including the circumnavigation of Australia in 1802–1803. Trim also accompanied his master to prison on the island of Mauritius, but one day disappeared and was never heard of again. Matthew Flinders wished for a monument to perpetuate the memory of his cat, and Trim now remains forever close to his master under the shady trees of Macquarie Street.

The Mitchell Wing, although not as old as some of the adjacent buildings, was first built in 1906 and added to later. The facade of classical columns and steps which fronts onto Bent Street opposite the Royal Botanic Gardens, and the elegant dark panelling and multi-tiered gallery of the interior, tell of an era gone by. Among the exhibits in this fine library are Captain Cook's diaries and the navigation instruments used by Matthew Flinders. In stark contrast to this classical building is the contemporary glass and concrete styling of the new State Library – the next building along Macquarie Street – where banks of flickering computers leave no doubt that technology has caught up with Sydney's premier library. This modern building stands incongruously among a row of historic buildings, some of which date back to the earliest days of the colony.

Walk on past the new library and step back once again into the past. **State Parliament House |8|**, while perhaps far less elegant than many of Sydney's historic buildings, nevertheless has its roots set deep in the city's history. The original Parliament House was part of the Rum Hospital. Built by convicts labour and paid for with 'rum money', it was completed in 1817 and partly adopted for the use of parliamentarians of the New South Wales Government in 1829. An extension on the northern side provided a seat for the Legislative Council, but in 1856 the Council moved into a unique structure on the south side of the main building referred to as 'the Box'. It is unique because it is the only remaining example of a prefabricated iron building in Sydney today. Originally shipped out from England as a church for Bendigo, it was later sent from Melbourne to Sydney and dedicated as the Legislative Council Chamber in Macquarie Street.

Next along this historic row of buildings is the **Sydney Hospital |9|**. Once the central building of a complex group known as the Rum Hospital, this was not the first hospital in the colony but was built by Governor Macquarie to replace the totally inadequate structure located on Dawes Point. It opened in 1816 and was used mainly for the care of sick convicts, but when transportation ceased it became Sydney's first civil hospital. It was demolished in 1879 and replaced in 1894 by the current buildings which, because of the numerous additions and alterations necessary for a busy contemporary hospital, are considerably changed from the original. However, the Macquarie Street entrance hall, with its wooden panelled walls, pressed metal ceilings, marble floor, baroque carved stairs and stained glass windows remain as a striking example of the workmanship of that era.

Continue walking along Macquarie Street, to the next building, the Mint. This fine structure was originally the southern wing of the Rum Hospital. It was converted to the Australian Mint in 1853 and currently houses the **Mint Museum |10|**. It has a huge strongroom, where gold from the goldfields was once stored, and a superbly restored facade. Between 10am and 5pm you can visit the Mint and examine its interior and historic displays. The next building is the adjacent **Hyde Park Barracks |11|**, which has also been sympathetically restored to its original appearance. It too is now a museum. Designed originally as a gaol by the convict architect Francis Greenway, the three-storey barracks, surrounded by high sandstone walls, stand in elegant isolation.

Refreshments are available from a cafe in the gravelled courtyard and this is perhaps a good time to take a breather and relax in the magnificently restored old world atmosphere of Sydney as it was in the days of soldiers and convicts.

St James Square

Leave the stately iron gates and arches of the barracks and walk past Prince Albert, whose statue stands on its pedestal looking across Macquarie Street to his queen in **St James Square |12|**. Cross the road and walk past Queen Victoria's statue to another Greenway masterpiece – St James Church. In fact, Greenway would probably turn in his grave if he could see the present church; it has been subject to so many alterations over the years that the original architect would probably hardly recognise his work. The steeple, the eastern porches, the tower doorway and most of the interior have been altered, some additions as late as 1907 when a new pulpit, the south portico chapel and a number of Edwardian picture windows were completed. The Law Courts Building, which lies behind the church, is also an original much-altered Greenway structure.

From St James Square walk back across Macquarie Street and down the side of Hyde Park Barracks, past the Registrar-General's building towards the prominent landmark of **St Mary's Cathedral |13|**. But before taking in the cathedral, bear left around the face of the Land Titles Office and into Art Gallery Road through the old sandstone gateposts at St Mary's Lodge, which have stood guard at the entrance to The Domain since 1835. Ignore Hospital Road, which branches off to the left, and follow the main road through The Domain to the **Art Gallery of NSW |14|**, the Ionic columns of which bear a resemblance to those of the old State Library just across the park. This was an architectural style favoured in the early 1900s and one that was well suited to the sandstone so popular with builders in Sydney.

After a visit to the Art Gallery to examine both the permanent and visiting exhibitions, return through The Domain to College Street and back to the imposing structure of St Mary's Cathedral. Designed in 1865 by William Wilkinson Wardell, the man who also designed Melbourne's St Patrick's Cathedral, and with its facade bearing a striking resemblance to the west front of the Notre Dame Cathedral in Paris, the solid block form of St Mary's dominates College Street. Both the interior and exterior of this building are elaborately decorated and the twin towers at the western end are soon to be crowned with long awaited spires, some 135 years after they were first planned.

Continue down College Street to the **Australian Museum |15|** building, a solid structure that has been built in many sections and in fact is still not complete according to the original 1861 plans of James Barnet who intended the building to take up the entire block. Like so many large buildings in the central city area it was completed in stages and the final result is a composite of different eras and different architects. The Sydney Grammar School buildings, adjacent to the museum, suffered a somewhat similar fate. Originally designed by Edward Hallen in 1831, the north and south wings were designed and built by Edmund Blacket in 1857. The major feature of the buildings is the 'Big Schoolroom' in Hallen's building. For many years it was the only large hall in the colony and many important public meetings were held beneath its flat wooden roof. This was also the birthplace of Sydney University in 1853 and has been the home of one of Sydney's leading private schools ever since.

Walk back to the Australian Museum building on the corner of Park and College streets and cross over to **Hyde Park |16|**. Part of Governor Macquarie's plans to design a comfortable environment in which to live, the park was originally a practice ground for military exercises. A pleasant and relaxing digression can take in the statue of Captain Cook on the corner opposite the museum and the Sandringham Memorial Gardens to the right, with their memorial to King George V and King George VI in the circular floral gardens.

Continue past these gardens, bearing right towards the northern end of Hyde Park where the eye-catching **Archibald Fountain |17|** dominates the scene. Approached by walkways from all different directions, the fountain is Sydney's equivalent of Rome's Trevi Fountain and equally popular with tourists. It was erected by J.F. Archibald, a well known Sydney publisher, to commemorate the association between France and Australia in World War 1. In more sombre contrast, at the southern end of the park is the Anzac Memorial, which honours the memory of the Australians and New Zealanders who fell in two world wars and numerous smaller conflicts. Opposite Bathurst Street, on the western fringe of the park, is another link with overseas monuments, this time London's Cleopatra's Needle. Although similar in appearance, the Obelisk, as the Hyde Park version is called, lacks the romance and intrigue that surrounds the London monument. Indeed, although perhaps significant in terms of local history, the Sydney column has the rather undignified background of having originally been erected in 1857 as a vent for the burgeoning Sydney sewerage system!

A magnificent avenue of fig trees extends the length of the park on the main walkway between Liverpool and Macquarie streets, and elsewhere green open spaces with scattered trees provide relief from offices and shops for busy city workers.

After this digression, return to Park Street and follow it down to George Street. From the corner of George and Park streets note the group of three fine buildings opposite, designed and strategically placed to provide character and open urban space in the heart of a city becoming desperately crowded with high rise office buildings. In front of you and slightly to the left is **Sydney Town Hall |18|**, a Classical Revival structure that creates the focus of the group with a facade comprising decorative attached columns, the lower level in the Ionic order and the upper level in the Corinthian order. The exterior is dominated by the clock tower while the interior is capable of seating over 2,500 people and contains one of the most powerful pipe organs in the world. Until the opening of the Opera House it was Sydney's main cultural centre but is now mostly used for meetings, exhibitions and concerts.

Cross over George Street and walk to the left past the steps of the Town Hall to the main Anglican centre of Sydney St Andrew's Cathedral |19| which was built between 1837 and 1886. Designed in Gothic Revival style and constructed from Sydney freestone, it is located right beside an open square studded with plane trees. A recessed area with a wall fountain marks the location of the old Sydney burial ground. In those days this area was on the outskirts of the settlement, and was used as a cemetery between 1792 and 1820. In 1869 the graves were cleared to make way for the Town Hall. Despite the input of many different designers, the cathedral buildings have an overall cohesive and pleasant appearance, creating an interesting contrast with the massive skyscrapers that now surround it.

Walk to the front of the Town Hall and on the opposite corner of George and Druitt streets is one of Sydney's most beautiful buildings. Colloquially known as the QVB, the **Queen Victoria Building |20|** was built between 1893 and 1898 and is a fine example of Late Victorian Romanesque architecture. It takes up an entire city block and while the exterior with its copper dome is an eye-catching feature, it is the interior that creates most interest. Designed as a shopping/office complex with covered markets below, it has gone through many changes until superbly restored and reopened in 1986. Stained glass windows, cantilevered stairways and tiled floors are all part of the magnificent interior which attracts as many visitors as the up-market shops that now line the different levels.

The history of the QVB is the history of Sydney Markets. In 1893 a recession had just ended and many of the city's 450,000 residents needed work. A forward-thinking Sydney City Council decided to replace the 1820 George Street Markets, which had fallen into disrepair and been an eyesore for over half a century, with a new market building next to the Town Hall. The flamboyant structure with its extravagant exterior and sumptuous arcades was completed in 1898 and immediately became a focal point for the central city area.

After a chequered career which at one time saw it on the brink of financial ruin, and even talk of demolition, a complete restoration returned the QVB to its original glory and once again made it Sydney's most revered shopping centre.

Walk key

1. Robertsons Point |
2. Mosman Bay |
3. Curraghbeena Point |
4. Mosman Rowing Club |
5. Reid Park |
6. The Rangers (site) |
7. The Barn |

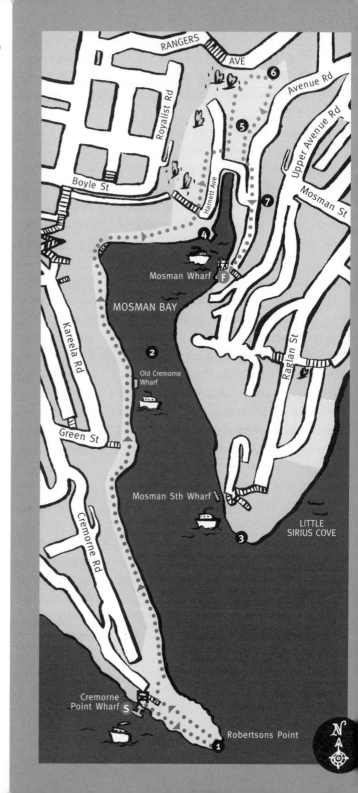

Cremorne to Mosman

An inlet steeped in maritime history

Start

Circular Quay ferry wharf.
Catch the Mosman Bay ferry.

Finish

Mosman Bay ferry wharf.
Catch the ferry to Circular Quay.

Length/Time

2.5 km/45 mins
(not including ferry trip)

Wheelchairs

Mostly good access with
a sealed footpath, but there
are a few short flights
of stairs in places.

As you walk along this foreshore track, it is not hard to visualise the old whaling ships moored in the bay with the smoke and steam and smell of the whaling industry swirling up over the high hills on either side. Tucked tightly into the head of the cove and well removed from the populated parts of Sydney Town, Mosman Bay was well suited to this obnoxious commercial activity. Some of the history of that early industry survives and can be enjoyed during this delightful foreshore walk.

Without question the most attractive way to approach this walk from the city is by water. The beauty of Sydney Harbour is legendary and nowhere is it better appreciated than from a ferry plying across the main arm of the harbour just downstream of the bridge. Head down to Circular Quay where most of the ferries leave for their scattered destinations and find which berth is catering for the Cremorne/Mosman run. As a general rule, they leave at half-hour intervals during the day although weekend timetables may change according to demand and the season. Information is available at the Quay as are tickets for the journey across.

The ferry run

Two of Sydney's great icons dominate the harbour scene as the ferry leaves the wharf – Sydney Harbour Bridge on the left and the Opera House on the right. The bridge is covered in walk 3, while the Opera House is included as part of walk 1. As the ferry pulls out of Sydney Cove the elegant residence of the Governor General – Admiralty House – is visible on Kirribilli Point. This magnificent sandstone building was one of the early mansions built on the north side of the harbour, and between 1849 and 1885 had a succession of wealthy owners. It was taken over by the British Admiralty in 1885 and, until 1913, housed fleet officers, mostly admirals. An Act of Parliament was passed in 1945 to establish Admiralty House as the official residence in Sydney of the Governor-General, although it had been previously used by both State and Commonwealth governments. Just to its right, also on Kirribilli Point, is the less grand but equally attractive Kirribilli House, residence of the Prime Minister when in Sydney. Both residences are surrounded by delightful gardens, possibly a legacy of the fertile soil of James Milson's farm which, in the early 19th century, supplied vegetables and dairy food to the visiting ships.

As the ferry sweeps around Bennelong Point and heads down the harbour, up ahead is a grim island sentinel that since the mid-19th century has guarded the approaches to the city. This is Fort Denison, more colourfully known as Pinchgut after the nautical term for a narrowing of the waterway, but known by the local Aborigines as the rocky islet *Mat-te-wa-ye*. This round, sandstone martello tower with its accompanying barracks was nothing more than a rocky island for the first forty or so years of settlement. It was used as a place of extreme punishment for incorrigible criminals who were banished to its treeless isolation without food or water and left to the mercy of wind, weather and the occasional passing boat that threw them food. In 1797 a convicted murderer called Morgan was hanged in chains on the island and his skeleton left for three years as a grim warning. This terrified the local Aborigines who associated the bleached skeleton with evil spirits.

The unexpected arrival in 1839 of some American warships triggered fears that the new settlement was not sufficiently protected against attack from the sea. During the 1840s the fort was built with sandstone walls 3.7 metres thick at the base and armed with a number of guns facing mainly down harbour. From 1906 a gun was fired at 1pm every day to check the town's clocks, but this was discontinued at the outbreak of the Second World War. Nowadays the fort is used mostly for recording tidal data and carries a navigation beacon on the top of the martello tower. It is open for inspection by guided tours and information can be obtained from the National Parks and Wildlife Service, located in Cadman's Cottage on West Circular Quay (see walk 2).

Cremorne Point

The only walking so far has been confined to the decks of the ferry, but Cremorne Point is the first stop and the starting point for the land side of the walk. Disembark onto the floating pontoon and walk up the ramp to the bus terminal at the top. Just to the right is a moderate flight of steps leading up to the footpath on Cremorne Point. Access for wheelchairs is via a road ramp off Milson Road some 100 metres or so to the left as you leave the ferry wharf. This ramp leads directly to the sealed footpath of the foreshore walk and from there on wheelchair access is fairly easy.

Before setting out on the main walk, make a small detour along the footpath which veers off to the right to **Robertsons Point |1|**, the official name for Cremorne

Opening Times

Ferry wharf shops: 8am–6pm.

Refreshments

Ferry wharf shops are located at Circular Quay and Mosman wharf. Water bubblers can be found at Cremorne Point and in Reid Park.

Point. This headland juts well out into the main reach of Sydney Harbour and offers superb views of the city, the foreshores and any activity on the water. Look back towards the CBD across Fort Denison and the Opera House. This is arguably the best angle on the city of Sydney as it creates an attractive vista with the greenery of the Botanic Gardens and The Domain around Farm Cove providing a natural and colourful foreground to the organ pipes of the city high-rise blocks stacked in an agreeable configuration up the hill from Circular Quay to the peak at Centrepoint Tower. This is a particularly good spot from which to photograph the city, especially at night, when the multi-coloured lights are reflected in the waters of the harbour.

Robertsons Point was named after James Robertson who was granted land there in 1823. His son, Sir John Robertson, became an important political figure serving as New South Wales premier on five occasions. Cremorne itself was named after the well-known parkland of Cremorne Gardens, in London, since one of the earliest developments on the point was a form of leisure gardens and amusement park for city dwellers. Ferries transported picnickers and revellers across the harbour where they enjoyed the pleasant ambience of the rocky headland with its natural as well as man-made entertainment.

Cremorne had a brief brush with industry when, in 1893, a viable coal seam was discovered nearby. Attempts to mine it, however, were abandoned after strong public opposition. A small lighthouse is located on the rocky foreshores as a navigation beacon for shipping moving up the harbour, while the neatly maintained grounds have a wide variety of native and exotic trees and shrubs which in turn attract numerous birds, notably currawongs. The point is a delightful quiet spot to sit and commune with nature and was popular with the local Aborigines who called the area *Goram-Bulla-Gong*. Apart from the relaxing nature of the headland itself, the eroded sandstone cliffs would have provided good shelters for them and the littoral zone was a major source of oysters and other marine foods.

After the short trek out to the point, return to the steps above the ferry where the main track leads off to the right towards **Mosman Bay |2|**. The path is fully sealed all the way and has only modest gradients in places with three short flights of steps, which should not make wheelchair access too difficult. It offers an easy walk even for unfit people and the entire length of the track is fringed by the rocky foreshores of Mosman Bay to the right and some interesting homes and gardens on the left. The bay itself is cluttered with yachts swinging to wind and tide on their moorings, all adding to the serene, relaxed atmosphere of a quite delightful waterfront scene. Some householders have extended their gardens into the reserve through which the path runs and in doing so have created an interesting mix of native and exotic flora. A plaque nearby recognises the

Yachts moor in Mosman Bay where whalers once careened their ships

beautification efforts of two local residents.

The walkway is generally very well cared for and makes for a very pleasant, leisurely stroll with no overhanging shrubs or rocky outcrops on the path, as is the case with many foreshore tracks. To the right the harbour extends beyond the moored yachts to distant Bradleys Head, which creates the dog-leg in the middle of the harbour and is covered by walk 6 page 61. On the other side of the harbour is the low lying suburb of Rose Bay which once formed the entrance to the harbour from

seaward until it gradually silted and formed a sand bar joining the island of South Head to the mainland. Further along the track the distant scenery is hidden by the high hill of **Curraghbeena Point** |3| guarding the entrance to Mosman Bay, originally named Great Sirius Cove because it was here, in 1789, that the flagship of the First Fleet, *HMS Sirius*, was careened. This bay is a deep, landlocked indentation in the harbour foreshores with steep, high sides, nowadays cluttered with a wide variety of residential buildings.

Mosman Bay

About halfway into Mosman Bay the footpath descends almost to the water's edge and steps lead down onto Old Cremorne Wharf. This is a regular ferry stopping point, and to the left steps lead up through the bush to the suburban streets of Cremorne, providing access through the reserve for ferry travellers. Skirt around a big rock just past the ferry steps and continue walking along the track towards the head of the bay. There may be a slight problem with wheelchairs here as there are a few steps to negotiate, but with a few willing arms – and there are always walkers along this track – these steps can be easily traversed as they are in short flights. The track continues past more gardens on the left, then descends to a point where a small stream runs down through a gully and into the bay. There are a few more steps here as the path swings to the right and across a small wooden bridge over the creek. A number of alternative tracks lead off to the left but these are merely access points and are of no interest unless you wish to cut short the walk.

Continue along the main track which bears right around the foreshores and into the head of Mosman Bay. First the track skirts behind a number of sailing and rowing clubs and although not visible through the undergrowth of the bush, this is the site of an old quarry which, in the mid-19th century, provided a great deal of the building stone used in major Sydney buildings. The sandstone wall which runs around Farm Cove and the Botanic Gardens (covered in walk 1) was quarried here and remains to this day as a testimony to both the stone and the stone masons of that time. The path leads past a marina which is established in the tight upper reaches of Mosman Bay and the famous **Mosman Rowing Club |4|**; haunt of many of Sydney's notable personalities, particularly those in the art world. The path then leads out into **Reid Park |5|** where an extensive open grassy area has been reclaimed from the mud flats and the creek that once formed the headwaters of the bay.

History is alive and well in this part of Mosman Bay. Walk into Reid Park and follow the old creek up through the high ravine to what were once the upper reaches of the bay. Just above the footbridge one of the first settlers in this area, Oswald Bloxsome, built a magnificent home high on the hillside and called it **The Rangers |6|**. He rowed across Mosman Bay, tied his boat to a rock now marked on the side of Reid Park, then walked up the path above the rock to his home. Rangers Road which runs from Mosman to Neutral Bay perpetuates the name now that the house has gone and Bloxsome's estate subdivided.

Although only four kilometres across the harbour from the CBD, the deeply indented bay with its high surrounding hills was, in the days of early settlement, far removed from the township in Sydney Cove. It was therefore an ideal location for less acceptable maritime activities where smell and noise were involved. It was here that ships were careened and repaired — the first being the flagship of the First Fleet — *HMS Sirius*. After the long journey out from England, her hull was in need of a 'shave and shampoo' so she was hauled over on the sand flats of the bay which was subsequently named Sirius Cove to commemorate the event. Whaling was another maritime activity that had unpleasant side effects, and in the early part of the 19th century the small northside bay underwent a change of industry as well as a change of name.

Sirius Cove was renamed Mosman Bay after Archibald Mosman who, together with his partner John Bell, acquired land in 1831 to set up a 'whaling allotment' with a stone wharf and a number of stone buildings on the eastern foreshore at the head of the bay. One of those buildings remains to this day and is believed to be the oldest surviving industrial building on Sydney's North Shore. Walk back from Reid Park across the head of the bay and follow the road leading down to the ferry wharf. On the left is **The Barn |7|**, as this building is now known, tucked hard up against the cliff. Mosman's whaling company prospered and at one stage the head of the bay was a hive of activity with stone storehouses, dwellings for ships' crews and a residence for Mosman himself. Rather than processing the whale products, the main undertaking was the repair and refurbishing of the whaling ships, for the sheltered bay was ideal for careening – the practice of hauling the ship over onto its side in order to clean and repair the bottom. Nowadays only the barn remains as silent witness to that pioneering venture.

With the harbour providing the only means of transport to and from the burgeoning city in Sydney Cove, it was obvious some form of ferry service was needed if the North Shore was to develop. The ferry to Mosman Bay began in 1871 and despite a number of failed ventures, to this day provides a regular service for commuters, residents and tourists. The present ferry wharf is close to the site of the original structure at the head of the bay, with two other jetties further downstream. There is a plaque commemorating HMS *Sirius* on the right and a few small shops adjacent to the main wharf. Here you can enjoy a well-earned rest and a cup of coffee after the walk from Cremorne and while waiting for the ferry back to Sydney. Children will find an attractive playground in nearby Reid Park and there are toilets located at the head of the ferry ramp. This is the end of the Cremorne to Mosman foreshore walk.

If you are continuing on to the next walk look across the road from the wharf and note the steep steps that climb up the hillside. That is the start of the walk between Mosman and Clifton Gardens and it is a tough call, so brace yourself for some energetic climbing. Otherwise relax and catch the next ferry back to the city.

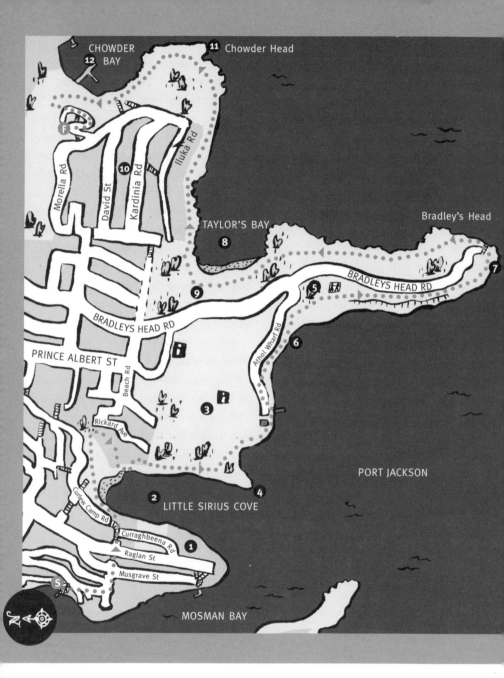

Walk key

1. Curraghbeena Point | 2. Little Sirius Cove | 3. Taronga Zoo | 4. Little Sirius Point | 5. Sydney Harbour National Park | 6. Athol Bay | 7. Bradleys Head | 8. Taylors Bay | 9. Ashton Park | 10. Clifton Gardens | 11. Chowder Head | 12. Chowder Bay

Mosman Bay to Clifton Gardens

Discover one of the most beautiful foreshores & Sydney Harbour National Park

Start

Mosman ferry wharf. A ferry from Circular Quay arrives at 30-minute intervals.

Finish

Clifton Gardens. Catch bus 228 from Clifton Gardens to Mosman Junction, thence any bus to the city.

Length/Time

6 km/2 hours

Wheelchairs

No access

Sydney Harbour has long been recognised as one of the most beautiful waterways in the world, but the full extent of its beauty can never be fully realised from a tourist bus, a ferry or a lookout. Only a walk around the foreshores through the Sydney Harbour National Park can reveal the enormous range of bush wildlife, the carpet of wildflowers in spring and the hidden sandy beaches that belong to a desert island, not a major city. This walk continues the foreshore track from Mosman, passing, as it does so, the world-renowned Taronga Zoo.

The first part of this walk is perhaps the most demanding and least appealing since far from plunging into unspoiled bushland it climbs up the steep streets and steps of **Curraghbeena Point |1|**, one of the encircling arms of Mosman Bay. The first flight of steps begins right opposite the entrance to the Mosman Wharf, so if you arrive from the city by ferry, walk straight up the ramp and across the car park to where the steps will be seen heading steeply upwards to join an even steeper road – Trumfield Lane. This is not a walk for the unfit or the elderly and quite definitely not for wheelchairs. Both the road and the steps are steep and Trumfield Lane winds up the hillside and continues into McLeod Street at a fierce gradient. Once at the top of this winding road, cross Musgrave Street and head for a red brick block of flats slightly to the left. A short cut runs between two buildings here; it is fairly obvious with a few steps and a concrete footpath leading across the crown of the hill and into Raglan Street on the other side.

This street, which runs along the ridge, is divided into two levels at this point, but wooden steps lead down to a short street, an extension of McLeod Street, and more steps wind down towards **Little Sirius Cove |2|**. It is all downhill now and a well marked footpath with steps ends at the attractive waterfront park known as Sirius Cove Reserve, which is mostly surrounded by bush and well suited to children as it has a small beach, a playground and toilets. For those who are not fit enough to make the climb over Curraghbeena Point, this reserve is a good access point from which to start the foreshore walk.

The foreshore track

The foreshore track begins on the eastern end of Sirius Cove Reserve. Walk past the toilet block and a few metres further on a path leads off into the bush on the left. Initially the walking is easy as the path is sealed and the gradients fairly modest. It follows the east shoreline of Little Sirius Cove through native bush that screens off the houses above and runs right down to the rocky foreshores of the bay, which is peppered with colourful yachts all swinging in unison to their moorings. There are a couple of flights of steps leading off to the left, but these only provide access from the suburban streets above. A little further on a timber house-like structure appears on the right; this is the local sea scout hall and is ideally located on the small beach fringing the edge of Little Sirius Cove. The Aboriginal Cammeraigal clan loved this area because of the abundance of shellfish in the sand flats of the shallow bay and wildlife in the bush surrounding it.

A few steps lifts the track to a slightly higher level where the stone boundary wall of **Taronga Zoo |3|** runs along on the left side for some distance. There is no public access to the zoo from the footpath although there are a couple of gates for staff. This is the maintenance section of the zoo and no animals are visible. Quite suddenly, the wall takes a sharp turn to the left and the footpath follows. But take time out here to digress, because a number of tracks lead off to the right. Follow the first down through the bush towards the foreshores along a track marked with posts and rope. Near the rocks of the shoreline where the track takes a sharp left turn is a plaque on a rock indicating the site of Curlew Camp. This was an artists' camp established during the late 1800s by such well-known Australian artists as Tom Roberts, Sir Arthur Streeton and Julian Ashton. Not surprisingly, it was once a favourite spot for these and other artists who set up tents on the foreshore to enjoy the pleasant atmosphere and capture the magnificent harbour scenery.

Return to the main track and a metre or so further on another track leads off to the right onto the bush-covered headland known as **Little Sirius Point |4|**. The frequent references to *HMS Sirius* in this area are reputed to have come about from her being careened in Sirius Cove (Mosman Bay) after her voyage with the First Fleet. The track out to the point is through native bush, although a few feral shrubs such as lantana have established a foothold. Tea tree, lilly pilly, coast wattle and melaleuca are here in profusion, as is pittosporum. Despite the introduced species, the bush here provides an ideal environment for birds ranging from rainbow lorikeets to willy wagtails, currawongs and even a few blue wrens. The path out to the point may be a little overgrown, but well worth pushing through to reach the excellent vantage point at the end.

Opening Times
Taronga Zoo: Daily 9am–5pm.

Refreshments
A kiosk is located at Mosman ferry wharf, and a kiosk and restaurant inside Taronga Zoo. Water bubblers can be found in Sirius Cove Reserve and Chowder Bay Park.

Return to the main path and yet another diversion to the right leads down steps to Whiting Beach. This white sandy beach almost totally surrounded by bush more resembles a remote spot on a tropical island than the shoreline of one of the busiest harbours in the Southern Hemisphere, with the CBD of Australia's largest city only three kilometres away. Being close to the zoo, wild birds of every description hang around in the foreshore trees hoping to glean a few scraps from the tables of their pampered relatives inside the zoo. Straw-necked ibis, pelicans and the ubiquitous seagulls are prominent among the wide variety of birds which, together with geckoes and the occasional frill-necked lizard, are constantly hovering around this beach and the adjacent bush.

Back up the path from the beach, turn right onto the main track again. Now the going starts to get a bit rugged. The sealed surface disappears, and although the dirt track is well constructed it might be somewhat boggy if the weather has been wet. However, it is normally quite accessible and makes for fairly easy walking even for unfit or elderly people although, of course, it is not for wheelchairs. At one point it descends steeply down the rocks to the water's edge and then climbs back up again with steps that are not difficult, but might try those who are a bit short of breath! It is just a case of taking it steadily and not overdoing the steep parts. In any case, relief is at hand, for soon after this rugged stretch the path levels out and reaches the ferry wharf, where it joins the main zoo road at the turning area where the tram lines once terminated. This spot became notorious as, unable to stop their headlong pace down the hill, trams frequently plunged through the barriers and into the harbour!

Taronga Zoo needs no introduction; the Aboriginal word 'taronga', meaning 'water view', says it all. This world-class zoo is built on the slopes overlooking the harbour; the stunning views can also be enjoyed from the foreshore track that runs along the lower zoo boundary wall. Originally located at Moore Park, the zoo created a sensation when it moved to Taronga by ferrying its elephants across the harbour on a punt! A visit to the zoo is a must, but since it is located on a fairly steep hillside, it is best to start at the top and walk down the slope through the exhibits. From the wharf a chairlift or bus carries passengers to the top of the hill and the main entrance. Access from the city is by direct ferry to the zoo wharf from Circular Quay or by 247 bus from Wynyard across the lower northern suburbs. At this point in our walk there is still a lot of ground to cover, so those who are feeling a little tired or would prefer to continue the walk at a later date can board the ferry or bus at the wharf and return to the city.

Sydney Harbour National Park

To continue along the next section, walk up the road from the ferry wharf until a path leading off into the bush appears on the right. This is the continuation of the foreshore track and runs through the bush of the **Sydney Harbour National Park |5|**, although the path is well cleared and creates no difficulties for good walkers. The terrain is moderately undulating although the track can get a little rough in places, but for walkers of average fitness it is accessible in most conditions. The bush here is typical of the Sydney coastal region with colourful angophora – the Sydney Red Gum – predominant among the larger trees, while coast banksias, tea tree, wattle and coast rosemary are the main shrubs in the undergrowth. In spring and summer the bush is alive with colour as scarlet bottlebrush flowers vie with a range of grevillea, golden glory pea, and the delightful native heath. Wildlife is also prolific here, with many small escapees from Taronga Zoo finding a pleasant bush home among local native wildlife. Sulphur-crested cockatoos are a common sight as are the ibis which fly in and out of the zoo all day – mostly at feeding time – while magpies, currawongs and wattle birds add their musical accompaniment to the bush atmosphere! All shapes and sizes of lizards scurry across the path or scramble around on the rocks.

The sizeable bay on the right is known as **Athol Bay |6|** and was for many years a major berthing point for laid-up naval ships. The ships and the jetties that serviced them have now been removed, as have the structures to which they were moored, but Athol Bay will always be remembered in naval history as the temporary anchorage during the Second World War of the majestic liners (then troopships) *Queen Mary* and *Queen Elizabeth*. In those days they were the largest vessels afloat and unable to pass under Sydney Harbour Bridge so they were moored in Athol Bay to await the Australian troops they would carry to various theatres of war.

After about ten minutes of walking the track leads out onto an open grassy area. This is **Bradleys Head |7|**, a grassy promontory which juts out into the harbour and divides the upper reaches from the lower, creating a dog-leg around which shipping must navigate. It is named after William Bradley who arrived in 1788 as a lieutenant aboard *HMS Sirius*. He assisted Captain Hunter in surveying Port Jackson, Broken Bay and Norfolk Island. His plan of Sydney Cove, now in the Mitchell Library in Sydney's Macquarie Street, is recognised as the earliest survey of the settlement cove.

In the 1840s it was decided to establish a military defence complex at Bradleys Head as part of a defence plan to counter fears of an invasion from sea. South Head, Middle Head and North Head provided the outer defences guarding the entrance, while Bradleys Head and Fort Denison were considered strategically important points around the harbour and a fortress established on each. On Bradleys Head the remains of the gun emplacements built from sandstone carved from the local rock are still in place, both on the headland itself and on the road above which runs along the ridge from North Sydney to both Bradleys Head and Middle Head. Because of the hilly terrain, the route for this road was originally chosen to create the most level path for the horse-drawn vehicles servicing the batteries. It was named Military Road and to this day provides the main traffic artery through the northern harbour suburbs. The old stone wharf on the headland is still in good condition, as are the gun emplacements themselves and the sandstone wall at the top with its rifle ports overlooking the approach road.

Bradleys Head is one of the best vantage points from which to watch harbour activities and when the weekend yacht races are in progress or when some well-known vessel is visiting Sydney, this promontory is crowded with sightseers. A tripod mast from *HMAS Sydney* is located right on the point over one of the original sandstone gun pits to commemorate that vessel's victory over the German raider *Emden* which she sank in the First World War, while in the water just off the headland is a stone pillar marking one end of the 'measured mile'. This is a measured distance of one nautical mile (1.852 kilometres) used for calibrating the speed of vessels on the water; the other end is the tower on Fort Denison.

The lower fortifications were never used for their intended purpose and in fact were stood down in 1888 and used only for training purposes. Having examined them, the upper battery can be reached by steps or a road leading up from the car park. Walk along the road to the point where it turns sharply up the hill. The continuation of the foreshore track is quite obvious, plunging once again into the thick foreshore bush. At the same spot a flight of stone steps leads down to a small but interesting beach on the edge of the harbour. This might make an interesting diversion and it is a prime spot for viewing harbour activities, but otherwise is of no significance.

Follow the track as it winds around the edge of **Taylors Bay |8|** through fine stands of angophoras and more typical Australian bush. This area is known as **Ashton Park |9|** and is also part of the Sydney Harbour National Park. The tall trees, many of which are different species of eucalypts, have been part of the foreshore scene for probably centuries, and create a very distinctly bush ambience with a wide variety of native shrubs and wildflowers – an ideal environment for the wildlife which is as prolific here as it is all along the foreshore walks. Every now and then a track will split

The city skyline seen from the foreshore track

off to the right from the main pathway and lead down to the rocky foreshore or to the occasional little sandy beach. Where the main track veers hard round to the left keep going straight ahead to a small headland where there is a rock platform with a seat, offering welcome spot for a brief rest and delightful bush and harbour views.

Clifton Gardens

Rejoin the main track and continue around Taylors Bay where signs of civilisation appear once again in the form of houses along the shoreline. A steep flight of steps leads off to the left providing access to Iluka

Street, **Clifton Gardens |10|**, and are of no interest unless you plan to cut short the walk at this point. Otherwise, follow the track as it leads in front of some quite large houses with attractive gardens growing right down to – and in some cases over – the path. The going gets a little rough here and in wet weather gum boots will be needed. But soon the track climbs back into bushland again as it rounds **Chowder Head |11|**. A track to the right is clearly marked and leads out to the extremity of this headland which is another fine vantage point from which to watch harbour activities. Be warned that the cliff is fairly high here and care will be needed if young children are present as there are no protective fences.

Other tracks lead off to right and left of the main path. Those to the right provide access to the rocky foreshores; those to the left lead back to Morella Road in suburban Clifton Gardens. The weathered sandstone rocks around this point provided excellent shelters for the Aborigines who first lived here, while the sandy bays provided them with an abundance of shellfish. At one time many middens bore witness to their feasts but these have for the most part disappeared or been destroyed, as have rock carvings that were reported to exist before the area became developed. Continue on along the main track which eventually ends in a steep flight of steps running down past houses and gardens to the foreshores at

Chowder Bay |12|. This spot will appeal to the young and young at heart as it is landscaped and laid out as a pleasant recreation area with a jetty, a swimming pool and a toddlers' playground.

Chowder Bay first caught the eye of an American whaling skipper, Captain Cliffe, when he anchored there and his crew made clam chowder on the beach. He was sufficiently impressed to purchase 15 acres of land and build a homestead which he called Cliffeton, from which the present name Clifton Gardens was derived.

Between 1863 and 1872 it was a popular picnic area with Sydneysiders and in 1885 was extended to include a swimming pool, a pier, a skating rink and a pavilion. Ferries brought crowds of inner-city residents to enjoy the open spaces, the beach and the bushland behind and apart from its attraction as an amusement centre, it became – and still is – a very popular family spot. Captain Cliffe's house, located on the slopes above the park, eventually became a hotel and well into the 20th century attracted weekend crowds. In 1967, however, the hotel was demolished and the park returned to its role as a quiet family picnic ground.

There is no regular ferry service from Chowder Bay, but walk up the steps or the road to a turning bay at the top of the hill where a 228 bus provides a service to Mosman Junction. From there, any number of buses provide a regular service to the city.

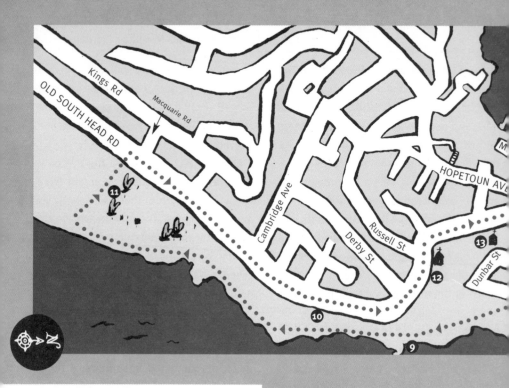

Walk key

1. Watsons Bay | 2. HMAS Watson |
3. Camp Cove | 4. Lady Bay | 5. South Head |
6. Hornby Lighthouse | 7. Naval chapel |
8. The Gap | 9. Jacob's Ladder | 10. Signal
station | 11. Macquarie Lighthouse |
12. St Peter's Anglican Church |
13. Our Lady of the Sea

Start

Watsons Bay bus terminal.
Take bus 324, 325 or L24
from Circular Quay.

Finish

Watsons Bay bus terminal.
Take bus 324, 325 or L24 to city.

Length/Time

5.5 km / 2 hours

Wheelchairs

No access to Camp Cove, but can be
bypassed. Access to South Head is
reasonable in most places. The Gap
walkway is very difficult due to the
steps, but these can be bypassed.

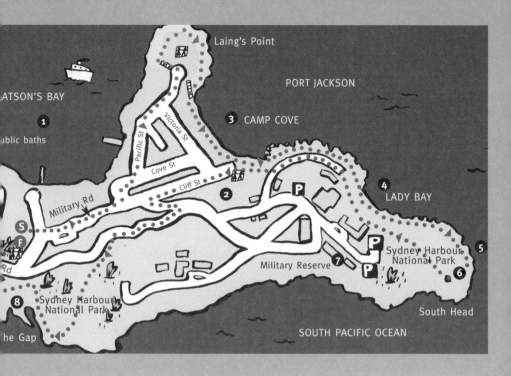

The Fortifications of South Head

Waiting for the enemy

Like North Head, the towering cliffs of South Head offer a perfect bastion for defending the harbour and the city against an attack from seaward. Between them, the pincer arms of these two high headlands have protected Port Jackson for well over two hundred years – through two world wars, several potential conflicts and innumerable scares. Yet neither of these fortifications have ever been tested in action. They do, however, make for an interesting walk in which to speculate on what might have happened had they ever been needed in their intended role.

Watsons Bay

The walk around South Head begins at **Watsons Bay |1|**, a pleasant little bay tucked under the headland at the far end of Sydney Harbour and named after the 1911 harbour master. Take the 324, 325 or L24 bus from Circular Quay and alight at Robertson Park at the terminus. This area, with its beach and stream, was once a popular meeting place for the Cadigal tribe of Aborigines who first inhabited it and who doubtless relished the food obtained from both the sea and the local bush. Today it is also known for its fine seafood restaurants as well as for The Gap – a high cliff overlooking the ocean and a favoured spot for suicides.

From the bus stop walk straight along Cliff Street towards South Head. On the right is the bush of the Sydney Harbour National Park behind which the first buildings of the naval establishment **HMAS Watson |2|** are visible. Turn left into Short Street, then right into Cove Street, then left again into Pacific Street, following these narrow, winding streets to Laings Point, also known as Green Point. This is a very old part of Watsons Bay as will be seen by the number of interesting old cottages along the way. The last house on the right at the end of Pacific Street is a timbered house partly clad with shingles and built in 1885 as the very first marine biological research station in Australia.

Take the steps to the right which lead down to the beach at **Camp Cove |3|** and on the left is a plaque which commemorates the first landing of white people in Port Jackson. Captain Arthur Phillip was dissatisfied with Captain Cook's choice of Botany Bay for the new settlement so he decided to examine Port Jackson, which Cook had mentioned in passing. Phillip's exploration party pulled their boats up onto this beach on January 21 1788, when they arrived to look for a potential landing site for the First Fleet.

South Head

Walk across the beach to the opposite side of Camp Cove and follow the steps up into a grove of coral trees. Here you will see a quite remarkable old cobbled road once used to service the military establishments of South Head. On the right is a wall fitted with gun ports to cover the possibility of a foreshore landing, while on the left is a large cannon, mounted in a gun pit to provide more powerful artillery.

There is a choice at this point of following the service road, which has now lost its attractive cobblestones and become sealed, or taking the footpath which winds around the cliff tops. The latter is obviously the more appealing, but is rather narrow and rough in places and would not be suitable for wheelchairs. It does, however, offer entrancing views of the water around the rocks beneath, and at times almost seems part of the old fortifications as low defence walls with gun ports replace the protective railings in places. About half a kilometre into the headland there are toilets, and a nearby steep flight of steps provides access down the cliff to **Lady Bay |4|**. This bay is a small indentation in the cliff line with about 100 metres of sand and superb clear water. Because of its isolation it became the first official nude beach in Australia when the government in 1976 bowed to public pressure and legalised nude bathing on two of Sydney Harbour's small beaches – Lady Bay and Reef Beach, near Manly.

Restoration and regeneration of **South Head |5|** has converted the once barren and unkempt headland into an attractive addition to Sydney Harbour National Park. Although there are still infestations of lantana and other feral weeds in places, native shrubs are springing up on either side of the walkway and converting the cliff top into a delightful arbour. Coastal species such as tea tree and banskia together with the bushy coastal wattle are replacing the exotic species and in so doing are attracting more native birds. An interesting transition is taking place at the very tip of the headland where thick lantana has for decades provided a secure shelter for a colony of blue wrens. The lantana is being removed in small segments and replaced with thick native shrubs in an effort to persuade the wrens to stay while at the same time removing the unwanted vegetation. Magpies are a common sight and, when the sun is out, lizards of different species can be seen scampering across the warm rocks.

Follow the footpath as it winds round the cliffs and at the very point of South Head stands **Hornby Lighthouse |6|**, which still provides a beacon to guide mariners through the Heads and into Sydney

Opening Times

Naval chapel: Inspection by special arrangement only.
Phone: (02) 9563 4444.

Refreshments

There are restaurants, bars and cafes in Watsons Bay and the surrounding streets. Water bubblers can be found in Robertson Park and Gap Park.

Harbour. This light came into being in 1858 as a result of two tragic shipwrecks – the *Dunbar* and the *Catherine Adamson* in the previous year. The painted sandstone tower is of classic lighthouse design with a light bronze balustrade surrounding the beacon. It was named after Sir Phipps Hornby who was commander-in-chief of the British Pacific Fleet in the 1860s. Adjacent are two sandstone cottages originally built to house the lighthouse keepers in 1858; both of these are being restored as part of the general preservation plans for the area.

Continue on along the track past a number of gun emplacements carved into the rock and built of local sandstone similar to those on Middle Head. These are located at strategic points around South Head, forming part of the total ring of defence around the entrance to the Sydne y port. The path curves away from the cliffs and completes the circuit around South Head by rejoining the roadway just above Lady Bay. Continue back to Camp Cove but on reaching the beach bear immediately left into Cliff Street and walk past more interesting old cottages, notably Nos. 12, 14, 15, 16 and 17, all of which are fine examples of weatherboard houses, mostly on sandstone foundations, common to the mid- and late Victorian periods.

Continue along Cliff Street to the junction with Short Street and on the left is a private road leading into the naval base of HMAS Watson. An interesting diversion at this stage is to continue into the base to inspect the **naval chapel |7|**, built as a memorial to the naval personnel who died in action. The east wall of this chapel is totally glass and the building so located that this glass wall frames the entrance to Sydney Harbour. Inspections are permitted at certain times; ask the gatekeeper. Otherwise take the fork to the right a few metres before the gatehouse. This leads past old military buildings including the officers' mess and married quarters which have been mostly restored, while a footpath leading from behind the white, two-storey officers' building joins the track which runs along the cliff tops over the infamous Gap.

The Gap

Walk back down the cliff top path and on towards **The Gap |8|**, well known to Sydneysiders as a suicide spot. Beneath the vertical cliffs, the rollers of the Pacific Ocean crash incessantly, providing a grim

Part of the fortifications on South Head

reminder to would-be suicides, that if the fall doesn't kill them the ocean will. The path follows the cliff line through the attractively landscaped native scrub of Gap Park as it climbs towards the higher cliffs behind Watsons Bay township. A lookout at the top provides another spectacular view of the cliffs. It was in the surging foam at the base of these cliffs that the sailing ship *Dunbar* came to grief in 1857. Unable to make the Heads, she was caught on a lee shore and driven onto the rocks in a gale with the loss of 121 crew and passengers. Only one survived and he was found the next morning clinging precariously to a ledge on the cliffs.

Follow the track across Gap Park, past remnants of more gun emplacements, until it climbs the hill and opens out into green lawn with the main road coming in from the right. This is Old South Head Road which follows the original road built in 1811 by 21 soldiers of Governor Macquarie's 73 Regiment who took only 10 weeks to complete the 13 kilometres from Sydney Town. Nearby is a cleft in the cliff down which intrepid rock fishermen would lower themselves on a rope ladder; the spot has become known as **Jacob's Ladder |9|** but is now no longer used and the ladders have long since been removed.

The track veers away to the left onto a coastal walkway, so follow this across the top of the cliffs where it leads past the **signal station |10|**, a four-storey white octagonal tower, convict built of sandstone in the 1840s. It replaced the first signal station established in 1790 – a timber structure which hoisted a signal flag, visible from Observatory Hill, in Sydney Cove, when a ship was sighted approaching from seaward. On 15 January 1793 a fire was lit on the cliffs at this point to guide the ship *Bellone* to safety as she lay off the Heads at night – the first recorded use of a coastal night navigation beacon in Australian maritime history.

Walk on along the track to more maritime history, this time the well-known and loved **Macquarie Lighthouse |11|**. This tall white tower is often credited to the convict architect Francis Greenway but in fact the present tower is an 1883 replica, by James Barnet, of Greenway's original lighthouse, although some remnants of Greenway's original walls remain around the structure. Macquarie Lighthouse to this day provides a beacon that can be seen 50 kilometres out to sea.

Continue past the lighthouse along the cliff top path to the open spaces of Christison Park. You can walk to the end of the park or follow the path to the right and rejoin Old South Head Road for the return to Watsons Bay. This gives a different perspective on Macquarie Lighthouse and the Signal Station, after which, instead of taking the path back into Gap Park, follow the road as it curves left and slopes down the hill. On the right is **St Peter's Anglican Church |12|**, a Gothic Revival chapel built of picked sandstone with a plain shingle roof completed in 1864, but with a loft and gallery added in 1939 to house an organ once owned by Napoleon Bonaparte. Keep walking down the hill and again on the right is the Roman Catholic Church appropriately named **Our Lady of the Sea |13|**. This is an American Romanesque structure, first built in 1910 but with a number of additions and alterations that have been made since then.

There are a few other interesting buildings along Old South Head Road as it turns down to the park and the bus terminus where our walk began. The Watsons Bay Hotel and Doyle's Fishermans Wharf offer welcome refreshments.

North Head

The island that became a headland

Start

Manly Wharf interchange.
Take a 171 or E71 bus from
Wynyard or Manly ferry or Jetcat
from Circular Quay.

Finish

Manly Wharf interchange.
Bus 171 or E71 direct to the city
or catch a Manly ferry or a
Jetcat to Circular Quay.

Length/Time

5 km/2 hours

Wheelchairs

Access to most parts of the
walk. No access to bush tracks
at Collins Beach and Fairy
Bower/Shelly Beach. These
can be bypassed.

North and South heads, the two bastions that guard the entrance to Sydney Harbour, were not always headlands; they were once islands. When rising sea levels at the end of the last Ice Age flooded the valley that became Sydney Harbour, the two headlands were surrounded by water. Time and tide, and a sand-moving phenomenon of the ocean known as longshore drift, gradually joined the islands to the mainland with sand spits. Nowadays, Manly sits astride the spit joining North Head; this walk takes in the interesting and changing scenery of this coastal promontory.

Walk key

1. Manly | 2. Manly Wharf | 3. Little Manly Point | 4. Collins Beach | 5. Quarantine Station |
6. North Fort | 7. North Head | 8. Fairfax Walk | 9. Parkhill Arch | 10. St Patrick's College |
11. Shelly Beach | 12. Fairy Bower | 13. Foreshore walking path | 14. Manly Beach

The walk begins in the heart of busy suburban **Manly |1|**, permanently established in the hearts of Sydneysiders as the holiday resort – in the words of the early advertisements – 'seven miles from a city and a million miles from care'. And it ends at one of the world's most famous beaches – Manly Beach – where, in 1914, Hawaiian Duke Kahanamoku introduced Australians to surfing. Access from the city is by bus, ferry or jetcat. All terminate at **Manly Wharf |2|** interchange, an interesting place to start the walk because here, on the beach immediately adjacent to the ferry wharf, is where Captain Phillip is thought to have landed in 1788, when surveying Port Jackson prior to bringing the First Fleet up from Botany Bay.

Phillip was impressed with the manly appearance of the Aborigines he encountered on the beach, and named the bay Manly Cove. He later had cause to rue his words, since on a subsequent trip to the area he was speared in the shoulder by one of them. Leaving the wharf interchange, turn right and walk along East Esplanade, past the fun pier and around the small bay crowded with moored yachts. The footpath leaves the water's edge at the sailing club and sweeps sharply to the left up Stuart Street. This is a modest gradient and runs through suburban houses over the top of the rise and down the other side to Little Manly and its adjacent headland.

Little Manly Point Park, which takes up the whole of **Little Manly Point |3|** and divides Little Manly Beach from Spring Cove and **Collins Beach |4|**, has an interesting, albeit relatively recent history. In 1883 a gasworks was built on this point to service Manly residents with an adjacent wharf for berthing coal-carrying ships. The gasworks was demolished when it reached the end of its useful life, but for many years afterwards the smell of gas was so strong that few people ever visited the area. In 1992 the site was deemed free of toxic fumes and converted into a waterfront park – an ideal spot for family picnics with an adjacent boat ramp for launching fishing or centreboard sailing boats.

After a stroll down into the park, walk back up to Stuart Street, turn right and follow it until it becomes a dead end. Leading off to the left is a small track which winds down through scrub to Collins Beach. While the walk so far has been suitable for wheelchairs, at this point the going gets too rough along the bush path and down steps, so those with wheelchairs wishing to continue to North Head – where the going is easy – will need to return along Stuart Street, turn right into Marshall Street and then right into Darley Road, which leads all the way to North Head where there is good access for wheelchairs.

Otherwise take the track down to Collins Beach, named after David Collins, first Judge-Advocate and Secretary of the Colony. It is a small, sandy beach prettily enclosed with bush where, although the exact spot is not known, Captain Phillip is thought to have been speared in the previously mentioned incident. Walk across the beach and a track into the bush appears on the opposite side. Follow this to the point where it joins a service road to the Police Institute of Management, a training establishment on the shores of Spring Cove. Continue along the road as it climbs the hill and bear hard right when it intercepts the main road. This road is the only means of access to North Head, so follow it until the next point of interest appears – the gatehouse for the North Head **Quarantine Station |5|**, about half a kilometre further on.

From the road, little can be seen of the group of buildings at Cannae Point (Inner North Head) that comprises the Quarantine Station, but they are one of Sydney's most fascinating historic features. Situated at the opposite end of the harbour, well away from the settlement, and buried deep in bush with no access other than by water, this was the ideal spot at which to quarantine new arrivals and thus protect the infant colony from the epidemics which periodically swept the Old World. Ships entering the harbour through the heads could be run into Quarantine Bay without coming anywhere near the settlement in Sydney Cove, and infected passengers and crew could be off-loaded and kept at a safe distance until they were cured. A permanent quarantine station was established on the headland in 1832 and relics of the many ships and people who had the misfortune to be isolated there can be seen to this day. Some 1500 rock engravings tell of an era when sailing ships

Opening Times

Quarantine Station: Guided tours only, enquire at the gatehouse or phone (02) 9977 6522.
North Fort & Artillery Museum: Sat, Sun and public holidays 12–4pm.

Refreshments

Cafes, restaurants, bars and hotels can be found along Manly Corso, The Esplanade and in many side streets. There are water bubblers on East Esplanade, in Little Manly Point Park, in Shelly Beach Park and along Manly Esplanade.

brought thousands of immigrants to the new land. The nearby, isolated burial ground holds the remains of those that made the journey but succumbed before they reached the town.

The hospital wards, the shower blocks and the disinfection rooms all carry a haunting aura of tragedy and suffering despite the fact that the setting is idyllic. Coming from the dark alleys of working class suburbs in England and Europe, many of the inmates here must have thought they had found heaven, with free food and accommodation in a location that could rival any millionaire's resort of today. The crystal clear water and sparkling sandy beaches, the stone jetty and the shell-encrusted rocks were quite a deceptive introduction to the squalor and hard work that awaited many of them when they were released into the harsh new colony.

The station remained in service until 1984, when one of the last major groups to be housed there were the passengers and crew of a jetliner who were quarantined as a result of a cholera scare on their flight. Today this very important historic feature is being faithfully restored. It is not open to the general public due to the fragile nature of the site but guided tours are arranged daily and there is a 'ghost walk' on certain nights when the tours encompass some of the more 'spooky' aspects of the station. Information about the Quarantine Station and the surrounding national park can be obtained from the National Parks and Wildlife Service in the gatehouse at the entrance.

View from North Head down Sydney Harbour to CBD

North Head

Continue along the road which runs through high stands of coastal scrub, mostly wattle, banskia and tea tree. Here the wildlife is prolific as the bush to the right runs down over the wide headland to the cliffs and rocky foreshores of **North Head |7|**. Lizards, bandicoots, bush rats, monitors and often a few foxes and rabbits appear here in summer, while many small bush birds flit in and out of the banksias. Wildflowers are not so prolific, possibly due to the constant salt-laden wind which drives over the headland directly from the ocean. But there are many varieties of grevillea and acacia in places across the undulating plateau of the headland which was severely burned out in a bushfire in the early 1990s. On the opposite side of the road is the now mostly disused Artillery Barracks.

After a further kilometre walk along the bush-lined road, the sandstone walled entrance to historic **North Fort |6|** appears on the left. Designed as the key fortification in Sydney's outer ring of defence, this military establishment was located in a commanding position to prevent unwelcome visitors from entering the harbour. The fort was built in 1938 and contained two 9.2 inch (23.4 cm) guns with a range of 26.5 km – capable of hitting an enemy as far away as Broken Bay to the north and the Royal National Park to the south – a formidable deterrent to any potential attack on Sydney from seaward. Together with similar fortifications on South and Middle heads, it controlled not only the water between the heads, but also the lower reaches of the harbour and the sea lanes of the eastern approaches. It is no longer used for its intended purpose but is retained as part of the nation's heritage estate and as a tourist attraction.

The Royal Australian Artillery Museum, which contains army exhibits reflecting the part the artillery has played in conflicts all over the world, is located within the walls of the fort, while an observation platform provides one of the most spectacular panoramas of the city and its harbour as well as the ocean and coastline to the north and south. A nearby monument is dedicated to all who played a part in the 'defence of Sydney' during the Second World War.

Return through the gate of North Fort and walk to the left along the scenic driveway that runs out to the car parks on North Head. The road terminates here but a footpath leads off towards the cliff edge where a lookout provides views across the almost two kilometre entrance to the harbour. From here the sandstone cliffs of South Head can be seen stepping out to sea in a series of rugged headlands that defy the constant battering of the ocean and protect the 'finest harbour in the world', as Captain Phillip described Port Jackson when bringing the First Fleet into Sydney Harbour. Over 100 metres below, at the foot of the sheer cliffs, the ocean surges restlessly, as though waiting for a victim to plunge over. And indeed, North Head, like most high cliffs, has seen its share of victims. In one incident, several decades ago, a young girl standing near the unfenced edge was lifted over by a sudden breeze which turned her skirt into an ineffective parachute. Murder-suicides with people driving their cars over the edge were not uncommon until fences were erected. And a young pilot once flew his light aircraft directly into the cliff as a unique but effective way of ending his life.

The track to the lookout is part of a circular walk known as the **Fairfax Walk |8|** which leads around the top of the cliffs to another lookout with equally spectacular views of the ocean and coastline. It offers easy walking through the clifftop scrub and also has easy wheelchair access. This is the outermost point of the walk, but there are still many interesting features to come, so follow the scenic road back past North Fort and the Quarantine Station to the arched sandstone gateway named the **Parkhill Arch |9|** after a local councillor who became a Federal minister. To the right a rough road leads off in the direction Blue Fish Point – not accessed by an official track but a spot loved by rock fishermen. At the time of writing this track was still closed as the sewage treatment plant blocks access to Blue Fish Point.

There probably will one day be a walking track that takes in Blue Fish Point and returns directly to **Shelly Beach |11|** along the north face of North Head, but since a number of government authorities are involved – notably the National Parks and Wildlife Service, Sydney Water and Manly Council – it is hard to visualise any substantial work being done for some years to come. To give credit where it is due, Manly Council have constructed a walking track from Shelly Beach to a rock lookout high on the north side of the headland, which is at least a start towards providing a track which would totally circumnavigate North Head, thereby creating one of the most spectacular walks on the north side of the harbour.

Shelly Beach

Continue down Darley Road from the arched gateway past Manly Hospital on the left and the magnificent building of **St Patrick's College |10|**, now the International College of Tourism and Hotel Management, on your right. This superb example of Gothic Revival architecture has long been a dominant feature of the Manly scene as its location on North Head makes it visible from some distance up the coast. Fine old sandstone walls on the left enclose St Paul's College behind which the bushland leads down to Collins Beach. Take a right into Vivian Street, left into Fairy Bower Road and right again into College Street as you follow the boundary of the tourism college down to Bower Street. Turn right and walk along the road around Shelly Beach Park until you reach the car park and coastal lookout on the cliffs. The view across to the northern beaches can be quite spectacular, particularly if a big sea is running. This is a favourite surfing spot and surfers risk their necks to ride the sensational waves directly beneath these cliffs, providing spectators at the lookouts with exciting, breathtaking action. Many of the legends of Australian surfing have developed their skills on these waves.

Follow a well-built path back up the hillside from the car park and enjoy even more spectacular views of the coastline from rock platforms set high up in the bush-covered headland. Then return to the car park and follow a similarly constructed path down to the promontory of **Fairy Bower |12|**. Apart from the views of Manly and more surfing action, this footpath provides an interesting variety of bush life on its circular tour of the headland that encloses the delightful bay of Shelly Beach. The path returns to the beach, where it joins the sealed **foreshore**

walking path |13| around the rocks past restaurants and cafes, where a welcome cup of coffee can be obtained before completing the walk at **Manly Beach |14|**. A short digression here is well worth while to take in one of Sydney's most famous beaches. Manly Beach comprises three separate sections although all three are part of the one beach. South Steyne is the southern end of the beach, North Steyne the central area and Queenscliff the northern corner. Huge crowds attracted to the delights of the beach made patrolling and lifesaving activities unmanageable, so each of the three sections has its own surf life-saving crews with separate clubhouses and equipment. In summer the waves, considered to be among some of the finest in the world, attract surfers from all parts of the globe, and international contests are an annual part of the surfing scene. In recent years the acceptance of beach volleyball as an Olympic event has resulted in volleyball courts, being established at South Steyne. A stroll along Manly's waterfront is a fine way to wrap up a pleasant walk around North Head.

To return to the city, walk across The Esplanade to The Corso, which leads to the ferry wharf and bus interchange.

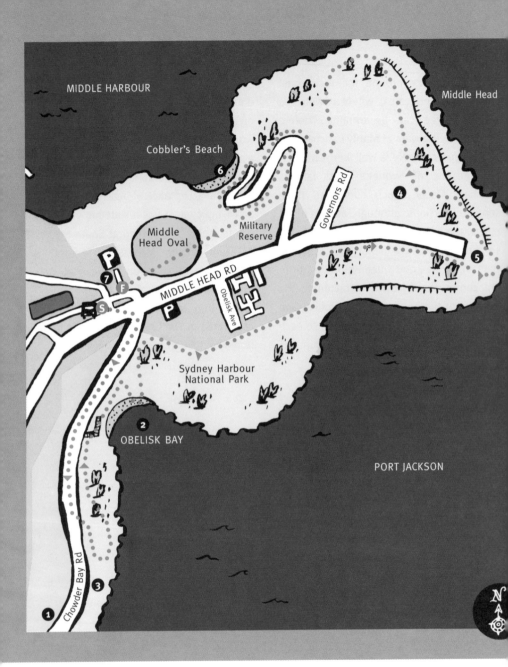

Walk key

1. Chowder Bay Army base | 2. Obelisk Beach | 3. Historic gun emplacements |
4. Middle Head | 5. Middle Head defence battery | 6. Cobblers Beach | 7. Naval hospital

Middle Head

Sydney's original first line of defence

Start

Balmoral Naval Hospital.
Take bus 244 from Wynyard.

Finish

Balmoral Naval Hospital.
Take bus 244 to the city.

Length/Time

2 km/45 mins

Wheelchairs

Road access to gun
emplacements on Chowder
Bay Road. No access
to Middle Head.

Middle Head is a high bastion at the entrance to Sydney Harbour, strategically located inside the protective arms of North and South heads. Small wonder, then, that it became a major feature in early Sydney's defence fortifications, for no ship could enter the harbour from seaward without passing directly under the guns on this headland. In the mid-1800s there was a perceived threat of invasion by the Russians and a series of forts and fortifications were hastily erected to counter the potential danger. Middle Head, with its unlimited field of fire covering the entrance to the harbour, was the focal point. This walk takes a look at these quite remarkable fortifications.

Middle Head was only one of a number of strategic points around Sydney Harbour to be equipped with gun emplacements. Others included Bradleys Head (described in walk 6), North Head (walk 8) and South Head (walk 7) as well as the island fortress of Fort Denison (Pinchgut).

An unintended but worthwhile legacy of those early fortifications is the natural bush and open space that surrounds most of them since for over a century these areas were sealed off by the military and out of bounds to the public. Now these almost untouched foreshore reserves form part of the Sydney Harbour National Park and offer some of the finest bushwalks in the metropolitan area. Currently the best route starts from the Balmoral Naval Hospital, which can be reached by bus 244 from Wynyard, in the city.

From the bus stop at the gates of the naval hospital, cross the road and bear right onto a sealed access road leading back along the foreshores towards the city. This leads to the army base at **Chowder Bay** |1| about one kilometre along one of the most delightful foreshore roads around the harbour. It runs along the cliff top above **Obelisk Beach** |2| with superb views out to sea through the heads, across to South Head and Camp Cove and along the south side of the harbour to Rose Bay and Point Piper. After about half a kilometre along this road look for concealed concrete structures in the bush on the left. These are some of the **historic gun emplacements** |3|

now almost overgrown and well hidden among the native vegetation.

A fairly obvious track leads off the road to the left and runs along the top of the cliffs across the face of the gun ports. Follow this path and discover not only the fortifications but also the delightful natural bush with its associated wildlife. The gun battery is a maze of tunnels and trenches cut into the sandstone rock linking excavated dugouts, magazines and gun pits. The guns were located inside hollowed-out rock cavities with the ports through which they were fired appearing merely as holes in the rock. The result from the outside was excellent natural camouflage which rendered the gun positions virtually invisible to an enemy entering the heads. The bush which surrounds and covers them added even more natural camouflage. Indeed, the guns were so well concealed it was necessary to cut away some of the surrounding bush in order to obtain a clear line of fire!

In complete contrast to the background of guns and war is the total peace and quiet of the native bush. Mostly untouched by humans, it extends across the hillside behind the gun emplacements with a wide variety of coastal species. The larger trees include angophoras and scribbly gums with wattle, tea tree and pittosporum providing a thick undergrowth beneath the canopy. In the sunny clearings lorikeets, wattlebirds and magpies chatter in the trees, while the constant music of water lapping against the rocks on the foreshore creates the perfect background.

Having examined the fortifications, walk back along the foreshore road, where a couple of tracks on the right lead down to Obelisk Beach. Just opposite the road junction outside the naval hospital gates is a natural car park set among a fine stand of eucalypts. Obelisk Bay is a delightful sandy cove tucked into an indentation on the rocky foreshore and completely encompassed by bushy hillsides. It is totally secluded and for this reason has become popular with nudists. The tracks down to the beach are steep and unmade and can be tricky to negotiate after rain as the path can become slippery. But the effort is well rewarded for once on the white sand you could be a million miles from anywhere, certainly not a few kilometres from a major city.

The road itself continues out to Middle Head but at the time of writing, this road was closed as it passes through a government establishment (AUSAID). However, there is access to Middle Head by footpath on either side of this complex. Probably the best route lies through the car park and the eucalypts on the right. Walk through this car park, which can be a bit muddy after rain, and along a track running beside the cyclone wire fence that encloses the buildings; a nearby sign indicates the route to Middle Head. Follow this path around the cyclone fence to a right-hand fork with a sign which says 'Obelisk', indicating a track down to the navigation beacons known as obelisks which gave the beach its name. The track here is very rough,

Opening Times

Sydney Harbour National Park:
Daily 5am–10pm.
Guided tours of the fortifications by arrangement. Phone (02) 9977 6229.

Refreshments

Water bubblers are located in the sports oval adjacent to Balmoral Naval Hospital. The kiosk is open if there is a sports event in progress.

winding down steep, rocky slopes and in places through dense bush; it is probably not really worth the effort, as the two obelisks can be seen from other viewpoints more comfortably.

Numerous other small tracks lead off to the right through thick bushland, but most of these only lead to the rocky foreshore below and are used mainly by fishermen. Like the obelisk paths, these tracks are unmarked, steep and overgrown, and it is easy to get lost or sustain injury in scrambling down them. Since they only lead to cliffs and rocky shorelines there seems little point in following them unless you intend fishing from the rocks and that, too, is a dangerous exercise! Also nearby is a blockhouse which during the Second World War controlled the western end of an anti-submarine net that stretched across the harbour to a similar blockhouse at Camp Cove (see walk 7).

The track continues along the cyclone wire fence until it has circled the government buildings, then rejoins the road coming out of the government establishment, where it divides at a fork. Bear right at this fork in the road. After passing through a barrier, continue along the right hand road towards the headland; the fortifications soon become visible to the right in a clearing on **Middle Head |4|**.

An 1877 gun emplacement on the cliff top

Fortress Sydney

The first section of the huge **Middle Head defence battery |5|** is a raised fort with two major gun platforms facing directly towards the heads. The guns mounted on these platforms would have been of the calibre of those located at North Fort on North Head and capable of engaging enemy ships well out to sea.

An intricate system of tunnels, magazines and shelters is built beneath the fort which is topped by a low control tower and other structures required to operate a totally self-contained and efficient fortification. Other sections of the battery are located at different points nearby, some with concealed gun posts, others with shelters, some even halfway down the 60 metre cliffs where light armaments and searchlights were located. Indeed, the whole headland bristles with gun emplacements. In the event of an invasion from sea, this headland would have been Sydney's front line fortress but fortunately such an invasion never occurred.

After inspecting the main fort structure, bear to the left and walk out onto the grassy headland where one of the more spectacular and certainly more interesting of the fortifications is located. Teetering on the edge of a high cliff, with the ocean pounding the rocks below, is a stone, circular gun pit which must have been one of the earliest installations of the battery. It has the royal insignia 'VR' etched into a circular niche in the stone with the date 1877. Adjacent to it, steep stone steps lead down through a cutting and straight over the cliff to service other gun emplacements set into the cliff face below. This hair raising path is closed off by a steel grille door, but just looking through the steel bars is sufficient to induce a severe attack of vertigo in anyone nervous of heights.

Rumour has it that the dark, damp tunnels carved into the sandstone of this headland were used during the Korean War to train soldiers to withstand the particularly vicious forms of brainwashing used by communist forces on their prisoners-of-war. Locals, particularly fishermen, talk of groans and screams echoing out from the caves and tunnels in the cliff face. At a number of places across the top of Middle Head, especially around the circumference, grille-covered holes appear in the ground at intervals; these are ventilation shafts for the tunnels in the sandstone.

Keeping the main battery on the left, walk back across the headland and veer right into the far corner of a clearing where a track into the bush is readily visible. Now the natural side of Middle Head takes over, for the headland here is cloaked with a wide range of scrub including coast wattle, tea tree, pittosporum and melaleuca. A community of ravens is usually in evidence here, together with lorikeets and magpies, while native mynahs and honeyeaters swirl around the bushes looking for nectar and insects. On a hot summer's day, lizards of all sizes and shapes scuttle from under your feet as you cross a hot rock. The path weaves its way through the bush to the west corner of the headland, where more gun emplacements appear on the right, both at the top and fixed precariously into the face of the cliff below.

Turn left at the T intersection with another track and continue through more native bush until the path comes out into the open again, this time at the corner of Govenor's Road (sic) and Battery Road, where a few of the cottages from the days of army occu-

pation are located. Walk past these towards a group of coral trees where a rough vehicle track leads down to the right; the sign indicates this is the way to **Cobblers Beach |6|**. Walk down this track through native trees and coastal bush badly infested with lantana and other introduced species until it opens out on another delightful cove similar in many respects to Obelisk Beach on the opposite side of the headland.

Like Obelisk Beach, Cobblers Beach has become a favourite spot for nudists, most of whom arrive by boat. Less exposed to the open sea and ocean winds, the cove is ideally suited for anchoring and the clear water makes for good snorkelling as well as swimming. The bush-covered slopes behind make it very secluded; despite the nudists, Cobblers Beach is popular with families.

Return up the track from Cobblers Beach to the cyclone fence surrounding the buildings of the AUSAID establishment and bear right along this fence. As with the track out to the headland, the track back follows the fence, but it is more overgrown on this side, and it may be necessary to push through high grass and weeds. Eventually the track reaches a sports oval adjacent to **the naval hospital |7|**, and a gate in the perimeter fence allows access to the playing fields. This oval doubles as a landing pad for naval helicopters bringing patients to the hospital. Walk across the oval towards the hospital where bus 244 provides transport back to the city.

PORT JACKSON

Vaucluse Point

13

SHARK BAY

VAUCLUSE BAY

10

Steel Point

9

12

14

Greycliffe Av

Coolong Rd

Fitzwilliam Rd

Wentworth Rd

11

Olola St

15

Milk Beach   **7**

8

VAUCLUSE RD

Carrara St

HOPETOUN RD

Hermit Point

6

5

4

3

NEW SOUTH HEAD RD

Clairvaux Rd

2

ROSE BAY

VAUCLUSE RD

Bayview
Hill Rd

1

F

Towns Rd

S

Rose Bay & Nielsen Park

Stately homes of Sydney

Start

Bayview Hill Road, Rose Bay, across from the Sacred Heart Convent School. Take bus 324, 325 or L24 from Circular Quay and alight at the school bus stop.

Finish

Sacred Heart Convent School, Rose Bay. Take bus 324, 325 or L24 to the city.

Length/Time

4.5 km/1hr 45 mins

Wheelchairs

No access to the foreshore walk. There is access via the road into Nielsen Park and around Vaucluse House. The steps up from Vaucluse house must be bypassed.

Despite its rugged beginnings, it took only a few years for the new settlement at Sydney Cove to develop its own breed of gentry. Wealthy merchants and entrepreneurs, isolated from the social lifestyle of their native European countries, set about creating an equivalent society in Australia. Large, elegant homes set in extensive estates began to appear around the fringes of the new colony, some of which survive to this day. The Heritage Walk takes in two of the best known – Greycliffe House and Vaucluse House – and passes a few others, as well as providing an interesting stroll along the harbour foreshores.

Walk key

1. Sacred Heart Convent School | 2. Rose Bay | 3. Queens Beach | 4. Shark Island | 5. The Hermitage | 6. Hermit Bay | 7. Milk Beach | 8. Strickland House | 9. Steel Point | 10. Shark Bay | 11. Nielsen Park | 12. Greycliffe House | 13. Vaucluse Point | 14. Vaucluse Bay | 15. Vaucluse House

The eastern suburbs of Sydney have always been known for their luxurious homes and affluent residents. Here there are also delightful, clean sandy beaches, green foreshore parks and views to die for. One of the most rewarding ways to take in this impressive lower harbour area is along the Heritage Walk, a few minutes by bus from the city but another world in terms of scenic delights.

Rose Bay

Catch a 324, 325 or L24 bus from Circular Quay and alight at Bayview Hill Road, adjacent to the **Sacred Heart Convent School |1|**. This prominent five-storey building is located in a prime position overlooking the harbour and city from the high slopes of Vaucluse. It was built in 1888 of sandstone quarried on the site and incorporated the original house Claremont, which was built in 1852. The Gothic Revival chapel with its ribbed, panel-vaulted stone roof is considered by experts to be an outstanding feature of the complex.

Walk down Bayview Hill Road to the bottom, where a clearly marked footpath leads off into the bush along the foreshores of **Rose Bay |2|**, once the preserve of the Cadigal people, who used the rock overhangs for shelter and the tidal rocks and sand flats as a source of food.

The going is easy along a dirt track with a few steps here and there which would prevent wheelchair access but otherwise they are not too demanding even for elderly walkers.

For the most part it runs through low coastal scrub with melaleuca, tea tree and wattle predominating, but the inimitable banksia is also in evidence, while here and there bamboo and banana stands – obviously escapees from the gardens just up the hill – clash with the native plants. There are some very fine homes in this area and every now and then one can be seen through the bush on the higher slopes. Previously mostly natural soil and rock, the track is now occasionally enhanced with a section of board-walk and steps carved from the rock.

Queens Beach |3| is the first significant break in the rocky foreshore on the left while on the right tracks and steps lead up to the streets above. Access to this small but pretty beach is down one of a number of bush tracks leading off to the left. There is a fine stand of coral trees along this section of the path and in summer lizards scatter ahead of walkers' feet. Watch out, however, for the odd blue-tongue which will be lying across the path every so often; they are not too inclined to move and, because of their natural camouflage, can easily be stepped on. Native birds add to the delights and every now and then a gap in the bush or a lookout point on a prominent rock offer views across to **Shark Island |4|** and up the magnificent lower harbour to the CBD, the Harbour Bridge and the Opera House.

Immediately across the water in the crescent of Rose Bay is Sydney's float plane base, and the roar of the aircraft taking off or landing punctuates the air at frequent intervals. This is a historically important base developed from a pre-Second World War flying boat base serving the Pacific islands, and a major RAAF base during the war years. After the war it became the Sydney terminal for the giant passenger flying boats and many a famous Australian flyer's name is associated with this base. Nowadays the light float planes run mostly joy flights up and down the coastline.

With such splendid views in all directions, it is hardly surprising this has always been known as the 'dress circle' of Sydney, an area as much sought after by the early home builders as it is today. On the right above the foreshore bush line are a number of exclusive homes, some old, some new, but they are mostly secluded behind dense garden shrubs and trees and often all that can be seen is the roof line. One such residence is the house which gives its name to the track – **The Hermitage |5|**. This fine example of a late Victorian harbourside villa was built of sandstone in 1878 and incorporated a smaller house first built in 1840. It was partially destroyed by fire in 1936, but was carefully reconstructed in its original form with steeply pitched gables, a three-storey castellated tower, and elaborately decorated barge boards and balconies. It is best seen from a distance when the steeply pitched roofs and elegantly decorated eaves rise above the trees and shrubs which all but bury it in greenery.

The track passes below The Hermitage to a small grassy reserve encompassing a quite delightful little sandy cove called

Opening Times

Vaucluse House:
Tue–Sun 10am–4.30pm.

Refreshments

A kiosk and restaurant are situated in Nielsen Park. Water bubblers are also located in Nielsen Park.

Hermit Bay |6|, named after the hermits who shared the foreshores with the Cadigal tribe in the early days when Rose Bay was little used by settlers. Here is a great deal of stonework in the form of sea walls and jetties as well as a slipway for pulling boats out of the water. The waterfront area is grassed and planted with clumps of banana palms and other trees, all of which create a very pleasant picnicking area. A small sandy beach and clear water add to the relaxed atmosphere and make for a quite delightful waterfront venue. Perhaps a good spot to take a refresher break before continuing the walk.

On the opposite side of the clearing the track continues up a few steps and then plunges once more into the bush. Here the walking can be a little more demanding as the path winds up and down some fairly steep stone steps and around small headlands although it is still not beyond the capabilities of the average walker. In any case, the bush section is brief and before long the track enters another open reserve. A few tracks lead off to the right here, but these only provide access to the foreshores from the streets above. Tracks to the left lead to two small beaches which lie at the base of the open area. These are Tingara Beach and **Milk Beach |7|** – two quite small crescents of clean white sand locked between colourful sandstone headlands and backed by bushy foreshores. These beaches were obviously enjoyed by the Aboriginal inhabitants, and shell middens on the foreshores attest to many a tribal feast. There are reputed to be interesting rock carvings below the high water mark if you can find them. Milk Beach earned its name as the delivery point for the boats delivering milk down harbour before roads were constructed.

Greycliffe House

The open grassy area above these beaches was formerly the estate of another fine old building known as **Strickland House |8|**, which dominates the scene as you walk out from the bush track. At one time one of the area's most notable residences, this fine old painted stone mansion was built in 1856 for John Hosking, Sydney's first Lord Mayor. Originally called Carrara after the Italian marble used for its fireplaces, it is set in spacious grounds with a coach house and stables as well as an extensive garden. It has a slate-clad hipped roof with a large bow front and verandahs with Doric columns and cast iron balconies. Prominent in the magnificent view across the main harbour from Strickland House is

Shark Island – so named not because of its shape, but because of the proliferation of sharks in the bay. Whaling ships entering Sydney Harbour in the early days of the colony discharged their offal overboard, thereby attracting large schools of sharks into the bays. In 1915 the buildings of Carrara estate became a hospital but now they are virtually unused.

The grounds of Strickland House are extensive and to continue the walk it will be necessary to return down the grassy slopes towards Milk Beach where a sign indicates the track leading off to the right into the foreshore bush. It is also accessible through a gate in the cyclone wire fence which surrounds much of the southern side of the estate. Now the bush becomes quite dense although the path is still easily accessible. Happily, much of the feral growth encountered earlier along the walk has disappeared and the bush now consists almost entirely of native shrubs and trees. Melaleuca are predominant here together with coast tea tree and wattle. A small but fine stand of angophoras add their colourful trunks to the delightful scene and also attract the native birds, particularly wattlebirds, which abound all along the bush-clad harbour foreshores. The rocks are visible through the bush on the left, with glimpses of the harbour through the trees. Every now and then a diversionary track leads off to the right, but these do not add significantly to the walk. Most simply provide access to the service road which converges on the walking track as it approaches **Steel Point |9|**; the two come together at a naval emplacement right on the point.

Nielsen Park

Walk across the road to concrete paths and steps leading down to the extensive horse-shoe beach of **Shark Bay |10|**, one of the most popular of beaches in this area. This wide crescent of sand is totally enclosed within the bushy environment of **Nielsen Park |11|** and is protected from its namesake by a shark-proof net. Pleasantly landscaped lawns, toilets and a kiosk, together with tables and shelters, all make this a pleasant recreation area within easy access of the nearby suburb of Vaucluse. In summer this popular beach and the surrounding park-lands are swamped with picnickers, especially families who appreciate not only the pleasant ambience of the foreshores but also the protection of the shark net. The kiosk dates back to the 1920s as do some of the nearby changing sheds – relics of the days when neck-to-knee costumes and segregated bathing were still a part of the beach scene in some places.

Bear round to the right along the service road to visit another fine old home, **Greycliffe House |12|** which, set among the trees behind the beach and lawns of Nielsen Park, resembles a film set from a period movie. This ornate sandstone house is the first of a number built by W. C. Wentworth, one of Australia's earliest and most revered explorers and one of the colony's leading statesmen. The house is not open for public inspection, but does contain Sydney Harbour National Park offices downstairs which are open to visitors. It was first built in the 1840s as a wedding present for Wentworth's daughter. The Gothic Revival structure has an unusual porch, ornately detailed barges, bay windows and a multiple gabled roof with more fretwork barge-boards. Like so many of the elite homes of the day, Greycliffe House was almost destroyed by fire in 1890 but has been painstakingly restored to its original condition and is now used by the National Parks and Wildlife Service.

After visiting Greycliffe House walk across Shark Bay, along either the beach or one of the many footpaths, and climb the steps which lead past the well-marked ladies' toilet. A service road curves around the northern headland but leave this and bear left along a track which leads to **Vaucluse Point |13|**. Once again the harbour views are spectacular, this time in the opposite direction as the city is behind and ahead are the open spaces of the lower harbour stretching to Manly and The Heads. Immediately beneath the low headland on the foreshore is an interesting group of rocks known as Bottle and Glass Rocks. Legend has it that in the very early days of settlement these rocks were used as targets for cannon practice in what was then a remote part of the harbour. Certainly the tumbled appearance of the rocks gives a degree of credence to the story – and yet another touch of colour to what must surely be one of the most colourful harbours in the world.

Vaucluse House

Follow the footpath back onto the service road and bear left until you reach the streets of suburban Vaucluse. Leaving the park, bear left again into Coolong Road and continue on for about 15 minutes, in the meantime taking in the elegant – but now mostly modern – homes that surround the waterfront on **Vaucluse Bay |14|**. Vaucluse is recognised as one of the most fashionable of Sydney suburbs and the luxurious houses that line the waterfront here are an indication of how it achieved that reputation. At the end of Coolong Street a small park on the left leads down to the head of the bay; while on the opposite side of Wentworth Road is a very exotic looking

estate with huge trees, tall palm stands and beautifully manicured grounds. Cross the road and enter Vaucluse Park, the setting for one of Sydney's most venerable and important historic houses.

William Charles Wentworth was born in 1793 – either in Sydney or in Norfolk Island or on board a ship between the two. He was to become the first native-born Australian to hold a high government position in the colony, but he was best known for his discovery, together with Blaxland and Lawson, of a route over the Blue Mountains to the interior of the country. He went on to distinguish himself in many fields of government and law and was the force behind the campaigns for self-government which eventually resulted in a new constitution for New South Wales in 1855. The magnificent residence known as **Vaucluse House |15|** was Wentworth's home and as you walk up the path towards the building, hidden from this angle by the trees, it is not hard to imagine the splendour of this estate when it stood alone on the bush covered foreshores of Sydney Harbour, a reproduction in Australia of one of the stately homes of England.

Walk towards the house from Wentworth Road past an impressive stand of tall palms, some 20 metres or more high, that scrape the clouds and lend an air of mystery to the house they conceal. Follow the garden path through an opening in the hedge and the main house is revealed behind a large undulating lawn with a central fountain.

The building is a three-storey Gothic mansion built in local sandstone with a turreted tower; it incorporates the original cottage which was built in 1803 for an ex-convict called Hayes. Wentworth completed the present building in 1827 and it was in the library of this building that he drew up the Constitution for New South Wales. On either side of the big bay window which dominates the front are wide stone-flagged verandahs with iron pillars supporting the roof, providing a cool exterior to the main rooms.

Continue across the lawn and bear right around the house to a building with arched windows that looks like a chapel but is in fact the stables. These are maintained as they were when the horse was as important to a family as the car is today, and the cobble floored stalls where the horses were stabled still have a 'horsey' aroma. Across from the stables are other outhouses – some of which were added after completion of the main building – and the entrance to the main house, which is open to visitors. It is well worth taking a break here to examine the interior of the house which, perhaps more than any building in Sydney, exudes the atmosphere of 19th century living as it was experienced by the colonial gentry.

The estate which surrounds the house once covered 500 acres (200 hectares) and included farm buildings, stable accommo-dation, free workers' cottages and convict barracks to accommodate a total work force of some 50 souls. Legend has it that Wentworth had a fear of snakes and know-ing that Ireland is free of snakes, arranged to have a large quantity of Irish soil shipped to Sydney which he then had placed in a trench around Vaucluse House to deter snakes from entering. Records do not show whether or not the tactic worked! Behind the house there is still an extensive open area, probably a paddock on the orig-inal estate. Follow a path that leads across this and a few metres along a plaque will become visible indicating the site of one of the workers' cottages. At the far end of the paddock, up a flight of steps, a stone dam creates a pool on the stream which runs down towards the house. No doubt this would have been the water supply for the animals, perhaps even for the residents, for it would, in those days, have provided clear, clean water.

Now climb a long flight of 107 steps up Petrarch Avenue to reach Hopetoun Avenue and return from the early 19th century to the present day. Turn right at the top of the steps and follow Hopetoun Avenue back to its junction with New South Head Road near the Sacred Heart Convent and the beginning of our Hermitage Walk. Cross the road to the bus stop from where a bus every 20 minutes or so provides transport back to the city.

Spit Bridge to Manly

Foreshores, ferries and flannel flowers

Start

Spit Bridge. Catch any Manly or Northern Beaches bus (there are about 40 services) from Wynyard (Carrington Street) and get off just before the bridge.

Finish

Transport interchange, Manly Beach. Take any bus, a Manly ferry or the Jetcat back to the city.

Length/Time

9 km/2.5 hours

Wheelchair

Only on the walkway from North Harbour Reserve to Manly. No access to the foreshore walk.

There are few walks in and around Sydney that can compare with this one in terms of natural beauty, interest and scenic appeal. The largest part of the walk is through native bush and along sparkling foreshores that could be a million miles from civilisation whereas in fact they are less than eight kilometres from the heart of one of the world's major cities. This walk has everything from points of historical interest, abundant wildlife and unique geology to indigenous art and quite stunning views through Sydney Heads to the Pacific Ocean.

Walk key

1. Clontarf Beach Reserve | 2. Castle Rock | 3. Grotto Point | 4. Dobroyd Head | 5. Crater Cove | 6. Reef Beach | 7. Forty Baskets | 8. North Harbour Park | 9. Fairlight rock pool | 10. Oceanworld | 11. Manly Wharf

Start this walk from a small park on the northern side of the Spit Bridge, just north of Mosman. The only public transport is the bus, but since this is the main route to the northern beaches there are plenty of buses and most stop at The Spit – just check with the driver to be sure. Northern beaches buses run every few minutes from Carrington Street (Wynyard) in the city. Get off at The Spit, just after the traffic lights, cross the road and walk over the bridge. A small park lies beneath the roadway and is reached by a service road immediately on the right as you leave the bridge. Walk down into this park and across to the far side where a clearly marked pathway leads off around the foreshore.

This track, which at first follows the old tram track to Manly, plunges into foreshore bushland, providing an exciting taste of what is to come. It is a dirt track but quite walkable and in places where it crosses creeks or foreshore swampy areas there are boardwalks and small bridges. Within a few minutes of starting the walk, the path dips down to a small rainforest area where a fascinating example of water gum can be seen on the left hand side, with its tangled roots and branches almost intruding across the path. Overhanging rocks and sandstone shelters add to the interest of this corner while to the right the shallow, sandy reaches of Fisher Bay (also called Mosquito Bay) sweep up into the corner where there are more species of swamp plants.

Continue along the footpath above the shoreline and around the next point. This is the site of an early Aboriginal midden, thought to have been used by the Guringai clan who lived in the area.

Aborigines gathered at specific points along the coast to collect shellfish and cook them, piling the empty shells into big mounds known as middens, and sheltered bays like this were favourite spots for such gatherings. The sand flats made it easy to collect the shellfish and the rock shelters provided a haven in times of bad weather or for night shelters.

Clontarf

Once around the small point, the footpath breaks out from the bushy foreshores and runs down to the edge of the next bay – Sandy Bay. Follow the path down onto the sand and then walk along the beach in front of the houses, joining the road where it rounds the next headland and passes Clontarf Marina.

The road runs into a reserve – **Clontarf Beach Reserve |1|**, a popular picnic place for families. There is a netted pool, an extensive beach and a restaurant under the big Moreton Bay figs which are prolific in the park and offer excellent shade for picnickers in summer. Across the water the sandy promontory of The Spit guards the entrance to the extensive upper reaches of Middle Harbour.

In 1834 the only means of transport across this narrow neck was a row boat service – a rather primitive and hazardous link with the northern shore, but one which lasted until 1889 when a punt was installed. As road transport developed and people began to commute to the city from their homes on the northern beaches, crossing The Spit became a bigger and bigger problem. Trams ran to the southern side, then passengers were transferred to the punt and transported across the water to other trams waiting on the northern side. This was a slow and uncomfortable business, especially in bad weather. The problem was solved in 1924 when a steel and timber bridge was built. This quickly became outdated, however, and the current lift span bridge was erected in the 1970s, but this is also now unable to cope with traffic demands.

Walk through Clontarf Reserve towards the beach and enjoy the peaceful ambience of this pleasant waterfront park – although it was not always as peaceful as it is today. In the mid-19th century this was a popular spot for day trippers who came by ferry from the city and inner suburbs. In 1868 this quiet little Sydney beachside suburb made world headlines when an attempt was made to assassinate Prince Alfred, Duke of Edinburgh, in Clontarf Reserve while he was visiting Australia. Although shot, the duke survived, and the would-be assassin, an Irishman, was executed at Darlinghurst Gaol.

From the reserve, walk along Clontarf Beach and follow the signposts which indicate the continuation of the footpath into thick bush that lines the foreshores and rounds the rocky headland to a cove known as **Castle Rock |2|**. On a clear day,

Opening Times

Oceanworld: Daily 10am–5.30pm.
Manly Art Gallery and Museum: Tue–Sun 10am–5pm
Water Funland: Open only weekends and school holidays in summer.

Refreshments

Cafes, restaurants and bars are situated at The Spit. There is a restaurant at Clontarf Reserve; shops at Balgowlah Marina; restaurants, cafes, takeaways, hotels and bars can be found in Manly. Water bubblers are located at The Spit, Clontarf Reserve, North Harbour Park, West Esplanade and Manly.

with the sparkling clear waters beneath, the colourful sandstone outcrops of the foreshores and the mass of native flora in the bush, this walk is a nature lover's delight. It is possible to climb down and walk along the rocky shoreline with its small indented beaches, as there is little in the way of surf waves to worry about. Tracks lead down at a number of points and steps lead back up to the path from the small beach in the corner of the cove. More energetic walkers, and those who like to scramble, can continue along the rocks as far as **Grotto Point |3|**.

The walking track, which runs through the bush above these low cliffs, is well maintained with boardwalks and bridges where walking would be otherwise difficult. At this point in time it is under the care of Manly Council which has provided interesting and educational information boards at intervals along the path. Above Castle Rock – named after a large rock in the cove which is meant to resemble a castle – steep steps cut into the rock climb the hillside and the walk moves into Sydney Harbour National Park where, of course, no dogs are permitted. The information boards are not continued after this point, which is unfortunate as the ridges to Grotto Point and adjacent **Dobroyd Head |4|** have a wide variety of interesting features. Most notable at this point is a fine stand of angophoras, or Sydney red gums.

Grotto Point

Follow the path upwards and along the ridge into one of the most prolific wildflower areas around Sydney Harbour. Velvety flannel flowers (*Actinotus helianthi*) in particular flourish on this headland and in early summer they are so numerous that some parts of the open coastal heath have the appearance of snow. Blue flax flowers are also in numbers as of course is the ubiquitous grevillea, different species of which are found along the full length of the walk. The larger trees begin to thin out as the track moves out onto the headland, for this area is exposed to the southerly and easterly winds off the

Grotto Point is renowned for its prolific flannel flowers

open sea which stunt most growth other than, perhaps, that of the hardy banksia.

Continue along the path until it reaches a three-way junction presenting three distinct options. The first is to take the right hand path down the ridge to Grotto Point with its interesting history and quaint little lighthouse. This point was thought to have been named by one of Governor Phillip's men sent from Botany Bay to explore the possibility of moving the First Fleet into Sydney Harbour in 1788. The expedition likened the caves on the point to a Mediterranean grotto and the name remained. The lighthouse is the lower of two 'leading' lights which, when lined up, provide guidance for shipping entering

Sydney Harbour. The second light is high on the hillside near The Spit.

Follow the path down to the foreshores at Grotto Point and take a breather on the rocks there. The outlook is quite delightful and although there is no beach, there is a stairway and ladder that was originally intended to provide access to the lighthouse for people and stores brought across by boat. The remains of an old jetty used for the same purpose are still visible. The coastal heath that covers the point makes the walk a pleasure, especially in springtime when the path is literally knee-deep in colourful blooms.

Return to the three-way junction by walking back up the footpath from Grotto Point to the junction and take the second option – the centre track – which leads down to the left of the ridge to a beach tucked underneath the cliffs sometimes called 'Washaway' or 'Wishy-washy'. Totally isolated from civilisation, except by the steep track down through dense undergrowth, this neat little beach faces the ocean directly through the Heads. As a result of the constant surge of ocean swell, the sand disappears at regular intervals, leaving nothing but a rocky foreshore. Then, due to currents and the phenomenon known as longshore drift, the sand miraculously returns and a beach some 150 to 200 metres long appears, enhancing the rugged beauty of the headland. Because of its isolation, this beach is sometimes used by nudists or fishermen, but on account of the difficult access, it is not common to find human footsteps in the sand.

Return again to the junction and take the third option, the left hand track which winds up the hill through shoulder-high coastal wattle and tea tree. This track can be a bit rough and slippery in wet weather, but it should not be dangerous for average walkers and in fine weather is relatively easy. Just before reaching the top a gap opens in the bushes to the right and what appears to be railway sleepers are laid in groups across a rock platform. Walk through the bushes and out onto the rock platform with commanding views over the ocean. Closer inspection will reveal that the baulks of timber are protecting Aboriginal rock carvings engraved into the face of the rock.

Take care when walking on this rocky outcrop not to step on any engravings as not all are protected and already they have been badly eroded by weathering and walking. Some are large and quite hard to distinguish, but among the more obvious are sharks, fish and kangaroos. It is interesting to contemplate just how these engravings came into being. Were they the casual art offerings of a group of Aborigines filling in time while relaxing as a family or neighbourhood group? Or do they carry more significance – perhaps a deliberate record of events laid down at a meeting of tribal elders gathered together to discuss neighbourhood business or to determine future activities of their people?

It seems that this flat area of rock, in its superb setting overlooking the entrance to the harbour and the ocean beyond, was some form of meeting place for the local clans. Similar carvings can be found at a number of places along the coastline; one very similar in content and location is situated on Port Hacking Point, covered in walk 19 page 160 of this book. But few, if any, have the unrivalled scenic splendour of this location on Dobroyd Head.

Dobroyd Head

Continue past the Aboriginal rock carvings as the track skirts the top of the headland. Here a major lookout point is located a few metres below the tourist road which runs around the top, offering spectacular views up the harbour, across to Manly and out to sea. This is a favourite tourist spot and the lookout is often crowded as tour buses line up along the road behind. From here the layout of Sydney's famous harbour is clearly visible. From the Heads, immediately in front, the main harbour sweeps away to the right past the southern suburbs of Watsons Bay and Vaucluse, while between Middle Head and Grotto Point the clear waters of Middle Harbour slide behind the headland. North Harbour disappears to the left around Dobroyd Point and across the Sound, tucked under North Head, is Little Manly Cove and Quarantine Beach.

Immediately below the lookout the headland is deeply indented by what is known as **Crater Cove** |5|. Here the rocky foreshores have for decades housed 'fringe' dwellers and fishermen living in huts made of rocks, driftwood and corrugated iron. Originally they were rumoured

to be smugglers, who set a lookout at the top of the headland to watch for excise officers. The lookouts used the raucous call of the crow as a warning, and as a result they became known as the Crow Tribe. The huts are also said to have provided a hideaway for draft dodgers in various conflicts, but currently they are under the care of the National Parks and Wildlife Service. Various attempts to move the occupants and demolish the huts failed for many years, even though the headland is part of the Sydney Harbour National Park.

If the sea is running, a spectacular water display will be visible on the Dobroyd bombora, just off the high cliffs of the outer point. A bombora is a steep and dangerous wave created by underwater undulations, in this case a rocky reef.

Take the path leading off to the north from the lookout and back into natural bush. Mostly low coastal scrub, the wildflowers are as prolific here as they are on the Grotto Point ridge. Flannel flowers are again in profusion as are native fuchsia, pink dog rose and 'bread and meat'. Everywhere there is a wide range of the delightful grevillea as well as coast tea tree. Onshore winds here keep the growth mostly to low shrubs, although as you round the corner of the headland and start to move back towards the mainland, a few eucalypts, also in many varieties, and casuarinas start to reappear. This walk is a nature lover's dream come true, for apart from the wide range of native vegetation the wildlife is quite exciting, albeit sometimes even a little startling.

Mostly confined to reptiles, with perhaps the odd bandicoot or rabbit, the common species are the small lizards which scamper from under your feet along the track and across the rocks. Occasionally monitors sun themselves on the big rocky outcrops; some of these are large and it can be quite alarming when what appeared to be a small log suddenly turns out to be a large monitor! Those unfamiliar with bush wildlife need have no fear, however, for despite their ferocious appearance, these magnificent creatures are harmless. Large birds, particularly currawongs, seem to be more populous in the stands of casuarinas or eucalypts, while honey eaters and wattle birds dive in and out the banksias and grevilleas.

A branch track to the right diverts along the cliff top to Crater Cove, while the main track reaches a junction where the signpost indicates the option of continuing down the hill and walking along the foreshores past **Reef Beach |6|**, or turning left and heading through the bush directly to the suburb of **Forty Baskets |7|**, so named on account of a catch of forty baskets of fish sent to a contingent of Sudan troops at the North Head Quarantine Station in 1885. The choice is governed by the state of the tide and your attitude towards nude bathing. If the tide is high the foreshore walk can be tricky; and although nude bathing is supposed to be illegal, it has been a feature of Reef Beach for so long that there is a

strong likelihood of running into a naked body somewhere along the foreshore. To avoid either of these possibilities take the left hand track through the bush

The track now becomes a wide, tree-lined walkway that leads directly to a street in Forty Baskets and the first houses since Clontarf. Follow the path onto Beatty Street, taking the right-hand fork and continuing to the end where steps lead down to Gourlay Avenue and a boatshed marina. Continue along the road as it winds around the head of the bay until on the right steps lead down to a delightful open area called **North Harbour Park |8|**. More toilets, a wide grassy area and two children's playgrounds make this an ideal rest stop or lunch venue for families.

Walk across the park, which has been reclaimed from the mud at the head of North Harbour, and climb the steps on the opposite side to King Avenue. Follow this street to the right where it joins Lauderdale Avenue, bear right again and a few metres further along the footpath leads off into a foreshore reserve. Proceed along Esplanade Park, past three small beaches to the **Fairlight rock pool |9|**. Then around the point to **Oceanworld |10|** on the right with its fine display of sharks and other marine denizens; there is also a water funland and a small art gallery. Walk along the esplanade to the transport interchange at **Manly Wharf |11|** and take your choice of bus or ferry to return to the city.

Blackwattle & Rozelle bays

Fish and ships

Start

Wentworth Park. Take the light rail car from Central Railway Station, which departs every 10–15 minutes, *or* walk from Market Street, across Pyrmont Bridge and down Pyrmont Bridge Road to Wentworth Park.

Finish

Wentworth Park. Take the light rail train back to Central Railway Station *or* walk back across Pyrmont Bridge Road to the CBD.

Length/Time

4.5 km/1.5 hours

Wheelchairs

Easy access throughout the full length of the walk.

Everyone knows the Sydney Fish Markets, but few know what lies beyond them around Blackwattle and Rozelle bays. Sitting under the umbrellas on the open deck of the markets, enjoying the seafood and the maritime activity, few realise that around the foreshores of these two bays is a walk that takes in a superb new bridge, restored old steam ships, nautical junkyards and boatshed lofts that accommodate arts and crafts studios. Eat well, then stroll back into maritime history on this walk around a little known part of Sydney Harbour.

Walk key

1. Sydney Fish Markets | 2. Blackwattle Bay | 3. Rozelle Bay | 4. ANZAC Bridge | 5. Glebe Island terminal | 6. Sydney's Heritage Fleet | 7. Maritime junkyard | 8. Leichhardt Bicentennial Park | 9. Pope Paul VI Reserve | 10. Blackwattle Bay Studios | 11. Forsyth Street | 12. Glebe Rowing Club

Start the walk at Wentworth Park, best known for its greyhound racing stadium, but also as the site for visiting circuses and other travelling shows. From the city, energetic walkers can stroll across Pyrmont Bridge then follow Pyrmont Bridge Road over the hill and down to Wattle Street, which runs beside Wentworth Park. An easier way is to catch the LRT (Light Rail Transport) from Central Station, alight at the Wattle Street stop and walk down the steps to the park. Turn right from the LRT station and follow the footpath beside the park to the intersection with Bridge Road, then cross over at the lights. Directly opposite is one of the entrances to the Sydney Fish Markets |1|.

The Sydney Fish Markets

You don't have to buy fish to visit the fish markets. Walk through the gateway and onto a broad quay fronting onto Blackwattle Bay |2| with a variety of marinas and jetties on the left, berthing an equally wide range of leisure and working craft. On the right is the main building which contains all sorts of markets – not just fish markets – while the quay itself is set up as a delightful outdoor rest area with tables, chairs and umbrellas creating a colourful foreground to the quiet waters of the bay. There is always plenty of maritime action going on here, with big commercial ships loading or unloading at a wharf across the bay, bustling activity nearby as the fishing boats come and go and yachts tying up to the marina. Then there is the busy market

scene to browse through with a variety of interesting products on sale, mostly with a maritime flavour.

The fish markets are a relatively new development on the edges of Blackwattle Bay, originally a swampy area from which wattles and reeds were gathered by the early settlers for house building, hence the name. It began to take on significance as a commercial waterway around 1890 when wharves were built to replace the ramshackle jetties that previously fringed the foreshores. Unlike adjacent Rozelle Bay |3|, which is deeper and hence became an important timber shipping area, Blackwattle Bay catered mostly for small coastal steamers which ran up and down the New South Wales coast and brought farm produce to the city. While it has always provided a haven for Sydney's fishing fleets, it was not until the 1980s and early 1990s that the foreshores underwent a major refurbishment which has made them a popular venue both as a fish market and a public relaxation area.

Towering over the waterfront is one of Sydney's newest icons – the ANZAC Bridge |4|, formerly the Glebe Island Bridge. Its tall towers and delicate cable tracery provide a splendid background to what is already a rewarding maritime scene. The entrance to the wide expanses of Blackwattle Bay and Rozelle Bay is beneath this bridge which opened to traffic in 1995, replacing the old iron swing bridge which had been in place for almost a century. From the marina, walk across the markets in the direction of the bridge and enter Jones Street via the main gateway. Turn left along this street and continue walking under the bridge approaches past a couple of waterfront industries until the Pink Panther sign appears on the opposite side of the road – the corner of Bank and Saunders streets. Cross the road under the bridge approach span and continue along Bank Street until, from a side street on the right, the attractively designed curving pedestrian access to the bridge walkway appears.

Set among a mass of new apartment and office buildings, this gently elevated pathway provides pedestrian and wheelchair access to the road level high above the busy waterfront streets. At one time this area was the scene of heavy industry, mostly associated with the Colonial Sugar Refinery, and at the time of writing, part of the old refinery building was still standing; if it is still there it will be visible on the right from the bridge walkway. An interesting feature close to the top of the access footpath is the seating of the massive stay cables that support the bridge. Underneath the main deck of the bridge, these cables are anchored by huge nuts, readily visible and resembling parts of a giant meccano set.

The ANZAC Bridge

This bridge, named as a tribute to those who fought under the ANZAC badge in several wars, is an eye-catching structure towering over the remains of the old ground-level bridge which is still visible from the deck of the new bridge. Founda-

Opening Times
Sydney Fish Markets (retail): 7am–4pm.
Blackwattle Bay Studios: Various times, depending on individual studio.
Sydney Heritage Fleet: Half-day tours and vintage cruises Tue and Thurs (all day).

Refreshments
Everything from coffee to full restaurant meals at one of the food outlets in the Sydney Fish Markets or at the shops on the corner of Glebe Point Road and Forsyth Street. There are restaurants in Glebe Rowing Club and Blackwattle Bay Studios. Water bubblers can be found in Bicentennial Park, Glebe High School grounds and Wentworth Park.

tions for the ANZAC bridge were begun in 1989 and the first vehicles crossed the roadway on 3 December 1995. The length of the main span is 345 metres, second only to the Sydney Harbour Bridge (503 metres), although the total length of the bridge structure is 805 metres. The deck is 27 metres above the water and the towers which support it reach 120 metres into the sky. These towers are hollow and there are 433 steps inside each to provide access to the top. Unlike the Sydney Harbour Bridge pylons, however, these pylons are not open to the public. Each of the massive stay cables, which create a delicate spider's web appearance when seen from afar, consist of bundles of 15.7mm diameter steel strands which are themselves made up of finer steel strands woven together like rope. If the stay cables were laid end to end they would reach from Sydney to Bourke.

The bridge spans Johnsons Bay, which forms the entrance to Rozelle and Black-wattle bays, and which was named after Australia's first chaplain, the Reverend Richard Johnson, who arrived with the first Fleet in 1788, complete with his library of 4200 religious books. He was granted 160 acres located 3 miles west of Sydney Cove which he called 'Glebe'. Just offshore from this land was a small, rocky islet which became known as Glebe Island.

From the bridge deck, look down on the western shoreline where currently there are a number of major wharves and a huge open space converted into **Glebe Island terminal |5|**. Until 1918 this area was not a vehicle terminal but Glebe Island, home to Sydney's main abattoir which was originally built in the 1850s and accessed by a causeway from Glebe mainland. But the residents of Glebe and nearby suburbs were not happy with cattle and sheep being driven through their main streets, so a timber bridge was built in 1857 to provide direct access to the eastern side of the island. This was the basic but effi-cient forerunner of the magnificent structure of today, and where once the stockyards of

The graceful ANZAC Bridge

the abattoir held cattle and sheep, now the huge terminal accommodates thousands of motor vehicles.

Beyond Glebe Island, seen across John-sons Bay, are the container terminals on the Balmain waterfront, yet another massive development of the once quiet waters of Sydney Harbour's upper reaches. This area is covered in walk 15. Behind, to the east, the city skyline is seen from a different perspective with the organ pipes of the CBD high-rise buildings rearing up behind the old terrace houses and wool stores of Pyrmont. Continue across the bridge walk-way, under the western tower to the end of the bridge span and take the access ramp that leads off to the right. This curls down through pleasant landscaping to the road beneath, past a row of huge grain silos. Turn right at the bottom and pass under the bridge approaches to reach James Craig Road, then cross over and walk outside the cyclone wire fence which encloses the Waterways main base and a number of maritime industries. Take care on this road because there is no footpath, only a white line indicating the demarcation between vehicle and pedestrian sections of the road.

James Craig Road

About 50 metres along you will come across a large sign indicating that this is the home of **Sydney's Heritage Fleet |6|**; a fine collection of vintage ships and boats that have been or are being restored to working condition. Old steam tugs, ferries and work boats that have long been retired are gradually being renovated by volunteers and brought back into service. Pride of this part of the fleet is the old steam pinnace that was once the governor's launch. Now fast approaching her 100th year of service, the stately *Lady Hopetoun* chuffs up and down the harbour catching the attention of visitors and locals alike with her cheery 'toot' on the steam whistle and her elegant appearance, just as she did when first launched in 1902. A guided tour of this fine display of antique vessels is available. Soon the fleet will also be located at Pyrmont, next to the National Maritime Museum. This is a place where it is very easy to lose a couple of fascinating hours.

It was here that the fine old barque *James Craig* was restored after being rescued from her watery grave in Tasmania.

She is now on display in Darling Harbour as part of the National Maritime Museum exhibits. This fine old windjammer is typical of the vessels known as the 'shopping baskets of the world' which in the mid-19th century played an important part in developing new colonies. Apart from providing a lifeline between the burgeoning industries of New South Wales and the markets of Europe these vessels were instrumental in bridging the isolation the new settlers felt after migrating to the other side of the world.

Launched in Sunderland, UK, in 1874 as the *Clan Macleod* the 55 metre (180 ft) barque was built of iron plates riveted onto iron frames and stringers. She had the usual barque configuration of three masts, the fore and main square rigged and the mizzen fore and aft rigged with a spanker. She carried a crew of 17 including the master's wife and three apprentices. In 1899 the ship was sold to the Craig Shipping Co of Auckland and she was renamed the *James Craig* shortly afterwards. For years she plied the trans-Tasman trade and survived World War One before being sold to an Australian company in 1918. A few years later, however, she was scuttled in Recherche Bay, Tasmania, after blowing ashore in a gale. For forty years she lay in the cold Tasmanian waters until a group of maritime enthusiasts from Sydney raised her and towed her back to Sydney where her restoration is now almost complete.

Nautical bric-a-brac

Continue walking along James Craig Road,

named after the old ship, for there is always something to catch the eye on these wharves, once the main timber importing centre for the port of Sydney. Nowadays it is a holding ground for every kind of vessel afloat, and although the ships that lie here change from time to time, there is always something of interest – big harbour cruise ships, working vessels, even sometimes a vessel that has been arrested or impounded at sea! James Craig Road is a fascinating spot for anyone interested in maritime activities, for there is always something unique on show in this mariner's treasure trove.

At the end of James Craig Road, veer left into The Crescent and left again, following the footpath around the corner, past more maritime bric-a-brac on the left. On the opposite side of the road, the first part of the railway viaduct begins with an ornately painted mural decorating the embankment, while opposite the railway bridge over Johnston Street, on the left is the 'Steptoe and Son' version of a **maritime junkyard |7|**. Stroll in the gate and find anything and everything from ropes and cordage to bits of boats to things you can use in the garden! Anyone addicted to junk yards, especially maritime junkyards, will find this the next best thing to paradise!

Glebe parklands

Leaving the junkyard, follow the short street to the left as it leads into **Leichhardt Bicentennial Park |8|**, also known as Federal Park, and an interesting change of scenery. Now the busy activity of the water-

front along James Craig Road is seen from the other side of Rozelle Bay and replaced by the peaceful environment of a delightful waterside park. Lots of open grassy areas with interesting native and exotic trees provide a total contrast to the bustling activity across the water, although the ships alongside the quay, now seen in profile from the other side of the bay, still offer an interesting talking point. Veer right as you enter the park and on your immediate right is a superb playground for children providing a variety of activities to complement the wide run-around spaces of the park itself.

Continue past the playground towards the railway viaduct and cross the bridge over the canal which divides the park from its counterpart on the other side known as Jubilee Park. Federation-style footpaths lead across to the built-up area of Glebe Point through a wide variety of trees, mostly figs or palms that are well grown. Follow the park to its waterfront corner at the bottom of Federal Road where a small section has been designated the **Pope Paul VI Reserve |9|**. The name commemorates the arrival there on 2 December 1970 of a launch carrying the Pope on his way to visit the Royal Alexandra Hospital for Children in Camperdown.

From this waterfront reserve Glebe Point Road runs up the hill to the right with remarkable old stone walls providing a frontage to cottages on the right, while the left side is dominated by what appear to be old, ramshackle iron-clad buildings. In fact these buildings, now known as the **Blackwattle Bay Studios |10|**, were once a major feature of

Sydney's maritime industry. Some were boat-sheds, some boat building establishments, some repair shops, some even factories. Sentenced to be demolished and rebuilt as apartment blocks, these old 'tin' buildings aroused the sympathies of local residents and historians, and were saved and converted into an arts and crafts centre. A stroll through the old timber and corrugated iron buildings is a delightful digression from the walk and will arouse nostalgia in anyone who remembers the woolsheds, hay barns, boatsheds and other old structures that with their timber supports and trusses and iron roofs and sides were so unsuited to Australia's climate. Yet these ramshackle old buildings were a mainstay in the development of the nation's early industries, especially the maritime and rural industries.

Continue up Glebe Point Road for four blocks and turn left into **Forsyth Street |11|**, which runs down the hill with views across Blackwattle Bay to the high rise buildings of the CBD. On the left of this delightful old street are fascinating little cottages with ornate Victorian decorations, mostly colourful ceramic tiles, along their street frontages. A classic corner shop and rows of terrace houses with their ubiquitous iron lace balconies bear witness to the origins of the suburb which has all the hallmarks of an early working-class area yet which, only a few hundred metres up the hill on Glebe Point Road, has magnificent Victorian upper-class homes to equal those of Paddington. Glebe, at one time, was considered one of Sydney's more elegant suburbs.

Turn right into Taylor Street and left into Ferry Road then continue down to the waterfront and the historic **Glebe Rowing Club |12|**, now used mostly by university crews. Turn right into a small park which then leads into the grounds of the modern and attractively designed Glebe High School. A footpath leads through the school grounds to rejoin Taylor Street. Follow this and turn left down Taylor Street, left again into Bridge Road and walk along the waterfront past an old coal loader to the point where our walk began at the entrance to the fish markets. You should have a good appetite after the walk, and nothing could be more conducive to satisfying that appetite than sitting looking over Blackwattle Bay enjoying a fresh seafood meal.

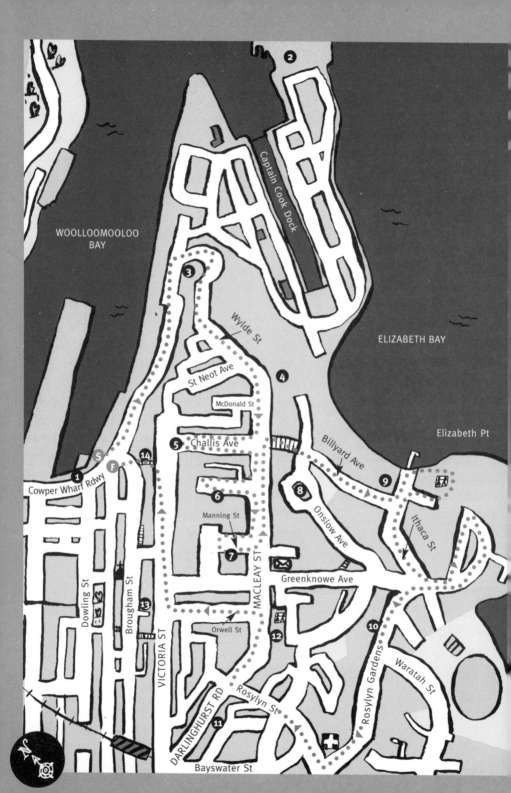

Potts Point & Kings Cross

Sophistication and sleaze

Start

Woolloomooloo Bay Finger Wharf. Bus 311 from Circular Quay or 312 from St James.

Finish

Woolloomooloo McElhone Steps. Bus 311 or 322 to the city.

Length/Time

3.5 km / 1.5 hours

Wheelchairs

The steps down to Elizabeth Bay House can be bypassed. The McElhone Stairs could be difficult to negotiate. Otherwise easy access.

In Sydney, the name Kings Cross is synonymous with strip joints, brothels and nightlife. Yet immediately adjoining it, and sharing the same postcode, are two of the most elegant and sophisticated suburbs in the city – Potts Point and Elizabeth Bay. This walk takes in both extremes – a visit to some of the finest and oldest of Sydney's elite mansions and a stroll through some of the boisterous but colourful streets which play host to less cultured activities.

Walk key

1. Harry's Café de Wheels | 2. Garden Island Dockyard | 3. Boomerah |
4. Jenner House | 5. Challis Avenue | 6. Rockwall | 7. Tusculum |
8. Elizabeth Bay House | 9. Boomerang | 10. Roslyn Gardens |
11. Darlinghurst Road | 12. Fitzroy Gardens | 13. Victoria Street |
14. Embarkation Park

Sydney is a very cosmopolitan city, but nowhere is it quite as cosmopolitan as at Kings Cross and Potts Point. In no other suburbs will you find such a wide spectrum of nationalities, such a contrast of cultures, religions and races. Within a few metres of some of the finest residences in the country you will encounter some of Sydney's worst slum alleys. Only a stone's throw from magnificent, elegant gardens, homeless people sleep under cardboard boxes in threadbare parks. Shady, tree-lined avenues exist side by side with narrow back lanes, repositories for discarded hypodermic needles and broken bottles. A mixture indeed, but an interesting mixture, for here in the elegant homes, in the back alleys, in the naval dockyard and in the box-like apartment buildings is a side of Sydney that is quite unique.

Because the walk takes in some of the less savoury areas, it should be taken as a daytime walk. Early on a summer morning is best, before the sun gets too hot and when 'the Cross' revellers have all gone home. Despite its reputation, parts of Kings Cross and the neighbouring suburbs of Darlinghurst, Elizabeth Bay and Potts Point are quite beautiful and considered by many city dwellers as the only place in Sydney to live. Hence the mansions that line the waterfront and the up-market apartments with views down the harbour to the Heads.

The naval presence

In order to cover all facets of this interesting area, the walk begins on the busy waterfront of Woolloomooloo Bay, orignally the home of the Cadigal people, and covered in more detail in walk 1. Cowper Wharf Road runs around the eastern side of the bay beneath the cliff face that once separated elegant Potts Point on the top of the ridge from the dockyard suburb of Woolloomooloo below. Energetic walkers can walk across from the city through The Domain or Botanic Gardens, otherwise bus 312 provides transport from St James in the city. Get off at the 'finger wharf', opposite the Woolloomooloo Bay Hotel, turn right (facing the water) and walk around the quay.

Almost immediately one of Sydney's most unusual icons appears – **Harry's Café de Wheels |1|**. This pie cart, as it once was, has been a part of the Woolloomooloo scene as far back as most locals can remember. It is still a pie cart but has come a long way from the ramshackle vehicle that first came to prominence as an all-night eatery. Its location at the head of the bay is ideal for its purpose of providing sustenance to the sailors of the naval base and the visiting freighters that once berthed along these wharves, and its 24-hour operation caters for late night revellers, from all over Sydney.

Walk on past Harry's Café de Wheels to the first entrance to the naval dockyard on the left. Entry is not permitted, of course, but the pride of Australia's fleet can be easily viewed from Cowper Wharf Road, since only iron railings separate the footpath from the missile destroyers, fleet tankers and frigates usually berthed along this wharf. On the right hand side of the road is an ugly concrete car park, built to cater for Defence Force vehicles but fortunately hidden by a screen of well-grown casuarinas. Apartment buildings are piled up along the skyline on top of the cliff which was formed by quarrying stone for the construction of the **Garden Island Dockyard |2|**.

About halfway along the quay on the left hand side of Cowper Wharf Road is a memorial to the men who set off from this wharf to fight in two world wars. Troopships loaded soldiers for both hemispheres and many theatres of war from this berth. The women of Australia, including many who waved them goodbye – often for the last time – erected this memorial to what was for many the blackest moment of their lives.

At the end of Cowper Wharf Road is the entrance to Garden Island Dockyard, the navy's main base in Sydney Harbour. It is possible to visit this very historic dockyard, but only as part of an organised tour. The dockyard was built by joining a small offshore island, Garden Island, to the mainland at a point originally known as Paddy's Point, but later renamed Potts Point after Joseph Potts, a wealthy bank official. Garden Island, as its name indicates, was first used for growing vegetables for the ship's company of *HMS Sirius* and this is noted in the ship's log. Building of the naval establishment began in 1886 and in 1913 was handed over to the Royal Australian Navy as its official base. The land reclamation which joined the island to Potts Point and

Opening Times

Harry's Café de Wheels: Open 24 hours.
Garden Island Dockyard:
Tours arranged. Phone the dockyard on (02) 9563 4444.
Elizabeth Bay House:
Tue–Sun 10am–4.30pm

Refreshments

Harry's Café de Wheels in Woolloomooloo. There are many restaurants, cafes, food outlets, hotels and bars along Macleay Street and Darlinghurst Road and in side streets. Water bubblers can be found in Beare Park and Fitzroy Gardens.

included a huge graving dock, was completed in 1942. Many of the first buildings on the naval establishment are still in existence.

Cross the road at the lights outside the dockyard gates and walk up the left hand side of Wylde Street, which winds up the hill past a fine old building atop the cliff on the right. This is **Boomerah |3|**. Now Fleet Headquarters, this mansion is typical of the huge homes built on Potts Point in the early 19th century when this was – and mostly still is – the dress circle of Sydney. Boomerah is a two-storey stone mansion including separate stables and servants' wing with articulated quoins and a slate roof, built around 1856 for a wealthy Sydney merchant. It has a sandstone bust of Lord Nelson in the grounds and before Garden Island became a major dockyard, must have boasted a view of Sydney Harbour second to none.

Potts Point

Continue on the left side footpath up the fairly steep hill past HMAS Kuttabul. This is a naval establishment of no historic interest, but which provides facilities for 400 sailors. Originally the site contained three stately homes built in the mid-19th century for wealthy merchants and which had beautifully landscaped gardens and superb views down the harbour. The only surviving feature is a mid-19th century gazebo located on a prominent rock in the grounds of Kuttabul. Crafted in the Classical style from stone with bay windows, wrought iron grilles and stone seats, it has a shallow domed roof and a floor of patterned white and black marble. On the opposite side of Wylde Street are the sandstone pillars and wrought iron gates marking the entrance to Boomerah, with a plaque and the ship's badge of *HMS Duke of York* adorning the wall in commemoration of the service of the British Pacific Fleet in this region during World War Two.

But all the graceful homes of Potts Point are not lost. Just past the main building of Kuttabul is **Jenner House |4|**, built in the 1860s for one of the Hordern family. The house itself is a delight, but it is probably better known for its grounds which are open for inspection by tour groups. This attractively terraced garden, like others nearby, is being restored from what was virtually total desecration following the construction of the naval dockyard. Head gardener of Kuttabul, Jack Gibbs, began the restoration in 1975 after researching the history of the demolished houses.

At the top of the hill Wylde Street becomes Macleay Street, an elegant avenue lined with plane trees that runs the length of the ridge towards Kings Cross. At the next traffic lights cross over and take the road to the right, **Challis Avenue |5|**, where there is a fine display of late Victorian architecture in a series of three-storey terrace houses, very painstakingly restored and maintained. Of particular note are the three buildings on the left: Slighclene, with an elaborately moulded ground floor colonnade and delicate cast iron balustrading on the upper balcony; Byrock, a magnificent paired terrace in Victorian Classical Revival style with colonnaded verandahs; and perhaps the most impressive of them all, Carmelita, a three-storey terrace with colonnaded facade in Romanesque style. Some 37 metres long, this fine building is owned by the Catholic Church and is impeccably maintained. At the bottom of Challis Avenue, cross over through the row of magnolia trees which runs down the centre of the street, and return along the opposite side to see more fine examples of 19th century Sydney's elegant terrace buildings.

At the top of Challis Avenue turn right

and walk up Macleay Street for one block then right again into Rockwall Crescent. At No. 7 is a fine example of a Regency style residence bearing the name of the street – Rockwall |6|. This was built during the 1830s and is one of the few surviving villas in the area. It has five bays, with an encircling verandah and Doric porches to the east and west facades – a superb example of the elegant Potts Point homes of the mid-1800s. Return to Macleay Street and walk to the right for another block to Manning Street where another example of the fine homes built by Sydney's wealthy residents dominates the street. **Tusculum** |7| is a two-storey stuccoed brick Regency mansion, similar in some ways to Rockwall and a fine example of the majestic villas that gave Potts Point its regal status. Erected between 1831 and 1835 this is one of the earliest and contains marble flooring brought from Tusculum in Italy, hence the name. It once housed the first Bishop of Australia, and is linked with many notable citizens of the early colonial era.

At this point it is necessary to return down Macleay Street to Challis Avenue, cross at the traffic lights then veer to the right a little, where a very narrow lane leads down between two apartment buildings. A signpost pointing down the lane indicates that this is the path to Elizabeth Bay House. Follow this lane down an alley and then steps, to the ultimate in elegant living – the homes of Elizabeth Bay. From the bottom of the steps, turn right into Billyard Avenue and just ahead on the right is one of the finest examples of the early Regency style architecture to be seen in Sydney today.

Elizabeth Bay

Elizabeth Bay House |8| is now owned by the people of Sydney, having been carefully and sympathetically restored to preserve it for future generations. It was originally built in the style of a Greek Revival villa between 1835 and 1838, and was located in 23 hectares of prime waterfront land granted to Colonial Secretary Alexander Macleay, whose name is perpetuated in the main street of Potts Point. The house was never totally completed although the interior is considered a masterpiece of the art of architect John Verge. The hall is a brilliant piece of design work, with concentric rings of wedge-shaped stones and the staircase flowing upwards in an elliptical sweep with ornate doorways of cedar on the ground level. The first floor balcony has a wrought iron balustrade supported on scrolled brackets – the trappings of a genteel era now long gone. The effect of spaciousness is enhanced by the doors being set back from the balcony behind a gallery of tall arches. This magnificent house is a highlight of the walk and an inspection of the beautiful interior a must.

The 23 hectares of garden have been whittled down to a small park in front of the building creating a haven of peace with its fish ponds and pleasant views. Walk across this park from the house and bear left to steps leading back down to Billyard Avenue. At this point it is worth stopping for a moment to look back at the buildings set in the steep hillside behind and beside Elizabeth Bay House. Mostly in the foreground are examples of architectural styles from different parts of the world, with the Mediterranean influence being particularly strong.

Keep walking along Billyard Avenue to an extensive wall running along the left hand footpath with wrought iron windows and a wrought iron gateway let into it. Behind this wall is one of the best-known mansions in Sydney – **Boomerang |9|**. It is not as historically important as some of the other houses in the area, although it represents an era which is architecturally important – the Hollywood style extravaganza of the 1920s. This exotic home was built in 1926 for Frank Albert, publisher of, among other works, the *Boomerang Song Book*, hence the name. With its beautifully landscaped gardens including stands of palm trees, fountains, a tennis court and boat house, and the extravagant styling of the pink stucco exterior and multi-coloured terracotta roof, it is a fine example of the influence of Hollywood on the local building scene in that period.

Turn left at the corner of Boomerang and walk down Ithaca Road to Beare Park and the Elizabeth Bay Marina. This is a pleasant little waterfront park with palms and large fig trees and a delightful cast iron drinking fountain dated 1857 – a good spot to take a break and enjoy the outlook over Sydney Harbour. Refreshed, now walk back up Ithaca Road and turn left into Elizabeth Bay Road. Across to the right are a couple of

Elizabeth Bay House

houses with timber shingle roofs; a number of other interesting buildings are also nearby.

Walk around the circular driveway which is the terminus of Elizabeth Bay Road and has a small park in the middle, then return down the hill to **Roslyn Gardens |10|**. Just opposite is a fine set of three-storey terrace houses with elaborate iron lacework balconies, strikingly typical of so many mid-19th century streetscapes across Sydney's inner-city suburbs. On the right as you climb the hill again is St Luke's Hospital, built in the grounds of another of the old estates that once were predominant in this area.

Kings Cross

Turn right around the corner of St Luke's and climb up Roslyn Street, which is fairly steep and narrow. A diversion along Kellett Street will reveal more interesting terrace houses, after which continue up Roslyn Street to Darlinghurst Road. To the left is the red light district that gives Kings Cross its unsavoury reputation. **Darlinghurst Road |11|** is the centre of the strip club area which comes alive at night, but which during the morning wears an innocent and pristine face! To visit this part of 'the Cross', turn left and detour for a few hundred metres up and back along Darlinghurst Road. Otherwise turn right and continue along Darlinghurst Road past bars, taverns and restaurants to **Fitzroy Gardens |12|** and the renowned El Alamein fountain, which commemorates the desert battle at El Alamein in during the Second World War. When operating, the fountain bears a remarkable resemblance to a dandelion seedball!

Cross the street at any point here and walk into one of the open courtyards, veering right to walk through Springfield Gardens into Orwell Street. This is backpackers' territory and both in Orwell Street and **Victoria Street |13|** there are numerous buildings converted into backpacker hostels. Points of interest worth noting in this area are the Wayside Chapel in Hughes Street, the legacy of the Rev. Ted Noffs who strove to minister to the needy, especially the street kids of the Cross, and the Metro Theatre (formerly the Minerva Theatre), where many young Australian actors began their careers. Turn right at the bottom of Orwell Street and walk along one of the most delightful of all Kings Cross thoroughfares – Victoria Street. Unlike some of the streets in this area, Victoria Street is known for its beautiful ambience; sun-dappled trees line the entire street, enhancing the rows of medium density Victorian cottages. The blend of Regency houses, Italianate terraces and the colourful plane trees have earned it a reputation as the 'Montmartre of Sydney'.

Near the end of Victoria Avenue on the left is an interesting roof-top park. This is **Embarkation Park |14|**, a small but well planned little recreational area on the roof of the Defence Forces car park building. Like the memorial on Cowper Wharf Road mentioned at the beginning of this walk, the park is a tribute to the men of the armed forces who embarked from the dockside below, en route to two world wars. It was built by the women and children they left behind.

At the left hand end of this park is a double flight of stone steps, McElhone Stairs, which like Butler Stairs and Hordern Stairs were built to provide pedestrian access to the cliff tops from suburban Woolloomooloo in the days before the roads were built. Follow McElhone Stairs down, cross the street and bear left back to Harry's Café de Wheels where our walk began and from where you can catch either bus 311 or 312 back into the city, or walk back through The Domain.

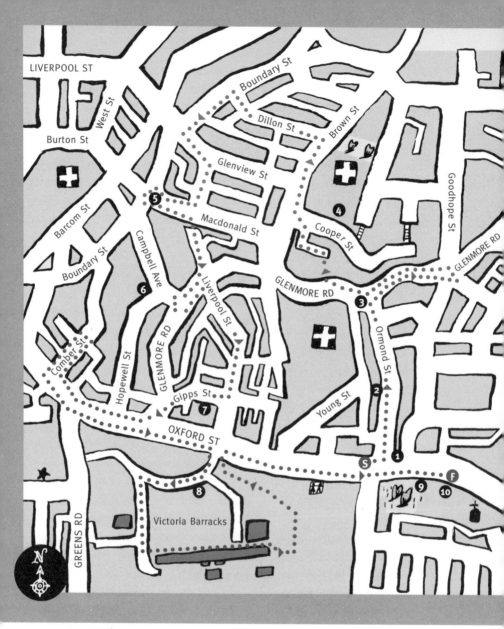

Walk key

1. Juniper Hall | 2. Engehurst | 3. Glenmore Road | 4. The Scottish Hospital |
5. Cutler Footbridge | 6. Corner shop | 7. Paddington Village | 8. Victoria Barracks |
9. Paddington Town Hall | 10. Paddington Reservoir

Paddington

Sydney's first gin distillery

Start

Paddington Town Hall.
Best buses are 380, 382
or 389 from Circular Quay.

Finish

Paddington Town Hall.
Most passing buses return
to the city.

Length/Time

2.5 km/1.5 hours

Wheelchairs

Easy access to all points
on the walk.

Paddington's claim to be Sydney's oldest suburb may be questioned by other inner-city suburbs, but certainly it is one of the most fascinating, and equally certainly, it dates back to Sydney's earliest days. South Head Road, now known as Oxford Street, was originally built by Governor Macquarie in 1811 to provide access to South Head where a signal station was established to advise when an incoming ship was sighted. The first land grant along this road was made in 1812 and while in part it became a fashionable area with some very elegant residences, in part it developed as a working-class suburb, mainly to house the workers building the Victoria Barracks.

Catch the 380, 382 or 389 bus from the Circular Quay in the city and alight opposite the Paddington Town Hall. Walk eastwards and on the corner of Ormond and Oxford streets is the first of many splendid residences in this area – a Georgian house called **Juniper Hall |1|**. This remarkable home is one of the oldest in Sydney and was built by an ex-convict who, two months after his arrival in the colony, was granted 100 acres of land on which to build a gin distillery! Robert Cooper, together with two companions, built and ran the Glenmore Gin Distillery close by. The venture was obviously profitable, and a further 3 acres was granted to Cooper on which to build his home, reputed to be the largest in the area for many years. He appropriately named the house Juniper Hall after the juniper berries used in making gin.

Cooper was a man of many talents and designed the huge house himself, completing it in 1825. It is built on a sandstone ridge with, as might be expected, extensive cellars. A magnificent front entrance is a feature of the house, with double front doors and fanlight flanked by two large multi-paned and shuttered windows on each side. Apart from his other achievements, Cooper had three wives and before his death fathered 23 children – perhaps one reason for the size of the house! In 1839 the distillery was sold to one of the partners who subdivided the land and created the new suburb of Paddington.

Walk down Ormond Street beside Juniper Hall, and on the left, cramped in between other buildings, is an indented alcove with what appears to be the facade of an old building. This is part of **Engehurst |2|**, built in 1835, another exclusive home in this gentlemen's residential area then known as Rushcutter Valley. In 1869 there were 14 houses of more than 10 rooms each in this select neighbourhood. Since those days the adjacent suburb of Woollahra has gained status and is now considered the more exclusive of the two.

A unique quality of Paddington is the steep, narrow streets and the Victorian terrace houses with their walk-up steps and tiled ground-floor verandahs, arched windows and doors. Most have lovely cast iron lacework around the upstairs verandahs with French doors opening onto a small balcony.

Glenmore Road |3|, which winds tortuously north-east from opposite the Victoria Barracks, was the original track used by bullock wagons hauling barrels of gin from Robert Cooper's distillery in Rushcutters Bay, hence its erratic path, following the contours of the hillsides to ease the load on the bullock teams. Turn right from Ormond Street into Glenmore Road and you will come to the well-known Five Ways junction with its statuesque Royal Hotel. Built around 1888, this imposing structure dominates the junction and is considered by many to be one of the finest hotel buildings in the district. Located on a corner between two street frontages, its fine display of iron lacework and wide first-floor balcony creates an eye-catching feature in an area saturated with eye-catching architecture.

Cross over and walk back along Glenmore Road, past just a few of the many styles of terrace houses which line this winding – although by Paddington standards, fairly wide – street. Keep a sharp eye out and between Nos. 194 and 196, on the right hand side, a narrow alleyway will appear – so narrow that two people would have to squeeze to get past one another, while the houses meet overhead. Such alleyways are more associated with the tiny lanes of Dickensian London and not common in Australia although a few may be seen in the older streets of Balmain and The Rocks. Walk through this laneway and turn left into narrow Cooper Lane then left again into Cooper Street. On the right is one of Paddington's best-known feature buildings – **the Scottish Hospital |4|**. Turn right down Brown Street and past the hospital grounds to appreciate the extensive landscaping and planting that must have taken place on this estate.

Built by Judge Kinsella in the 1840s, the original estate and mansion once known as The Terraces was considered to be one of the finest homes in the area, set among superbly terraced gardens. When the mansion became part of the Scottish Hospital, which was then extended across the grounds, great care was taken to preserve some of the well-established trees in the gardens. As a result many survive to this day and are more than a hundred years old. Stand inside the entrance to the hospital at

Opening Times

Juniper Hall: Daily 10am–5.30pm
Victoria Barracks: Thurs 10am–3pm

Refreshments

Cafes, restaurants, hotels and bars are situated along Oxford Street and at Five Ways as well as in some side streets.

the corner of Cooper and Brown streets and see the fine display of Australian rainforest species, palms, Norfolk Island pines and nettle trees.

From the hospital entrance cross Brown Street and enter Dillon Street. Along this suburban road are some excellent examples of Victorian and Edwardian terraces – some of which are among the last of this type to be built in Paddington. At the end of Dillon Street turn left into Boundary Road, walk up the hill and turn left again into Glenview Street, then right into Liverpool Street. Where Liverpool Street crosses Macdonald Street, take a diversion to the right to the **Cutler Footbridge |5|**, which was not a footbridge originally, but a viaduct built in 1908 to carry trams. The footbridge was added in 1940 to provide easy access for Paddington residents heading towards St Vincent's Hospital. From this footbridge, which crosses Boundary Street at rooftop height, you obtain a backyard overview of the maze of terrace houses beneath, with their steep roofs and square chimneys, tiny patchwork gardens and the narrow 'dunny' lanes behind them which provided access for the night soil carters.

Walk back over from Cutler Footbridge and turn right into Liverpool Street again where a wide variety of magnificent trees almost meet overhead, providing shade from the summer sun and a dappled light to enhance the old-world atmosphere of the terrace houses behind them. For an interesting diversion here, turn right along Glenmore Road, walk one block to Campbell Avenue and turn right again. Almost opposite, on the corner of Hopewell Street, is a classic **corner shop |6|** of the type that existed in suburban Sydney in the Victorian era. Paddington, in those days, was a commuter suburb and on the way to or from work, residents picked up their daily needs from these small mixed businesses on the corner of their street or adjacent to their tram stop. These grocer's shops became an important part of the community, providing not only the daily necessities but a focal point for neighbourhood interaction, much along the lines of the local store in country villages. In 1890 there was one corner shop to every 45 houses in Paddington; most are now converted to residences or offices.

Return to Liverpool Street and continue right up the hill to the corner of Gipps Street. Known as **Paddington Village |7|**, here is the quaint community that is so

Dominant landmark of the area – Paddington Town Hall

popular with tourists. Centred around Gipps Street, it contains some of the oldest buildings in the area. Turn right down Gipps Street from Shadforth Street along what is little more than a lane; the doors of the tiny houses mostly open straight onto the street and the footpath is barely wide enough to accommodate one pedestrian. Continue on down Gipps Street to the corner of Prospect Street to two small, single-storey sandstock brick cottages built in the 1840s which are reputed to be among the oldest surviving cottages in Paddington. Like the village itself, these buildings were erected in the 1850s as homes for labourers building the

Victoria Barracks, over on the opposite side of Oxford Street.

Cross over and follow the 3 metre high, 30 centimetre thick sandstone wall to the arched entrance gateway of **Victoria Barracks |8|**. Construction of the barracks was begun in 1841 and completed in 1848, using convict labour as well as workmen and tradesmen from nearby Paddington Village. It is totally surrounded by the stone perimeter wall which in some places has foundations 10 metres deep to ensure a secure footing. Immediately inside the main gate stands the guardhouse, punishment cells and a stone-flagged exercise yard. The spacious parade ground is dominated by the two-storey late Georgian style main barracks which are flanked by other similar sandstone buildings. The centrally located, arched entrance of the main building is surmounted by a clock while on either side a wide verandah extends across the face.

On the eastern side of the parade ground is the officers' mess, a fine structure. From its two-storey verandah extensive views of Sydney Town could be obtained. It is some-what more ornate than other buildings in the complex with a finely carved stone gable. Stables are located behind this building, which was the first in the complex to be completed in 1842. In the north-west corner is the commandant's residence, together with stables, kitchen and carriage house. The gaol and quartermaster's store, enclosed by a separate 3 metre wall, are maintained faithfully as are many of the associated buildings. Return to Oxford Street and turn right towards the main shopping centre which is dominated by the Classic Revival Post Office and **Paddington Town Hall |9|** which was completed in 1885. Then proceed along to the remains of the old **Paddington Reservoir |10|**, only the second reservoir to be built in Sydney and one which served local citizens for over 30 years from 1864. The brickwork arches make it an interesting archaeological feature, as do the vents with their cast iron lace grilles on the reservoir roof. Unfortu-nately the reservoir has been neglected and at the time of writing access is not possible as the structure is in a dangerous state.

An interesting little cameo of life from those early days is associated with the Paddington Reservoir. The water it stored was pumped from the pumping station at Botany, and a stand pipe, with its top at the same level as the top of the reservoir, was located close by, near the Victoria Barracks. The pump operator at Botany focused his telescope on the stand pipe and when he saw it overflow, stopped the pumps, knowing that the reservoir was full!

There is, of course, much more to Paddington and this walk barely scratches the surface of one of Sydney's oldest and most interesting suburbs. But to take in any more at this stage would make our walk too long and unwieldy, so the rest of 'Paddo' will have to keep for another day. To return to the city catch a 380, 382 or 389 bus from any stop along Oxford Street.

Birchgrove & Balmain

A walk along a piece of string

Start

Corner Victoria Road and Darling Street. Take bus 432, 433, 434, 441 or 442 from the city.

Finish

Corner Victoria Road and Darling Street. Catch any city-bound bus along Victoria Road.

Length/Time

10.5 km/3.5 hours

Wheelchairs

Access to all areas with the exception of the steps in the Illoura Reserve and Ballast Point (which can be circumvented).

On either side of the main road that runs down the ridge of the Balmain peninsula is a maze of narrow lanes lined with buildings from another era. An elderly Balmain resident, when asked how far an interesting walk around Balmain would go, replied, 'How long is a piece of string?' And how true that is; you could walk the full length of this suburb along Darling Street in forty minutes, but you could equally spend forty hours exploring the hundreds of roads, cul-de-sacs and laneways that lie on either side. This walk takes in some of the main features of this delightful suburb.

Walk key

1. White Horse Point | **2.** Cockatoo Island | **3.** Dawn Fraser Pool | **4.** Balmain Colliery site | **5.** Longnose Point | **6.** Mort Dock | **7.** Watch House | **8.** Shipwright's cottage | **9.** St Mary's Church | **10.** Illoura Reserve | **11.** Dolphin Hotel | **12.** Clontarf Cottage | **13.** Old St Augustine's Church | **14.** Gladstone Park | **15.** Balmain Town Hall

A lot of Sydney's history was conceived in this waterfront suburb just upstream from the Harbour Bridge, and it is this history which makes the walk so fascinating. Locked between Iron Cove and Johnstons Bay, initially the peninsula was part of a grant of 222 hectares to Scottish surgeon William Balmain, who arrived with the First Fleet in 1788. Its close proximity to the settlement at Sydney Cove attracted a mixed population as the colony developed; waterfront industries claimed much of the foreshore slopes for their workmen's cottages, while high on the ridge wealthy merchants and professionals built elegant homes. In time, the wealthier residents moved on to greener areas on the North Shore and in the Eastern Suburbs and the homes they left behind were often divided into apartments and lodging houses for city workers.

Like Paddington, time and trend saw Balmain reduced almost to a slum area for a while, then it became an 'arty' place where poets and artists starved in garrets. Now the wheel has turned full circle and Balmain is one of the most sought after residential locations in the inner-city area. House prices are escalating at an astonishing rate as the rich, the famous and the 'in' crowd rejuvenate the old suburb, returning it to its former up-market status yet retaining much of its past working-class history to give it an added dimension. As an elderly resident pointed out, you can walk through Balmain streets almost forever and still find interest on every corner.

Start the walk at the corner of Darling Street and Victoria Road. A number of buses from the city service this area. The 432 (Birchgrove), 433 and 434 (Balmain) run from Millers Point while services 441 and 442 run from the city. The 434 service runs down through Balmain to the ferry wharf at the bottom of Darling Street, which can be handy for the return journey up the hill.

From Victoria Road head north through Rozelle along Darling Street, which is renowned for its cosmopolitan ambience, with a wide range of street cafes, coffee shops and restaurants creating a European atmosphere. But before reaching the shopping centre of Balmain village, take a diversion down to the water's edge at Birchgrove where once heavy maritime industries were located, but which has now been returned to the public in the form of attractive foreshore parks and headlands.

Birchgrove

About ten minutes walk down Darling Street, turn left into Young Street and continue down the hill to where Elkington Park runs out onto **White Horse Point |1|**. Apart from the attractive park itself, the headland offers sweeping views of the upper harbour, notably **Cockatoo Island |2|**, once a major naval shipbuilding establishment, now gradually being returned to its natural state. Cockatoo Island is the largest island in Sydney Harbour and before it was taken over as a dockyard in the 1850s, was a maximum security gaol. Legend has it that the notorious Frederick Ward, alias Captain Thunderbolt, risked the sharks to escape by swimming from the island, while equally notorious Jackey Jackey failed in a similar attempt. Convicts were put to work excavating the sandstone rock of the island in order to build large underground storage pits for grain – a common practice in the early days of the colony.

Walk back from White Horse Point and on the left is the **Dawn Fraser Pool |3|**, one of many shark-proof enclosures which once fringed the harbour foreshores. This public pool, first built in 1883, was renamed in 1964 after one of Australia's best-known Olympic swimming champions, Dawn Fraser, who won eight Olympic and eight Commonwealth Games medals. On the right as you leave Elkington Park is a small caretaker's cottage c.1885 and on the left a service road which runs down to a small waterfront park and disused jetty. Walk into Fitzroy Avenue, on a cliff overlooking the park, where a row of fine terraced houses, mostly late 19th century, look out across the water. Turn right into Punch Street, left along Glassop Street, and left again into Birchgrove Road, where most of the houses are also turn-of-the-century. Continue past Birchgrove Public School to the corner of Water Street where a new housing estate has been built.

This was once the site of the **Balmain Colliery |4|** from which, between 1897 and 1931, coal was mined 1,000 metres below the water of the harbour. The coal seam is thought to have run under the harbour as

Opening Times

Balmain Watch House: Sat 1pm–3pm.
Dawn Fraser Pool:
Daily 7.15am–5.30pm.
Closed April to October.
For opening times of other historic buildings contact The Balmain Association, PO Box 57, Balmain NSW 2041.

Refreshments

Cafes, restaurants, bars, hotels and numerous shops can be found along Darling Street and in some side streets. There are water bubblers in Elkington Park, Birchgrove Park, Mort Bay Park and Illoura Reserve.

far as Cremorne, where another coal mine was once planned, but never came to fruition. Walk down Water Street and turn right into River Street, where the houses on the left seem to hang precipitously at levels along the cliff face. Follow narrow River Street to its end in Cove Street, where steep steps on the left lead down to a jetty. Across from River Street is Louisa Road, the main route along the peninsula known as **Longnose Point |5|**.

At one time the 'dress circle' of the area, there are many interesting old homes along this road. Of particular note is Keba, opposite Rose Street, and No. 67, regrettably now an uninteresting block of flats, but which was the site of Birchgrove House, c.1810, the first house built in the locality and the only house on the Birchgrove Estate until 1860. It was demolished in 1967. Continue out to the delightful park at the end of Longnose Point which was once a shipyard, resumed and renovated in 1970 for public use. This park has been renamed Yurulbin, the Aboriginal term for 'swift running waters'. This headland was once the home of the Wangal clan, reputedly the tribe to which Bennelong – the Aboriginal boy who accompanied Captain Phillip back to Britain – belonged. The views of the city from this pleasantly landscaped point are unusual; rarely seen on postcards or calendars they provide a very different perspective of the CBD.

Return back along Louisa Street and walk down the steps leading left to Deloitte Avenue, named after Q. L. Deloitte, a local sportsman at the turn of the century. On the right is Birchgrove Park, an expansive area reclaimed from the mud flats of Snails Bay between 1882 and 1904.

Follow the footpath around the foreshore and on emerging from the park turn left into Grove Street then right into Wharf Road. Scattered along the length of this road, and indeed throughout the whole of this area, is an amazing range of homes, mostly built between 1870 and 1900.

At the end of Wharf Road is an oil terminal, but continue past this and down to the foreshore on the other side via a flight of steps which will bring you out to Yeend Street Wharf.

Mort Bay

Up until now the views across the water from Birchgrove mostly have involved only yachts and other pleasure craft, but here in Mort Bay, commercial maritime activities take over. Across the water from Yeend Street Wharf is the service depot for State ferries and a marina on which big ocean going tugs are berthed. However, these are merely the survivors of the massive maritime industry which once dominated this waterfront. To relive a little of this interesting maritime past walk along the foreshores from Yeend Street jetty around a neatly landscaped part of the bay that was once the site of huge shipbuilding, railway locomotive and heavy engineering works. Behind the park is a modern housing development which covers the remainder of the site known as **Mort Dock |6|**.

One of the most significant figures in Australia's commercial – especially maritime – history was Thomas Sutcliffe Mort. He came to the colony in 1838 at the age of 22. As a woolbuyer, he immediately saw the potential for industrial development in the new land. By 1841 he was foundation shareholder in the Hunter River Steam Navigation Company. He soon realised that there was no dry dock in Sydney large enough for many of the ships that traded here. In 1854 he built Mort Dock – 122 metres (400 feet) long and 15.5 metres (50 feet) wide – in the corner of Mort Bay, and in 1855 the first ship was docked there. Not content with just docking visiting vessels, Mort started a shipbuilding yard beside the dock which subsequently became the birthplace of many ships trading around the coastline and a number of warships commissioned by the Royal Australian Navy. Mort later expanded into heavy engineering, producing machinery and railway locomotives in workshops adjacent to the shipbuilding yards.

In Mort Bay Park, which now replaces much of his waterfront complex, the historic dry dock remains. It is now filled and grassed over to form part of the park, but the sandstone perimeter walls and the original dock gate are still in evidence. Walk through this park and enjoy the pleasant landscaping, mostly with young Port Jackson fig trees, then cross to the far side where an old iron shed surmounts the Thames Street Wharf where once the dockyard workers disembarked from the ferries. Many thousands of men would have passed through this shed, built in 1860, to begin their arduous day's work in the shipyards.

Balmain

From the jetty bear left up the footpath which joins Thames Street and turn left again into Trouton Street. All around this area are wonderful relics of those heady dockyard days and it is worth taking time out to just stroll back in time for a short while in these narrow, nostalgic streets. On the next corner is an interesting group of workers' cottages and corner shop c. 1875,

while across the street at No. 33 Campbell Street is one of the original cottages in the area, built c.1844. Turn left from Trouton into Campbell Street and immediately right into narrow Wells Street, so named because a well had to be moved in order to build the road. Turn right from Wells Street into Waterview Street and then left into Caroline Street. On the corner of this street and Colgate Avenue is the site of the first house built in Balmain, c.1835, but regrettably demolished in the 1890s. On the opposite corner (Colgate Avenue and St John Street) is Broomoo House, the lower level of which is the original structure, built in 1844. Continue up Colgate Avenue to rejoin Darling Street.

On the corner here is the **Watch House** |7|, which is well worth inspecting. It is open to the public between 10am and 5pm. Now fully restored, this original police station is built from solid sandstone and dates back to 1854; reputedly it is the oldest lock-up in Sydney. It served as the focal point of Balmain law enforcement until the 1920s. Immediately adjacent is a sandstone house and shop said to have been built in 1843 for a barrel of rum.

Walk on to the Waverley Hotel, on the corner of Cooper and Darling streets, and visualise the raucous, bawdy singing of drunken sailors emanating from within its sandstone walls. This was the favourite haunt of whaler crews who anchored in the nearby bays after months at sea under horrendous conditions. Perhaps there was more to the location of the Watch House than meets the eye, being just a few steps up the street from this old sailors' pub! Take a moment to detour down Cooper Street to see a quite delightful relic of Balmain's early days – a **shipwright's cottage |8|** built in 1844. With thick walls of solid sandstone, a low-pitched roof and enclosed verandah, this little cottage is the epitome of early Australian harbourside buildings.

Continue up the rise in Darling Street and on the left, at the corner of Stack Street, is **St Mary's Church |9|**, originally built by Edmund Blacket in 1845 and the first church in the area. Although rebuilt in 1858, the original Blacket chancel remains. Cross over the road to No. 86 Darling Street, to a fine residence built in 1842 and subsequently enlarged in 1888; note the colonial fanlight. Then turn right into a narrow lane called Union Street and walk down to No. 17; the original home of John Cavill c.1853. Most of the old stone houses in Balmain were built by this Cornish stonemason and there are many similar houses further down this street and steps which lead into Hosking Street.

Walk left along Hosking then take a quick right into Johnston Street and left into William Street. No. 18 William Street is the one-time residence of boat builder William Gardner who lived here and for many years built his boats from this waterfront house, c.1844. From William Street walk into Edward Street which leads to a park – **Illoura Reserve |10|** – with stunning views of the CBD high rise buildings and the upper reaches of the harbour.

Shipwright's cottage, Balmain

Climb down the timber steps and turn left through the park towards the ferry wharf at the foot of Darling Street, where on the left are some of the old waterfront buildings, mostly hotels which, in their heyday, catered for the sailors of the ships moored in Darling Harbour or Mort Bay. Opposite the wharf is the one-time **Dolphin Hotel |11|** and next to that a few old stone cottages from the 1840s, one of which was owned by the boatman who plied across Darling Harbour to Millers Point. No. 50 Darling Street, Cahermore, on the left as you walk up the hill, was once the Marquis of Waterford Hotel while on the opposite corner is the former Unity Hotel, built it 1848, which is now the Oddfellows Hall. Since the waterfront here was a hive of maritime activity in the early days, it is small wonder so many pubs thrived, later to become residences or offices as the shipping trade moved across to Walsh Bay and Pyrmont.

For those who have walked far enough, a ferry or bus ride back to the city from Darling Street Wharf will round out the walk nicely. For the stayers, there is the long but rewarding haul back up to the top of the hill. Start by walking back up Darling Road then turn right down Duke Street where there are some significant old houses on the right, notably No. 33 Duke Street and No. 2 Duke Place. Bear left into Gilchrist Place and follow it through to the waterfront park which is on the site of Captain Rowntree's original workshops and wharf. Captain Rowntree was a prominent figure in early Balmain activities and the first meeting of Balmain Council was held in his warehouse on this site in 1860. Continue across the park to Hart Street, once aptly named Slipway Road, and follow it up the hill to rejoin Darling Street.

Cross over and walk down Ewenton Street then right into Charles Street. On the left hand side at No. 6 is the oldest brick house still standing in Balmain; it was built in 1839 with extensive gardens, some of which now form the greens of the Balmain Bowling Club. From Charles Street turn left into Wallace Lane then right into Wallace Street; immediately opposite is **Clontarf Cottage |12|**, a beautiful home built in 1844 and preserved as part of the National Trust. Continue through to Adolphus Street and turn left. On the corner of Adolphus and Vincent streets is the Rob Roy Hotel, an old

sailors' pub, c.1855. Turn right into Vincent and enjoy the views of the busy Glebe Shipping Terminal across White Bay Park.

At the end of Vincent Street turn right into Jane Street, which leads back up to Darling Street past some interesting houses and **Old St Augustine's Church |13|**, first built in 1848, the New St Augustine church being built in 1907. On the opposite side of the street is the Convent of the Immaculate Conception (1876). Most of the homes in this street and the London Hotel at the end date between the 1860s and the 1870s. Turn left at Gladstone Street and walk into **Gladstone Park |14|**, which was once the water reservoir for the area, excavated in 1917 with a capacity of over 10 million litres, but which is now used as a fire stand-by. There are toilets here and a children's playground and nearby is the main Balmain shopping centre with street cafes and pubs to provide all that weary walkers might need.

Continue south along Darling Street past the administration centre of the suburb with notable buildings such as the **Balmain Town Hall |15|**, built in 1888, the Working-men's Institute, constructed in 1896, and the Balmain Fire Station which dates from 1894. From this point it is only a 10 or 15 minute walk back to Victoria Road, where our walk through Birchgrove and Balmain ends and from where a frequent bus service runs back to the city. Buses from Darling Street Wharf, mentioned earlier, run up Darling Street to Victoria Road.

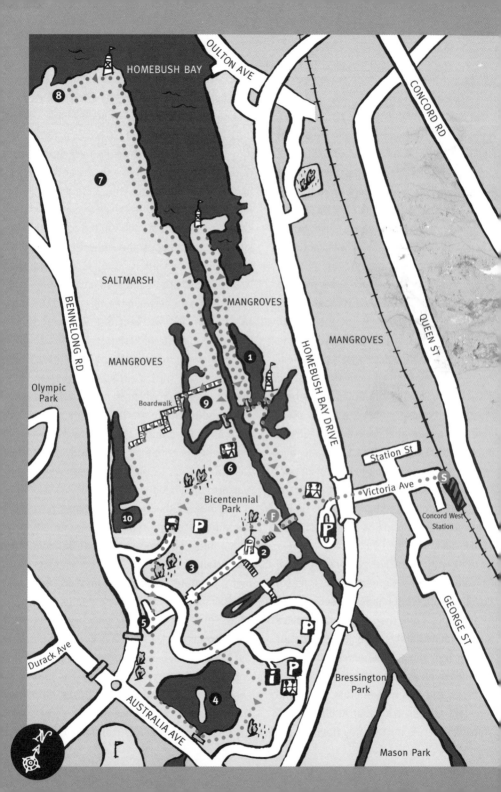

Bicentennial Park

Preserving the National Heritage of Sydney's foreshores

Start

Concord West railway station. Catch a train from Central Railway.

Finish

Concord West railway station. Catch a train back to the city.

Length/Time

7 km/2 hours

Wheelchairs

Easy access throughout the entire park.

Walk key

1. Billabong | 2. Treillage | 3. Peace Monument | 4. Lake Belvedere | 5. Sculpture | 6. Field Studies Centre | 7. Waterbird refuge | 8. Bird hide | 9. Boardwalk | 10. Bennelong Pond

There are many threats to the environment in the modern world, and the mangroves that once crowded the banks of the Parramatta River have been among numerous species endangered by industrial development in the bays and creeks along this waterway. But two hundred years after the first settlers struggled upstream from Sydney Town, one of these bays was dedicated to preserving the natural heritage. This walk through Bicentennial Park reveals the remarkable hidden life of the mangrove environment. Boardwalks across the mud flats and through the mangrove forests themselves offer an exciting experience of a world perhaps previously only seen in photographs.

Long before Parramatta Road became the main route between Sydney Town and its developing agricultural centre at Rose Hill (now Parramatta), much of the travel between the two centres was by water. The Parramatta River was the first 'highway' and for some time after settlement quite sizeable boats plied its quiet waters carrying personnel and goods to the new rural settlement at Rosehill.

Captain Hunter of *HMS Sirius* first explored the river in 1788 and commented in his journal on the wide open bay at what he then thought was the 'head of navigation'. Described by Hunter as having mud flats and mangroves everywhere, this bay was thought to be the extensive inlet now known as Homebush Bay. It was a prime hunting and fishing ground for the Aboriginal inhabitants who lived in the nearby woodlands and along the shoreline.

But mud and mangroves were not considered a very hospitable environment by the white settlers, and as the western suburbs of Sydney began to sprawl out from the city the mud flats and mangroves were at first by-passed and considered of little value for anything other than as a dumping ground for unwanted spoil, or as a fishing ground for river fishermen. This situation obviously suited the natural wildlife of the river. Undisturbed by anything more than the occasional passing boat, birds, mammals and fish flourished in the safe and bountiful refuge of the unwanted bay. Even as Australia became an industrialised nation, nothing more threatening than an

abattoir occupied the land nearby, and although the water became polluted, the mangroves survived – which in turn helped the wildlife to survive. But as the end of the 20th century closed in and the population increased, a cloud began to form over the muddy bay. Technology was giving greedy developers the means to build on impossible terrain and the wildlife of Homebush Bay was threatened.

However, dedicated and fast-moving nature lovers saved the day, persuading the government to declare the wetlands a nature reserve. With the bicentennial year approaching, they argued, it would make a major statement to the world that Australia did, after all, value its natural heritage. The outcome was the construction of the Bicentennial Park, a superb wonderland taking in the mangroves and mud flats of Homebush Bay together with Powells Creek and the marshes and wetlands to the west. The land was reclaimed from two council tips and landscaped to provide pleasant undulating hillocks and open grassy areas to complement the wetlands and mangrove forests which stretch out across Homebush Bay. Overall, the park covers some 100 hectares – 60 hectares of wetlands and 40 hectares of landscaped foreshores – in what is widely considered to be one of the most impressive nature reserves of its type.

The walk through Bicentennial Park can be approached in two ways. Energetic walkers who have already undertaken the walk through the adjacent Olympic Games complex can continue that walk by crossing the footbridge into Bicentennial Park. However, the two walks together create something of a marathon effort and it is probably best to do them separately. As a separate walk the Bicentennial Park is best approached from a different direction. Start by catching a train from Central Railway in the city and get off at Concord West station. Walk left up over the footbridge and then down across King Street to Victoria Avenue. Continue down this avenue, pass under the elevated roadway and immediately ahead will be the park gates.

Powells Creek

Once through the gates, ignore the first footpath to the right as it runs beside Homebush Drive and is part of a cycling track which leads out of the park en route to Ryde. Instead, take the second path on the right past the children's playground and picnic area into the mangroves on the eastern side of Powells Creek and to a couple of observation towers. If it is low tide, the mangroves will be sitting in a broad expanse of damp mud with their aerial roots protruding like a fakir's bed of nails. At high tide these are mostly covered but the twisted mass of mangrove trunks creates a fascinating network of patterns on the calm surface of the water. Only a few metres into the forest the path crosses a small offshoot creek and shortly afterwards a diversion track leads off to the right to a nearby observation tower overlooking the **Billabong |1|**. Climb this tower and observe the layout of the mangroves on either side

Opening Times

Bicentennial Park: Daily 9am–7.45pm.

Refreshments

There is a kiosk adjacent to the Information Centre. Water bubblers are found throughout the parklands. Shops can be found adjacent to Concord West railway station.

of the billabong and to the north and west. A veritable sea of olive green reaches out in all directions, broken only by an occasional glimpse of water. Some wildfowl will probably be visible, speckling the open spaces.

The principal mangrove here is the grey mangrove (*Avicennia marina*) which although growing to only a modest height compared to some mangroves, creates a very dense forest in places. Mangroves adapt very well to their seemingly hostile environment. Because of the waterlogged mud in which they grow, the roots are adapted as respiratory organs as well as providing a firm grip in the slime to hold the tree in place. From some of the roots grow embryo plants which push up through the mud, often reaching maturity while still part of the mother plant. Most species of mangroves also reproduce by means of fruit or seeds which drop from the mother plant and float off, sometimes across oceans, before settling on a distant shore and germinating. In this way the canny mangrove is able to reproduce itself through its roots at home, and at the same time populate distant beaches and mud flats with its seed.

Return from the first tower to the intersection with the main pathway, turn right and continue out past the billabong to the second tower, about a 15 minute walk. Through the mangroves wildfowl, usually ducks, moorhens or coots, can be seen fossicking in the mud; and from the second tower, at the end of the track, other birds, particularly pelicans, are usually visible enjoying undisturbed respite on the waters of Homebush Bay and the distant Parramatta River.

The parklands

The path out to the bay does not cross Powells Creek at any point so it will be necessary to return almost to the gates in order to turn right and cross the bridge over the creek. Continue up a modest gradient to an interesting structure at the crown of the hill. This is known as the **treillage |2|**, a French term roughly translated as 'trellis structure'. The name is very descriptive since the treillage is effectively a tower constructed with wooden trellis as the sides.

Climb to the top and enjoy extensive views of the park, including the mangrove forest, wetlands and open parkland. Beyond the suburbs on the eastern side the distant towers of the city stubble the

The Symbol of Multiculturalism sculpture

horizon, while to the west, the Olympic structures create a very dramatic skyline.

Surrounding the foot of the tower is a moat in which 199 small fountains discharge water which flows down a 200 metre low-gradient race to where the two-hundredth fountain is located. This rather unique structure represents the two hundred years of white settlement to the Bicentennial year of 1988. Walk down the slope beside the water race to the bottom where twin columns, originally mounted in Macquarie Street as part of the Bicentennial decorations, mark the end beside a small pool. A row of plane trees on either side of the race complete the peaceful picture, and seats are provided along the full length for visitors to sit in the shade and contemplate as the water flows past.

Leaving the treillage, walk straight down the hill towards the service road and note the stainless steel sculptures on the right. This is the **Peace Monument |3|** which was commissioned in 1986 by the NSW State Government as part of the International Year of Peace. It is a three-dimensional map illustrating what it might be like to be out in space looking back at Earth and is intended to remind us of our fragile place in the solar system. The abbreviated inscription on the monument reads: 'Peace on Earth, on the Moon and in Space Between and Beyond.'

Follow the service road down to the left to the expanse of water known as **Lake Belvedere |4|**, an artificial pond specifically designed to attract a wide species of waterfowl. Many waterbirds will only inhabit waters that are akin to their natural habitat, so this lake had to be specifically constructed to accommodate as many species as possible by meeting the individual requirements of those species.

There are deep areas, shallow areas, foreshores which dry out at times, reed-encrusted areas, sand banks, a small creek and an island in the centre. Those species attracted to the lake can be observed from the elevated surrounding grassy areas or from jetties.

Continue past Lake Belvedere and immediately ahead, at the top of the rise, is the Information Centre. At this stage it might be a good idea to call in and get some information about the park before setting off on the main part of the walk. There are toilets here and a children's playground as well as barbecues and a cafe, all surrounded by sweeping lawns and undulating hillsides, making it an ideal picnic ground for families.

Walk down to the edge of Lake Belvedere again and then trek out around the western shoreline. The path will eventually lead past a **sculpture |5|** dedicated to multiculturalism. This bas relief is a replica of the oldest intact sculpture of Ahura Mazda, the winged god of Persian religion, and was presented by the Persian Cultural Society in 1994 to celebrate multiculturalism. Now bear right and walk across the road and up over the grassy slope, past a sundial. The grassy open spaces start to give way to mangroves here, but keep heading over the rise towards a building among the trees at the bottom of the slope. This is the **Field Studies Centre |6|**, used mainly by schools and organised groups.

A pathway leads past the Field Studies Centre and into the mangroves through planted stands of casuarinas and other native shrubs. Not far along an information board advises that in late summer and autumn golden orb spiders weave their webs among the mangroves, sometimes creating a tunnel effect over the path in this area. This can be somewhat disconcerting for walkers who are not familiar with the spider, but it is quite harmless to humans and at worst a sticky strand of web – which is easily wiped away – may wrap around your face. On the right of the sealed path the mangroves start to thin out and glimpses of Powells Creek appear. Wildfowl, mostly moorhens and ducks, favour the cover provided by the mangroves, but in the open water pelicans and sometimes black swans swim regally, anchoring against the breeze.

The waterbird refuge

Along the last section of the walk the mangrove forest on the left gives way first to saltmarsh areas and then to a large, landlocked expanse of open water forming a giant pond. This provides a fine **waterbird refuge |7|**. Black-winged stilts, ducks, coot, black swans and pelicans are here in large numbers while frogs and other amphibians enjoy the reeds around the edges. Acacia, melaleucas, grevilleas and even a few eucalypts are in evidence around the shoreline, while in the swampy wetlands mirror bush, salt water couch, sea rush and wallaby grass thrive. Information sheets or books obtained at the information centre will help identify the enormous range of native plants in the park.

Before the path reaches the observation tower on the point, on the right through a gap in the mangroves a couple of rusting hulks introduce an unnatural element to the environment. These are relics of an era when Homebush Bay, and in particular the mangroves, were used as a dumping ground.

Indeed, one of the greatest problems in building the nearby Olympic venue was the removal of toxic waste which, after years of industrial dumping, had permeated the shoreline. Fortunately, the area is responding to the clean-up and the hardy mangroves, having survived the onslaught of the past century, are thriving again in relatively clean, unpolluted water.

The path reaches its furthest point at a small observation tower which provides a fine view of the open waters of Homebush Bay and the Parramatta River beyond. Depending on weather and environmental conditions, there is usually a wealth of wildfowl in these open waters; if not they are certain to be in the lagoon behind. Between them these two waterways offer great scope to observe the overall activities of the mangrove forest and swamp dwellers under almost all conditions. Also visible from the top of the tower are the developments along the shorelines on either side of Homebush Bay. To the west are the striking structures of the Olympic complex and the undulating slopes of the Millennium Parklands which, when completed in 2010, will be one of the most significant man-made parks in the world. It will cover 450 hectares, making it bigger that New York's Central Park. Its construction involves planting over 2 million new plants and some 65,000 native trees.

Descend from the tower and head west across the top of the waterbird refuge along a short road lined with bottlebrush and other native shrubs. Where this road terminates a **bird hide |8|** has been built from which you can watch the wildfowl on the lake without disturbing them. Over 140 species of water bird have been recorded here, some of which make an annual migration to and from Siberia – a quite remarkable feat of endurance as well as navigation. This is the end of the track and it will be necessary to return down the side of the lake, past the saltmarsh and back into the mangrove forest. After about 10 minutes a **boardwalk |9|** through the mangroves leads off to the right.

The mangrove forest

Now comes the most interesting part of the walk, through the fantasy land of the twisted trunks and spiky pneumatophores (aerial roots) of the mangroves. Despite its somewhat barren appearance, the mangrove forest is teeming with life. When the tide is in, swarms of fingerlings can be seen weaving through the mangrove roots, darting here and there through the clear water as enemies, real and imagined, chase them. In early summer, coots, moorhens and ducks lead their tiny offspring through the channels looking for food, quacking or honking as the tiny chicks rev their 'outboard motors' to keep up with mum. Dragonflies hover before darting off between the trunks, while the ubiquitous flies persistently make them-

selves known, especially when the tide is out and the mud appears. The boardwalk twists and turns as it weaves between the trunks of the mangroves only a few centimetres above the mud and under a canopy of branches and leaves. Small crabs appear and quickly disappear on dried mud banks, and although there are happily none present, it takes little imagination to visualise the horny outline of a crocodile sneaking through the swampy environment.

Take a right turn at the intersection of two boardwalks and follow it out onto dry land again. A raised path leads back through the mangroves with **Bennelong Pond |10|** on the right containing more interesting bird life; wildflowers bordering the path provide a contrast with the mangroves. This path leads out past the administration building, completing the circuit of the wetland area by returning to the undulating grassy slopes of the parkland. Walk to the left up the hill towards the treillage tower and down the other side to cross Powells Creek; return to the gates and thence to Concord West railways station for a train back to the city.

It is exciting to know that this, one of the most interesting of all the walks, is totally accessible to those in wheelchairs. Even the meandering boardwalk through the mangroves, while perhaps calling for a little pushing and shoving, should not present any great problems.

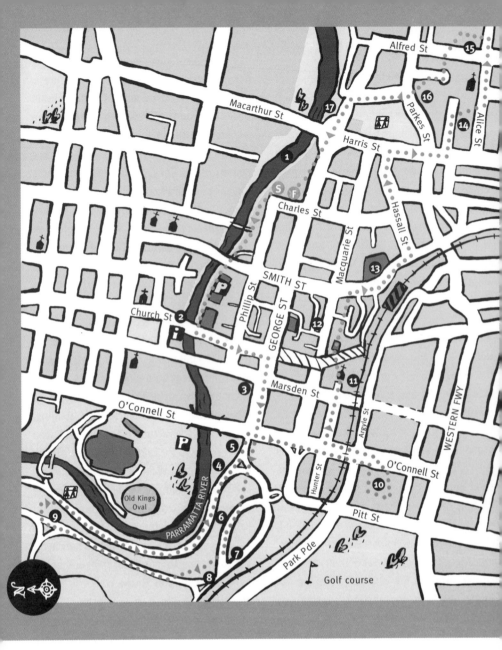

Walk key

1. Parramatta River | **2.** Lennox Bridge | **3.** Brislington | **4.** Parramatta Park | **5.** Gatehouse | **6.** Old Government House | **7.** Observatory | **8.** Bath house | **9.** Dairy cottage | **10.** St John's Cemetery | **11.** St John's Cathedral | **12.** Houison Cottage | **13.** Lancer Barracks | **14.** Experimental Farm Cottage | **15.** Elizabeth Farm House | **16.** Hambledon | **17.** Queens Wharf

Historic Parramatta

'Where the eels lie down'

Start

Rivercat ferry wharf, Parramatta.
Catch the Rivercat from
Circular Quay.

Finish

Rivercat ferry wharf, Parramatta.
Catch the ferry back to the city.

Length/Time

6.5 km/2 hours

Wheelchairs

There are steps at Lennox
Bridge, but these can be
bypassed. Easy access to
all other points on this walk.

Few people realise that Parramatta was once destined to be the capital city of New South Wales. The unproductive land around Sydney Cove would not support the new colony so within weeks of the First Fleet's arrival a search was begun for more fertile, productive land. Parramatta – then called Rose Hill – was decided on as the best location for the main centre of the colony and the first land grant issued in Australia was to James Ruse at Parramatta. This walk includes many of the historic buildings, including Ruse's farm, that formed the foundation of the city which might well have been the capital of Australia today.

The site on the shores of Sydney Cove chosen as the landing place for the First Fleet was well suited in terms of a sheltered harbour and a good supply of fresh water. But the land around it offered only limited agricultural resources and it was obvious to Governor Phillip that unless suitable soil was found quickly, the people he had brought to the colony would soon starve. After a quick foray around the nearby bays and harbours he headed up the Parramatta River and, at the head of this winding and narrow waterway, discovered exactly what he wanted – fertile land on which crops could be grown.

So urgent was the need to find suitable land, that an exploratory crew landed at the head of the river in April 1788, only three months after the arrival of the First Fleet in Sydney Cove. By November of that year a settlement was well established and land had been cleared on a rise known as Rose Hill, which is now part of Parramatta Park. A year later Australia's first grain crop was harvested – 200 bushels of wheat and 35 bushels of barley – and by 1791 Parramatta was rapidly taking over as the main centre of the new colony. Captain Watkin Tench recorded in his diary that year: 'Sydney has long been considered as only a depot for stores … cultivation of the ground is abandoned, and all our strength transferred to Rose Hill.'

Small wonder, then, that with such a background the present city of Parramatta (the named was changed in June 1791) is alive with history. Indeed many of the early buildings are still in their original location, mostly well preserved and restored. A walk through Parramatta is a walk back into that challenging era when the first rural development in Australia's history began – when the first crops were sown and harvested, the first farms established, and the foundations of what was heading to be the capital of New South Wales were laid on the river flats 25 kilometres from Sydney Town.

Parramatta River

The best way to begin this walk is to follow in the footsteps of those early pioneers – along the **Parramatta River** |1|. It is also possible to travel by train or bus, but the trip up river provides a more adventurous atmosphere and the changing tableaux of riverside activities add interest to the trip. While the early settlers in their inefficient boats worked upstream against strong tides and fluky winds, taking probably days to reach the head of the river, today's fast Rivercat ferries streak up through the mangroves in exactly one hour.

Start by catching the Rivercat at Circular Quay. On a fine day an open-air seat is preferable, for despite the wind created by the ferry's speed, a much better view of the passing river scene is obtained from the outside than through the tinted windows of the cabin. The Rivercat – each of these is named after an Australian sporting champion – backs out of the wharf and heads straight under the massive arch of Sydney Harbour Bridge, covered in walk 3. The first few kilometres of the upper reaches of

Sydney Harbour bustle with maritime activity. On the left as you head past Goat Island are the major shipping container wharves of Balmain and Glebe, backed by the elegant tracery of the ANZAC Bridge, covered in walk 12. On the right, in stark contrast, are the tree-covered headlands of Balls Head, Berry Island and Manns Point and the elegant residences of Hunters Hill (walk 18).

Under the concrete arch of the Gladesville Bridge and heading due west, the shorelines are covered with residential development, some old, some very new. Much of the heavy industry, such as oil depots, gasworks and shipbuilding yards, have now been demolished and replaced with toy-town type housing developments. The Olympic complex with its still-to-be-completed Millennium Park, is a notable feature on the left.

Now the ubiquitous mangroves start to close in from either bank and while there is still a great deal of industrial development behind them on either shore, as the upper reaches approach, the river narrows and the mangrove forest discreetly hides the less salubrious factory installations. Indeed, it is time now for the ferry to slow as the mangroves almost brush the sides and make navigation difficult. Like a modern-day *African Queen* the Rivercat pushes through the mud and the mangroves until suddenly, round the last bend, the high rise buildings of Parramatta appear and the mangroves are gone. The ferry berths alongside a jetty and the walk begins in earnest.

Opening Times

Brislington: 1st and 3rd Sun, 2nd and last Thurs of each month 10.30am–3.30pm.

Gatehouse Art Gallery: Tue–Fri 11am–3pm, Sun 11am–4.30pm.

Old Government House: Tue–Fri 10am–4pm; Sat, Sun and public holidays 11am–4pm.

St John's Cathedral: Guided tours Thurs and Fri 10am–2.30pm.

Linden House (Lancer Barracks): Sun 10am–4pm.

Experiment Farm Cottage: Tue–Thurs 10am–4pm; Sun and public holidays 11am–4pm.

Elizabeth Farm: Daily 10am–5pm.

Hambledon Cottage: Wed, Thurs, Sat, Sun and public holidays 11am–4pm.

Refreshments

Restaurants, cafes, kiosks, shops, hotels and bars are throughout Parramatta centre. There are restaurants at the Rivercat wharf and Old Government House and water bubblers in most parks and malls.

Parramatta city

Walk up the ferry ramp and bear right along the river bank; a footpath leads to a distant stone bridge over a stretch of still water locked behind a weir. This weir was originally built in 1818 to retain the fresh water upstream for drinking purposes by preventing it from mixing with the brackish estuarine water below. Continue along the footpath above the weir under one road bridge and on to the next, which is **Lennox Bridge |2|**, an attractive sandstone arch built between 1836 and 1839 by David Lennox, the first Superintendent of Bridges in the colony. Take the steps to the top of the bridge and turn left along Church Street, one of the two first streets laid out in Governor Phillip's 1790 plans for the new settlement. At first called Rose Hill, in 1791 the name was changed to the Aboriginal name Parramatta, meaning 'head of the river' or 'where the eels lie down'!

On the opposite side of Lennox Bridge, the relatively modern Riverside Theatres can be seen. This cultural centre was built as part of the Bicentennial celebrations in 1988, exactly 200 years after the first white settlers landed on the river bank here. Walk along Church Street past the street cafes and restaurants to George Street, then turn right and continue along George Street to the next intersection with Marsden Street, named after pioneer clergyman and farmer Samuel Marsden. Although an unpopular person in the colony, Marsden was a central figure in developing its agriculture, particularly wool. On one visit to

Old Government House, completed by Governor Macquarie in 1815

London he took with him the first parcel of commercial quality wool ever to leave Australia. He is buried in Parramatta and the street perpetuates his name.

On the corner of Marsden and George streets are two fine buildings; the Woolpack Hotel (c.1800), which holds the longest continuous licence in the country, although not always in its present location, and **Brislington |3|**, a red-brick Georgian residence with a slate hipped roof built in 1820. Currently used as part of the local health system, this fine old structure was built for ex-convict John Hodges, possibly as a hotel, but it was later confiscated when he ran into trouble with the law and became a convict again! It was later owned and occupied by three generations of doctors. The tradition of this house being associated with the medical profession was continued when it was purchased by the Parramatta District Hospital.

Parramatta Park (Rose Hill)

Continue walking along George Street and cross O'Connell Street to enter the area where Parramatta's history began – Rose Hill, now known as **Parramatta Park |4|**. The unusual **gatehouse |5|** has the appearance of a child's toy fort, with its red and white face brick, stuccoed facade and castellated tower. The arched entrance comprises two ornate iron gates with an unusual bay window over the top. The gatehouse was completed in 1885, replacing the original stone lodge built by Governor Macquarie in 1810. Just inside, on the right as you enter the grounds, is an obelisk commemorating the spot where Governor Fitzroy's wife died after a horse carriage accident in 1847.

From the gatehouse, the original entrance to the estate, look up the hill towards one of the finest examples of Australia's heritage – **Old Government House |6|**. It was on this hill that the first substantial crop of grain was grown – grain that was to save the small colony from starvation and start Australia on the path to becoming one of the world's major agricultural countries. Small wonder it was later chosen to house the seat of government. Walk up the grassy slope to the left of this splendid building, first erected by Governor Hunter in 1799 –

although it was preceded by a lath and plaster structure – and developed to its present state by Governor Macquarie between 1815 and 1818.

It consists of a central two-storey Georgian block with two linked single storey buildings, one on each side. Small-paned windows with shutters, an elliptical fanlight and side panels around the central doorway, all add to the Classical Georgian styling, while the timber portico is thought to have been designed by Francis Greenway. In the days when it was at its prime, it must have made a wonderful sight, standing proudly on the crest of the hill surrounded by sloping vegetable gardens, fields of wheat and barley, orchards and vineyards. This fine building is the oldest remaining public structure on the Australian mainland.

Old Government House is open to the public. After walking through continue on up the hill keeping the buildings on your right. Immediately across the road is perhaps one of the most fascinating of all relics of the early settlement at Rose Hill. Marked by an obelisk, this is the site of Governor Brisbane's former **observatory |7|**, built in 1822 and the first observatory to be erected in Australia. Even more interesting are the two stones which stand beside it, for these are the remnants of the transit instrument that was housed in the observatory and appear to this day to be aligned for a sighting.

On the right hand side of the road is the circular stuccoed brick edifice with a steeply pitched conical roof which was originally Governor Brisbane's **bath house** |8|. It had a flagstoned floor and central Roman style sunken bath, with cubicles around the circumference to provide some privacy. The water was pumped from the river below and stored in a dam nearby. Later the building was converted to a pavilion. To the right of the bath house an unusual grouping becomes visible across the top of the ridge. Dominant is the Boer War Memorial, a Greek Revival portico built in 1837 as part of Parramatta's courthouse, and re-erected as a memorial to Australian soldiers who died in the Boer War. Cannons on either side of the memorial are dated 1806 and 1810.

Nearby is one of the few remaining boundary stones put in place to mark the boundary of Parramatta in 1839. Stonemason David Lennox, builder of the Lennox Bridge, was instructed to lay these stones by Governor Gipps. Continue on past the Boer Memorial and follow the road for about one kilometre until a small, white stuccoed brick cottage appears to the right. There are in fact two cottages which formed the original dairy, but the older of the two was the **dairy cottage** |9| for the Parramatta Government Farm and as such is one of the oldest dairy cottages of its type in the country. Probably built in the 1790s it has a verandah supported by timber posts with an iron hipped roof.

This is the furthest extent of the walk through Rose Hill history, so turn back and walk beside the river to the gatehouse where we began. Now bear right along

O'Connell Street. Continue on this street under the railway bridge to **St John's Cemetery** |10|. This is a cemetery of great historic importance, for among the graves, which date back to 1790, are some of the early pioneers such as David Lennox and Samuel Marsden, John Batman, founder of Melbourne, and John Blaxland, considered to be the father of Australia's cattle industry. A number of other important people, some of whom arrived with the First Fleet, are also buried here. This cemetery, the oldest in Australia, is surrounded by a convict-hewn stone wall built during the early 1820s.

After visiting the cemetery, return under the railway bridge and along O'Connell Street then turn right into Hunter Street, cross Marsden Street and enter the forecourt of **St John's Cathedral** |11|. The original chapel was built between 1799 and 1803 and the twin square towers added in 1820, each with its clock face and spire.

The chapel was demolished and replaced with a sandstone nave in 1852. Samuel Marsden was the first minister to preach in the cathedral; previously he had used the wooden huts which were Parramatta's first churches from which to deliver his fire and brimstone sermons.

There are so many interesting historic buildings in this part of the city that it is hard to determine which to include as part of the walk and which to bypass. From St John's Cathedral walk left through the mall and right along Macquarie Street where on the right you will pass the Leigh Memorial Uniting Church (1839) and on the opposite side **Houison Cottage** |12|, a beautifully restored family home built in 1842. Turn right from Macquarie into Smith Street and cross over to the other side where on the corner stands the Gothic Revival Arthur Phillip High School. A little further down Smith Street is the **Lancer Barracks** |13|; the oldest military buildings in continuous use in Australia.

The three original buildings in this group were designed by Governor Macquarie's aide-de-camp John Watts. They are arranged around a parade ground and were built between 1822 and 1888. An excellent example of Georgian architecture, the barracks also contains Linden House, built in 1828 in Macquarie Street and moved to the barracks where it is now used as a military museum. From the Lancer Barracks continue along Smith Street and take the first left around the Commercial Hotel into Hassall Street. Although not historic, St Ioannis Greek Orthodox Church is an interesting feature on the right, while a little further on is the Rowland Hassell Public School on the left. Turn right into Harris Street, cross Parkes Street then turn left into Ruse Street.

Early homesteads

A few metres along Ruse Street on the right is **Experimental Farm Cottage** |14|. While the cottage itself is not so significant, the land on which it stands could perhaps be described as the cradle of Australian agriculture. James Ruse arrived in Sydney as a convict with the First Fleet and claimed to be the first British subject to set foot on Australian soil. While this may be debatable, he certainly could legitimately claim to be the first recipient of a land grant in the new colony. Despite his conviction and subsequent transportation, Ruse was a well-behaved worker and skilled farmer. When his sentence ran out in 1789, Governor Phillip gave him a small block of land on the understanding that if he could make the land self-supporting, he would be granted a large block. By 1791 Ruse had succeeded, and the block of land in Ruse Street was made part of a 30 acre grant. He subsequently went on to obtain and farm many new land grants in Windsor, Bankstown and Riverstone.

Walk past the house and bear right through the grounds of the Experimental Farm to Alice Street, then left past Our Lady of Lebanon Church whose striking modern architecture creates a vivid contrast to the historic houses in the Parramatta area. Continue down the hill and across Alfred Street to arguably the most significant of all historic homesteads in Australia – **Elizabeth Farm House** |15|. This single storey rendered house was built by John Macarthur in 1793. It was, in Macarthur's own words, 'a most excellent brick house, 68 feet in front and 18 feet in breadth... the house is surrounded by a vineyard and garden of about three acres.' The original building was an English style cottage, which evolved to a distinctive Australian bungalow with deep verandahs as time went by and Macarthur's fortunes improved. Much of the early house can still be seen when entering the front door from the garden.

Stand on the front verandah of this fine old house and appreciate the site Macarthur chose. Before suburban Parramatta grew up around it, the view down the hill to the river and across the river flats would have been superb. Since the river was, in those days, the main access route, it is not hard to visualise the Macarthur family watching the approach of a boat and the disembarking of their visitors at the foot of what must have been a magnificent hillside estate. Some of that magnificence can still be enjoyed in the garden where a variety of fine old trees, exotic plants and giant cactuses give the homestead its true old world ambience. Take time to look around this excellent example of the earliest colonial structures; then walk around to the right of the buildings to leave by the front gate and stroll down through the remaining section of the estate grounds to rejoin Alfred Street at the creek.

Cross Alfred Street and follow a footpath leading off to the left beside the creek to Gregory Place. Then cross the road towards a corner garden with a superb stand of trees, buried among which is another historic old homestead. This is **Hambledon |16|**, a beautifully restored home set among a grove of stately old oaks mixed quite sympathetically with a few eucalypts, jacarandas and even a cork tree, most of which were planted by John Macarthur. Hambledon was built by Macarthur in the early 1820s for his children's governess, Penelope Lucas, hence its close

proximity to Elizabeth Farm. The walls are stuccoed brick with French windows. There is a stone-flagged verandah and the house, being close to the river, was used often as accommodation for the Macarthurs' vice-regal visitors.

Immediately across from Hambledon, Purchase Street leads down to George Street and the banks of the Parramatta River. This stretch of the river bank is preserved as a park to commemorate the original landing place for boats plying upstream with supplies for the first pioneer settlers. **Queens Wharf |17|** was originally built by convicts from local timber, and the first steamship from Sydney berthed here in 1831. In 1835 David Lennox replaced the timber structure with a fine sandstone quay, part of which is still visible to this day. There are also memorials in this park to the three naval ships that were named 'Parramatta' and which served in both world wars.

Although at the time David Lennox rebuilt this wharf Parramatta was still flourishing as the prime location in the new colony, its fortunes were beginning to wane. In 1813 a route across the Blue Mountains was discovered by explorers Wentworth, Blaxland and Lawson and in 1815 the road built by convicts under the direction of William Cox opened up the fertile plains that finally gave the farmers the land they had so desperately looked for. Ironically, the party which found the way across the ridges prepared for their journey in Parramatta, little knowing that their massive discovery would end the dominance of the thriving settlement on the banks of the Parramatta River.

Although the town retained its importance as the country seat of the governor until 1855, a plague of rust decimated the crops to the point where wheat growing became unprofitable. The huge plains to the west of the Blue Mountains and in the Hunter Valley were proving suitable for cropping as well as grazing and soon took over as the food bowl of the colony. Parramatta's prosperity also suffered because of its lack of a suitable port to accommodate overseas ships. Despite Lennox's new stone quay, the shallow tidal waters of the river were no match for the deep water berthing facilities at Sydney Cove, and gradually Sydney Town began to regain its status as the capital of the new colony.

Despite this, Parramatta continued to grow and small farming settlements in what are now the suburbs of Toongabbie, Castle Hill and Prospect flourished as fruit-growing and market vegetable centres. In 1861 Parramatta was incorporated as a town and in 1948 became a city in its own right. Rail and road took over from the river and the elegant mangrove-encrusted waterway, along which those early intrepid explorers journeyed to discover the first fertile lands on the continent, no longer carried the trade which had made Parramatta a major player in the founding of New South Wales.

From the riverside park veer back onto George Street and on the right is the last historic building of our walk – Harrisford, the original building of the Kings School, which opened it 1832. It was later sold to a Surgeon Harris, who gave it its current name. A footpath on the right just past Harrisford leads down to the ferry wharf and the end of our walk. Although fairly extensive, the walk covers only a limited number of the fine historic features of Parramatta. Perhaps the others can be covered on another walk; certainly there are too many to be covered in one day.

Start

Circular Quay. Catch the Woolwich ferry to Valentia Street wharf or a 506 bus from Circular Quay, then the Northern & Western 538 bus to the wharf.

Finish

Top of Joubert Street, Hunters Hill. Catch a 506 bus back to the city, or a Northern & Western 538 bus down to the wharf, then a ferry back to the city.

Length/Time

5 km/1.5 hours

Wheelchairs

Easy access around the streets. Access is difficult to Kellys Bush and Mornington Reserve but these can be bypassed.

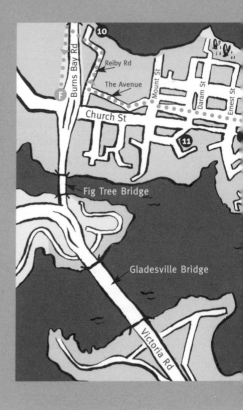

Walk key

1. Valentia Street Wharf | **2.** Woolwich |
3. Woolwich Dock | **4.** Kellys Bush |
5. Cockatoo Island | **6.** Mornington Reserve |
7. Passy | **8.** All Saints Anglican Church |
9. Old buildings | **10.** Figtree House |
11. Hunters Hill

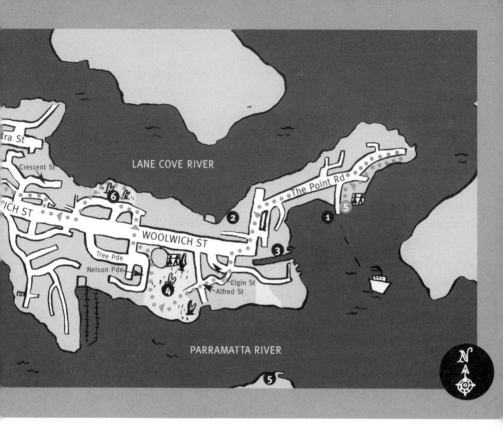

LANE COVE RIVER

Crescent St

The Point Rd

WOOLWICH ST

Tree Pde
Nelson Pde

Elgin St
Alfred St

PARRAMATTA RIVER

N

Walk No. 18

Elegant Hunters Hill
Gracious homes and the Great North Walk

Despite commencing life as a poverty-stricken penal colony, the untouched riches of the newly settled land ensured that Sydney Town soon fostered a breed of wealthy merchants. Sparing no expense – probably because there was nowhere else to spend their money – they built lavish homes, mostly around the foreshores of Sydney Harbour. A cluster of these magnificent old homesteads survives in Hunters Hill, one of Australia's oldest suburban areas. This walk, which is the first section of the Great North Walk, takes in some of these gracious homes.

Hunters Hill was just far enough away from the working-class suburbs of 19th century Sydney and the noise and grime of the industrial centres to make it a suitable residential area for wealthy merchants and professionals. Unlike Birchgrove, Potts Point and other recognised affluent suburbs, Hunters Hill was on the other side of the harbour which gave it added appeal as an isolated, peaceful refuge, well away from the machinations of busy city life.

Before white people set foot on the Hunters Hill peninsula it was popular with local Aborigines, probably the Gamaraigal tribe who inhabited much of the land around the Lane Cove River. Its foreshores were a rich source of shellfish and its bush-clad slopes offered a wide variety of wildlife, while the rocky terrain provided good shelters. The original occupants were displaced when the land became an important agricultural area with a number of small farms providing produce for the growing colony. The ferries, which began running up the Parramatta River in the 1830s, created new interest in the area and by 1844 all the land had been purchased and the peninsula was ripe for development.

Credit for the early development of Hunters Hill is probably due to two French brothers – Didier and Joules Joubert. During the 1850s and 1860s they encouraged Italian stonemasons to emigrate and build houses for them, gradually transforming the peninsula into a suburb of villas and elegant homesteads with Victorian stone houses predominating. The Joubert brothers

were also active in other ventures. Not least of these was establishing a permanent ferry service that not only provided access for residents, but also brought weekend trippers to picnic on the foreshores or to enjoy Seymour's Pleasure Gardens, a popular picnic and fairground venue.

Woolwich

To this day the ferry is the most convenient way to visit Hunters Hill, although this mode of transport has improved somewhat on the Joubert brothers' old steam vessel. Catch the ferry at Circular Quay to Valentia Street, Woolwich, or catch the 506 bus, also from Circular Quay, and get off at Church Street, then transfer to the Northern and Western bus 538 for the run down to the ferry wharf. Since the ferry is quicker and more pleasant, most walkers prefer this approach so our walk will start from the **Valentia Street Wharf |1|**. This is the suburb of **Woolwich |2|**, which adjoins Hunters Hill, and the ferry wharf services both suburbs. Walk up Valentia Street and turn right into The Point Road and immediately examples of the stone residences that are a feature of this area appear on the opposite side at Nos. 38 and 40. Continue along The Point Road past many interesting residences of which perhaps the most significant is at No. 55–57 on the right hand side as the road dips down to Onions Point. A stone wall surrounds a large sandstone building, Reinga. This was originally an eight-room stone house built in 1889 for Charles

Twemlow, a jeweller, but it has been extended, including the addition of a stone chapel, by the Church of Christ, the owner of the property from 1942 to 1980.

Walk back from the scout shed at Onions Point and enjoy the gardens and the homesteads on either side of the road; some are just interesting old cottages, some superb examples of the stone builders' art. Continue past Valentia Street for about 10 minutes then bear left into Gale Street and up the hill to the popular Woolwich Pier Hotel. On the opposite side of the road is a small park; walk down towards the water and on the left is a spectacular view of the quite remarkable **Woolwich Dock |3|**.

In 1888 a maritime complex was established on the foreshores here to provide dry docking and maintenance facilities for large ocean-going ships. A floating dock was imported from Britain and a large engineering factory erected. This enterprise was unsuccessful and was later taken over by the Mort Dock Company of Balmain who then excavated a huge graving dock from the sandstone foreshores. At one time one of the biggest in the world, this dock is 260 metres long, 24 metres wide and has a depth of almost 8 metres. It was opened in 1902 and was most recently used by the army's Water Transport Squadron. Seemingly located in a deep quarry cut into the coastal hillside, it is an impressive sight when viewed from the lookout above.

Walk on down the hill through the small reserve and take a right then left turn onto

Opening Times

As most of the buildings of interest mentioned in this walk are private residences they are not open for public inspection.

Refreshments

Restaurants, shops and cafes can be found near the intersection of Alexandra Street and Woolwich Road.

Franki Road which, in turn, runs into Edgecliff Road and Alfred Street in front of some 'dolls-house' single storey terraces. On the left is Clarkes Point Reserve and the Hunters Hill Sailing Club, as well as a large area of unused ground which at one time was an important shipbuilding yard where some of the Manly ferries were built. Continue on along Alfred Street and cross over Margaret Street following Alfred Street into a well known reserve – **Kellys Bush |4|**. On the left at the entrance to this reserve is Woodstock, believed to be one of the oldest buildings in Hunters Hill and once the home of John Clarke who, in 1835, acquired more than 16 hectares of land in this area. Unfortunately the old house has been almost totally engulfed by a rather garish pink building, and inspection, even from the outside, is not possible.

Kellys Bush

In 1967 a plan was floated to develop 8 hectares of this area, including the natural vegetation of Kellys Bush, for town houses and units. The residents of Hunters Hill have long been in the forefront of conservation activities and a group of 13 women banded together under the banner of 'Battlers for Kellys Bush' to fight development and keep the area in its natural state. They made history by enlisting the aide of a notorious union – The Builders' Labourers' Federation, headed by Jack Mundey – who imposed the world's first 'Green Ban' on the site in 1971. After a tough and emotional fight, the Battlers won and on 3 September 1983, Kellys Bush was purchased by the NSW Government and handed over to the local residents. The victory was considered a major stepping stone for the conservation movement in Australia.

A typical Hunters Hill cottage

Walk through the gateway and bask in the success of the Kellys Bush battlers. There are a number of paths, one leading through the park from Alfred Street, and one leading down to a foreshore lookout and from there along a foreshore walk. The park is not very big and the path, after winding through the bush, leads out onto Prince George Parade. But small though it may be, Kellys Bush has some interesting features. There is a wide range of native shrubs and trees, and wildlife is reputed to exist (dogs must be kept on leads) although it is not very obvious apart from a few lizards scampering over the rocks on hot days and the usual noisy mynahs, lorikeets and magpies in the trees. The view from the lookout is excellent, taking in much of the upper reaches of Sydney Harbour and in particular **Cockatoo Island |5|**.

Walk out of Kellys Bush into Prince George Parade and turn right into Gladstone Avenue. This runs up over the hill and across Woolwich Road, then down towards the harbour on the other side of the ridge. Follow it to where it ends in steps that lead down to Vernon Street and **Mornington Reserve |6|** on the foreshore. These steps are extremely narrow and steep and frequently covered with water, which makes the descent to Vernon Road very hazardous. Elderly or unfit walkers might be better advised to take the access from Serpentine Street, which is the next street along Woolwich Road.

However, the Gladstone Road steps are well worth the effort to get to the bottom, because where they end a track leads to the left into a narrow but interesting lane that runs behind some old waterfront homes with a sheer rock face on the left and old stone walls on the right – rather reminiscent of the narrow streets of Cornish and other British villages. At one point the lane almost becomes a tunnel as branches of figs on the top of the rock face create an overhead canopy that covers the laneway. Shortly the lane leading down from Serpentine Street appears on the left – this is the alternative route down from Woolwich Road mentioned earlier – and about 100 metres further on the right a post appears indicating a laneway and steps known as Mornington Steps. These also lead down to Mornington Reserve. Mornington House – a stately old stone residence – is on the right of the steps; the reserve to which it gave its name was once a right-of-way providing access to what was the Mornington Ferry Wharf.

At the foot of the steps another post indicates the pathway leading off to the left. Walk along the Mornington Reserve keeping close to the fences of the houses above and take in the views across the Lane Cover River. Another short flight of steps at the end of the reserve leads back onto Vernon Street and back up the hill to Woolwich Road. This part of the walk through the residential area starts to become rather intricate, but happily every corner is marked with a direction post, indicating where to turn for the next leg. Some posts are marked with a small engraved plate indicating that you are following the Great North Walk.

Hunters Hill

The Great North Walk is a 250 kilometre walking track from Sydney to the Hunter Valley. It began as a Bicentennial project, linking sections of established walks with sections of specially constructed walking track. The full walk starts at Governor Macquarie's obelisk in Macquarie Place and follows our route on the ferry to Valentia Street Wharf and through the elegant residences of Hunters Hill. It continues through Lane Cove National Park to Thornleigh, then north to Brooklyn, across the Hawkesbury River to Yarramalong, Paxton and the Hunter Valley. The full walk takes about 14 days and camping sites are provided en route.

Continue along Woolwich Road past a wide architectural range of homes, mostly stone and mostly dating back to Victorian times. The next street to the right is Futuna Street; turn down this and follow it round to the left, passing St Peter's Catholic Church (1890) on the right. Turn right into Crescent Street then left into Garrick Avenue (following the posts) and walk through the narrow lane at the end of this street into Passy Avenue. As you walk along this narrow laneway, peer through the undergrowth on the right to take in one of the most impressive sights on the peninsula. Seen across open lawns and gardens is a two-storey period home that could have been part of a Hollywood film set.

This beautiful residence called **Passy |7|** is a fine example of the French-influenced style of building favoured by Jules Joubert, who has often been called the 'father' of Hunters Hill. The eastern façade, which is little changed from the original, is classical Georgian style, with shuttered, small-paned windows, hipped roof and an elegant verandah. The house was built between 1855 and 1857 for the French Consul but was later sold to the owners of the Parramatta River ferry service. The main entrance, which has a wide paved forecourt with striking wrought iron gates, is in Passy Avenue on the corner of the laneway. Continue down Passy Avenue and turn left into Ambrose Street, at which point one of Hunters Hill's most notable buildings comes into view – **All Saints Anglican Church |8|**.

Built between 1884 and 1888, the church was not totally completed until a bay to the nave and the bell tower were added in 1938. Of particular note are the stained glass windows, considered to be among the finest in Australia. Adjacent to the church is an interesting rectory. This is a fine two-storey house in the Victorian Italianate style and it also features some very beautiful examples of stained glass, mostly in the fanlights. The site on which All Saints is built was once Seymour's Pleasure Gardens, a popular picnic spot for groups that arrived by ferry at a nearby wharf.

Turn right into Ferry Street and right again into Alexandra Street where there are more interesting cottages, most of which were built in the late 19th century and display typical features of colonial homes of those days, notably the wide bullnose verandahs. A hundred metres or so is all that is required to examine these cottages, then turn back along Alexandra Street to the intersection with Ferry Street. Here the streetscape is effectively that of the 19th century, for this is the focal point of Hunters Hill and contains so many wonderful buildings that it would be impossible to describe them all. On the corner of Alexandra and Ferry streets is the impressive Garibaldi, the first inn to be built in the area. Initially it was built c.1861 but was improved in 1862 with further additions in 1869. It was named after the famous Italian patriot and was said to house many of the Italian stonemasons that worked in the area in the 1860s and 1870s. It had a chequered career as a residence and shops, as well as a hotel.

Walk past the Garibaldi and on the left are a number of **old buildings |9|** now mostly restored and converted to art galleries, restaurants and boutique shops. Continue along the left side of Alexandra Street and the next point of interest is the Old Bakery which, unfortunately, is not the original building as that was destroyed by fire. But adjacent at No. 29 is the baker's cottage, Allee which, like the bakery, was originally built around 1867. The front of the cottage has been changed, but the structure itself is original. There are similar fascinating cottages along this street as well as on the opposite side.

On the corner of Alexandra and Ernest streets is the Post Office, built in 1890 to take over from a smaller building on the opposite side of the street. Further along more notable municipal buildings are ranged along the right hand side of the street. These include the Town Hall, which was virtually destroyed by fire in 1978 and was rebuilt using the stone façade of the original building. On the left two fine residences are worth examining. No. 21 was, around 1872, the home of Supreme Court Judge Charles Manning, while No. 19, Merilbah, built c.1850, is an excellent example of the use of wide verandahs in colonial architecture.

Further along, on the corner of Mount and Alexandra Streets, is the striking Victorian style of the two-storey Gladstone, formerly the Gladstone Hotel, which was built in 1882 as a boarding house. Verandahs and balconies, each with ornate iron lacework and pillars, run across the Mount Street face of the building at both levels.

Cross over Mount Street and bear left at the fork into The Avenue (once again look for the guide post) and walk down beside the grounds of Hunters Hill High School. At the embankment of the elevated Burns Bay Road, turn right into Reiby Street and follow it round towards Fig Tree Bridge. The road comes to an end under the bridge, adjacent to what is arguably the most historically important building in Hunters Hill – **Figtree House |10|**.

The first part of the present Figtree House was built as two stone cottages in 1836 by Mary Reiby, probably to house convict farm labourers for her farm, which covered a large tract of the surrounding area. She named it after the Port Jackson figs which grew in profusion close by and used it as a sanctuary from her hectic business life in Sydney Town. In 1847 Jules Joubert's brother Didier purchased the farm from Reiby and immediately added a two-storey stone wing and paved verandah, joining the two cottages into one substantial house. A pavilion facing the river and the timber tower were built in 1895 by Didier's son, Numa Joubert. A plaque in St Malo Reserve describes the influence Mary Reiby – ex-convict and wealthy merchant – had on the colony when she lived here on her beloved farm.

Walk under the road bridge, turn left and climb through the park to the top of the hill at the Hunters Hill Hotel. From here you have a number of options: you can catch a 506 bus back to Circular Quay, or you can catch the local North and Western bus 538 down to Valentia Street Wharf and return to Circular Quay on the ferry. Or, if you are still feeling energetic, you can walk back down the ridge to the ferry wharf, enjoying even more of the historic buildings of **Hunters Hill |11|** before catching the ferry back to the city.

Walk key

1. Gunnamatta Bay | 2. Port Hacking | 3. Jibbon Beach | 4. Bundeena | 5. Royal National Park |
6. Aboriginal rock carvings | 7. Port Hacking Point | 8. Jibbon Bombora

Royal National Park
A right royal walk

Start

Cronulla Railway station. Take the train from Central Station.

Finish

Cronulla Railway station. Take the train back to the city.

Length/Time

4.5 km/ferry 0.5 hours; walk 1 hour.

Wheelchairs

No access to the Royal National Park

A vintage ferry ride, a stroll along a deserted beach, a visit to an Aboriginal rock carving site and a bush walk – surely a recipe for a pleasant day out and all within easy reach of the city. Add to that an interesting touch of maritime history and lots of natural history and the day is made even better. This walk provides a chance to shake off city cobwebs and breathe deeply the clean air of coastal breezes as they blow in from the ocean, picking up the inimitable scent of the bush.

Public parklands have been around since 1872 when the American conservationist Cornelius Hedges successfully argued for Yellowstone Park to be gazetted as a 'public place ... never to be changed'. In Australia in 1879 the first national park in the world was established south of Port Hacking, near Sydney – the Royal National Park. Although covering only 14,900 hectares, which is small compared to the likes of Kosciuszko National Park (627,200 hectares), the Royal National Park has a wealth of natural features which annually attracts hundreds of thousands of visitors. There are, of course, numerous and widely varying walks through this natural wonderland, but just by way of a taste of what is on offer, this pleasant little walk takes in a corner of the park of particular interest.

Catch the train from Central Station to Cronulla and turn left as you leave the station. Walk down Cronulla Street and turn left again through the tunnel which runs under the railway. Bear left from the tunnel and walk through the car park to the waterfront and the main public jetty, which lies beside a restaurant named Mariner's Cove. These are located at the head of **Gunnamatta Bay** |1|, a deep inlet which provides access across the shallow waters of Port Hacking to the Royal National Park. The ferry to Bundeena leaves the main jetty at half past the hour both on weekdays and weekends. It costs $2.60 for a very pleasant half-hour run across the inlet aboard a traditional old wooden ferryboat; this ride in itself is a most appealing part of the adventure.

Port Hacking |2| is a delightful open inlet some ten kilometres south of the entrance to Botany Bay. It is shallow, particularly in the lower reaches, with sandy shoals restricting the use of all but relatively shallow draught vessels. But the water is clean and clear, with sandy banks and beaches around its perimeter, making the area a pleasant environment for family holidays.

The native bush of the Royal National Park blankets the southern shoreline except for one small settlement just inside the entrance. As the ferry leaves Gunnamatta Bay to cross Port Hacking, the open ocean is visible on the left as is the long stretch of **Jibbon Beach** |3| which is the first part of our walk.

Port Hacking was first discovered by Matthew Flinders and George Bass, two young adventurers on *HMS Reliance* who, in 1796, were bored with sitting around in Sydney Harbour. Already showing great promise as navigators and explorers, the two rigged up a small boat – reputed to be an 11 foot (3.3 m) dinghy – and requested permission to explore the coast south of Botany Bay. In the tiny *Tom Thumb*, no bigger than a child's sailing dinghy today, they explored and charted the coast, including Port Hacking, which they named after Henry Hacking, quartermaster of *HMS Sirius*.

The only settlement on the southern shore is **Bundeena** |4|, and it is here that the ferry berths. Bundeena is surrounded on three sides by the Royal National Park as can be seen by the fact that except for a few houses along the shoreline, the foreshores are all covered in thick bush. Leave the ferry and walk along the jetty to the quiet streets of Bundeena, bearing left up Loftus Street past the RSL Club. Since there are no kiosks or even water bubblers in the course of the bush walk, now is a good time to stock up as there are a few shops just to the right of the jetty. Continue along Loftus Street until it turns hard right up the hill then bear left and follow Eric Street a short distance down to the corner where a signboard indicates the start of Jibbon Beach.

Royal National Park

Jibbon Beach is a long, wide stretch of sandy beach backed by the **Royal National Park |5|**. On most days the beach is totally deserted, and even in the mid-summer holidays there is never more than a handful of people scattered along its 1 kilometre length. The water here is crystal clear and the sand littered with shells.

Behind the beach the Royal National Park does its part to add to the natural beauty of the place. Straggling banksias rise out of a wealth of native shrubs, mostly melalueca, coast wattle and tea tree. In the denser undergrowth grevillea, ferns and sedges create a dense understorey by allowing very few wild flowers to poke through. But the beach is clean and untainted except for a few creeping pig-face attempting to suck sustenance from the dry sand.

Walk the length of the beach, either in the soft white sand or in the firmer wet sand along the water's edge. A number of footpaths weave through the bush which

Refreshments

Shops are located near Bundeena wharf. There are no water bubblers on the walk.

provides access from the houses in Bundeena, but the walk along the beach is by far the most pleasant.

Towards the end of the beach, restoration and regeneration of the bush is under way in an attempt to get rid of some of the introduced weeds that are starting to take over, notably the asparagus fern and lantana. The beach terminates in a rocky outcrop where a couple of tracks lead off into the bush behind. The best track to take is the one that follows the headland around; it can be seen quite clearly running along the seaward side of the bush. Walking is easy and the path follows the rocky foreshore for a short distance before cutting inland across a grassy open space and then plunging into thick coast wattle. Follow this track as it winds through the bush and climbs a rise. Now the sea becomes visible again through the trees. Although a little rough in places, the path is still quite clear; occasionally steps are provided where there are rocks to be traversed.

After about 150 metres, the track reaches the edge of a cliff overhanging a quite delightful little bay. It is well sheltered and has a small beach, while the water that swirls around the rocks is so clear you can see the bottom for some way out. Take the path that leads to the right at this point and winds through the bush around the edge of the little cove before coming to a short flight of rock steps. Here the bush opens out into a wide open space surrounding a large rock platform, and an information board indicates that this is the site of **Aboriginal rock carvings |6|**. The board is very faded and barely legible, but says the carvings are visible about 20 metres in over the rock platform. There are also a few explanatory notes provided, but these have faded in the sun and unfortunately cannot be read.

Walk delicately around the carvings because, although still very visible, they are already badly eroded. They are most likely the work of the Dharawal people, who inhabited the area before the arrival of white settlers. The artwork depicts fish and animals, possibly recording events of fishing or hunting that took place along the foreshores or in the bush. Most distinct are the turtle and the stingray, but look across the far section and sharks, whales, kangaroo and what might be a dugong are also very obvious. Interestingly these carvings are almost identical both in terms of subject and execution to those on the rock platform of Dobroyd Point, in Sydney Harbour, covered in walk 11. Even the rock platform chosen for the carvings is similar. Both are close to the coast and both are surrounded by thick bush.

Aboriginal rock carvings at Port Hacking Point

After examining the rock engravings return to the main track and continue on towards the headland of **Port Hacking Point |7|**. Another, even more delightful small cove appears below as the path winds around the top of the cliffs. The clean, freshly washed sand has not a human footprint in it and the encircling cliffs hide it from all but immediate eyes. This is the stuff of boys' adventure stories, for it is not hard to imagine smugglers landing their contraband on such a secluded beach. Nor is it difficult perhaps to conjure up images of the Aborigines who helped to carve the rock platform above, camped here and launched their canoes off this lovely beach to spear fish in the crystal clear water.

Soon the banksias and melaleucas give way to low coastal heath as the path reaches the end of the headland and the horizon appears. Exposed to the fierce southerly winds, the stunted undergrowth has a hard time surviving on the bleak promontory. But what is lost in the native bush is gained in the rocks which radiate brilliant colours as the waves scour away the moss and grime, carving the rocks into fascinating shapes and leaving the striated colours of the Hawkesbury sandstone glowing like some surrealist painting.

On the tip of the headland a sign indicates the direction back to the Aboriginal carvings as well as a path southwards to **Jibbon Bombora |8|**. Take this latter path, which runs along the edge of the cliffs and follows the curve of the coast as it begins its run southward towards Wollongong – a formidable, rugged coastline with only one small break in the endless procession of dramatic cliffs which mark the eastern boundary of the Royal National Park. It is possible to walk the full length of this coast, as well as divert inland to various features of the park such as the rainforest and the wetlands. But to cover the full length of the coastal track would take a few days and is beyond the extent of this book. Full details on all walks are available from the National Parks and Wildlife Service.

From Port Hacking Point follow the track for about half a kilometre along the coast until it comes to a small beach, then pause a while and look out to sea. About five hundred metres offshore, if the swell is up, the Jibbon Bombora will put on a fine display. A bombora is a rearing wave created by a sudden undulation on the sea bed – usually a reef or some other obstruction on the bottom – and it can be very spectacular when a big sea is running. Even in a small swell there is often a white water display, but when the big seas move in on the coast, the Jibbon Bombora is an awesome sight. Feared by mariners, but often sought after by surfers, bomboras are to be found at many points along Sydney's coastline.

From the sea back to the bush. Follow the well-marked track away from the small beach and note again the change in vegetation. The coast banksia and tall wattle take over from the low coastal heath of the shoreline, and even a few eucalypts will start to appear as the track moves further inland. Before long, glimpses of blue water again appear through the trees. Shortly afterwards the track opens out onto Jibbon Beach and the circuit of the headland is completed. Walk back along the beach and the roads of Bundeena to the jetty, where the old ferry will appear on the hour to provide transport to Cronulla and the train back to the city.

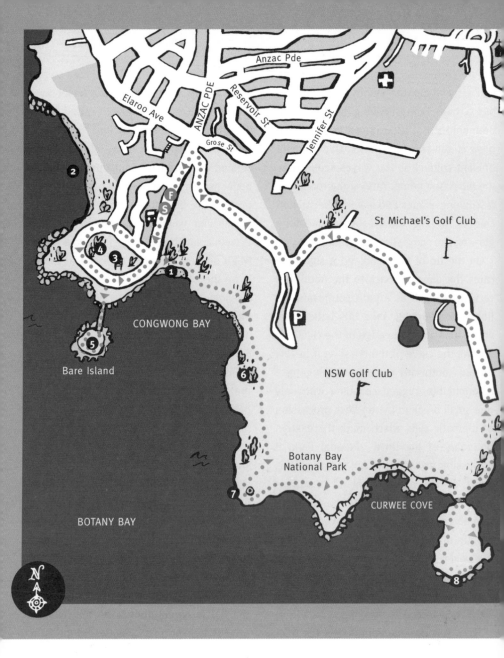

Walk key

1. Congwong Bay Beach | 2. Frenchmans Bay | 3. Watchtower | 4. Cable Station |
5. Bare Island Fort | 6. Botany Bay National Park | 7. Henry Head | 8. Cape Banks

La Perouse

A French foothold on Australian soil

Start

La Perouse. Take bus 394 or L94 to the La Perouse terminus.

Finish

La Perouse. Catch the 394 or L94 bus from the La Perouse terminal, direct to the city

Length/Time

8 km/2 hours

Wheelchairs

Access to La Perouse headland and museum; no access to the coastal walk, Henry Head or Cape Banks.

The French navigator Comte de La Pérouse arrived in Botany Bay in January 1788 intending to annex for France any part of New Holland that Captain Cook had not taken possession. But he was too late – for Captain Phillip had just moved his First Fleet to Port Jackson, where he claimed the whole of New South Wales for the British Crown. La Pérouse sailed away in disgust on 10 March 1788, but his name lives on in the southern Sydney suburb where he pitched his camp and established a brief French foothold on Australian soil.

Great explorers like Lieutenant James Cook made a practice of naming many of their discoveries after the men who served with them. On the south side of Botany Bay is Cape Solander, named after a botanist on Cook's ship *Endeavour*; and Cape Banks on the north side is named after the man who financed the expedition. The grave of Forby Sutherland, Cook's seaman who had the doubtful honour of being the first Britisher to die in Australia, is located on the south side of the entrance to the bay. Although the French explorer Comte de La Pérouse was greatly frustrated in his efforts to claim part of Australia for his country, his memory and that of some of his crew are also perpetuated in names around Botany Bay. The first Frenchman to die on Australian soil, Pere Receveur, is, like Sutherland, given pride of place with his grave on the north side of the bay. The memory of La Pérouse himself is perpetuated in the name of the suburb adjacent to the original site of his camp.

The south side of the entrance to Botany Bay and Cape Solander are covered in walk 21. This walk around Cape Banks begins at La Perouse and takes in the coastline around the north side, which is probably better known to most people as a major golfing venue. In fact there are no less than three golf courses here – the New South Wales Golf Club is situated furthest south, below St Michael's Golf Club and the Coast Golf Recreational Club. Fortunately these are inland from the coast and do not interfere with the walk.

La Perouse

Catch bus 394 or L94 from Circular Quay to its terminus at La Perouse and walk down the road to the headland and Bare Island. A circular drive runs out around the headland between two beaches and offers access to the island across a footbridge. On the left is **Congwong Bay Beach |1|** and beyond that the bushy headland of Henry Head and beyond that again Cape Banks. On the right is **Frenchmans Bay |2|**, reputedly the bay in which La Perouse anchored his ship *L'Astrolabe*. Centrally located in the circular drive is an octagonal sandstone **watchtower |3|** built around 1820 which, despite the extensive military fortifications in the area, was not part of the military emplacement but was instead used to counter the smuggling that was rife in the then unguarded Botany Bay. It later became the first school in the area.

Also within the grassy park created by the circular road is the historic **Cable Station |4|** which was built around 1882 as part of the infrastructure for laying the first ocean telegraph cable from Australia to New Zealand, one link in a world-wide project which would connect all continents. The north wing now houses a striking gallery of Aboriginal arts and crafts from local artists as well as some from other parts of Australia. Also housed in this building is the La Perouse Museum which, among other exhibits, contains unique relics from the ill-fated French explorer's last voyage when his ship disappeared, seemingly off the face of the Earth. Take time out to look around this world-class museum which sympathetically blends the histories of both white and Aboriginal cultures. Demonstrations of snake handling and boomerang throwing are given by local Aborigines, usually on weekends.

Close to the Cable Station building and the grave of Pere Receveur, is the La Pérouse monument. This obelisk was erected by another Frenchman, Captain B. H. de Bougainville, in 1825 to commemorate the visit to Botany Bay of *L'Astrolabe* and *La Boussole*, the other ship in La Pérouse's expedition.

Bare Island Fort |5| is a massive defence structure built in the 1880s, like so many of Sydney's fortifications, to counter an expected invasion by the Russian Pacific Fleet. Strategically located off the tip of La Perouse peninsula, the fort is one of the most extensive remnants of those paranoid days. The rocky island is honeycombed with tunnels, gun emplacements, magazines and barracks and so designed that its weapons could deliver a hail of fire across the entire entrance to Botany Bay. Soon after it was completed, faults were found in the structure and the fort was downgraded from a prime defence fort to a home for war veterans! Access from the mainland is across a frail looking 100-year-old wooden bridge and the regular guided tours provide information on the intriguing history, secrets and scandals that surround this quite remarkable island fortress.

Back on the headland after a visit to Bare Island, walk around the eastern side of the

Opening Times
Cable Station (museum): Wed–Sun 10am–4.30pm. Tours available.
Bare Island Fort: Guided tours only. Sat, Sun, public holidays or by request. Four tours per day.

Refreshments
There is a cafe and restaurant adjacent to Cable Station.

circular drive and return to the main car park overlooking Congwong Bay. Walk across the beach to the far end, where a constructed walkway appears, leading into the foreshore scrub with a sign indicating that you are entering part of **Botany Bay National Park |6|**. This particular walkway leads around the bay and the rocks to another beach – Little Congwong Beach – an isolated sandy indent in the foreshore which is well screened by the bush behind and therefore favoured by nudists. You can follow this track and then climb up through the bush from the beach, but an easier track goes off behind the main part of Congwong Beach and up into the bushland slopes.

This area was once known ironically as Happy Valley when, during the Great Depression, hundreds of homeless people set up a 'tent city' in the area. Nowadays the track winds through interesting bush with a wide variety of coastal species but which unfortunately is also infested with bitou bush and other weeds. Small swampy areas and watercourses provide more variety, with rushes, native broom and bottlebrush in evidence. The slopes are mostly scrub covered sand dunes and here coastal wattle, tea tree and melaleuca dominate.

Cape Banks

The track winds up the hillside to a point where it almost joins the service road to the golf clubs. A number of tracks lead off in different directions, but the main path to **Henry Head |7|** is clearly marked. Between the trees you get fine views of Bare Island and the wide sweep of Botany Bay, the huge container terminal on the north side and the oil jetty on the south. Botany Bay is now a major shipping port. It also supports Sydney's main airport and although the twin runways of the airport that project into the bay are mostly concealed behind the container terminal, the constant flying over of aircraft on take-off and landing leaves no doubt as to where the airport is!

Keep walking along the path, where the vegetation, now more exposed to the winds from the sea, becomes more stunted. Wildflowers are in abundance here in spring and summer, especially the white flannel flower, which can be seen in large clumps across the hillsides. Eventually the path comes out onto a rough service track for Henry Head, so turn right and follow this until it reaches the cliff and the small white lighthouse that provides guidance for ship-

The watchtower

ping. Gun emplacements and fortifications built to supplement those at Bare Island cover most of Henry Head.

Unfortunately this area is rather neglected, although moves are afoot to revegetate and regenerate the headland. The gun emplacements have been vandalised and there is a great deal of rubbish in the area. However, despite their unattractive condition, the massive gun emplacements and blockhouses are impressive and well worth examining, and their unbroken view of the ocean beyond the entrance to Botany Bay shows how effective they would have been had an enemy tried to enter the bay from seawards. This whole region is part of the Botany Bay National Park, which is divided into two sections covering the north and south headlands. A serious bushfire devastated the northern headland in 1998 but as is usual after bushfires, regrowth has been fast and the coastal scrub has regenerated, covering the blackened areas.

From Henry Head walk eastwards along a well-made path across the top of the cliffs. This peters out after a while and the track is not so obvious although the rock platform at the cliff top makes for easy walking in most places. The scrub here is mostly low to medium height melaleuca and coast wattle, home to a great range of bird life. Particularly noticeable are the Sydney ravens which seem to have established a sizeable colony above the windswept rocks. Smaller bush birds are also in evidence as are lizards. There is also the odd snake, so walk carefully. Follow the track around the corner and an ocean vista of the coastline on both sides of the entrance, from **Cape Banks |8|** to Cape Baily, opens up. As with so many of the coastal cliffs in this region, high sandstone bluffs provide solid protection against the ravages of the ocean and make Botany Bay a well-sheltered anchorage.

As the path through the bush becomes rather hard to follow, climb down over the rocks and onto a small beach where the walking is easy. A few of the greens belonging to the NSW Golf Club appear on the left, having a very manicured appearance in contrast to the scruffy wildness of the native bush; this is a spectacular location for a golf course. For the last few metres before reaching Cape Banks itself, there is a choice of a path up through the bush or a walk across the rocks at the end of the beach. The outermost green of the golf club lies just above the rocks behind Cape Banks and beside it is a footbridge across a rocky gully to the island-like Cape Banks headland. Walk out across the bridge and onto the cape, which is a low, flat rocky protrusion into the Tasman Sea covered in sparse vegetation, mostly rushes and pigface with a few hardy natives clinging precariously to the ledges The wreck of the *Minmi*, which ran aground in 1937, is still visible on the southern side and there are some interesting rock formations on the windswept promontory.

Walk back over the bridge and veer right. The path now winds up scrub-covered dunes and over the top to more military establishments, where it becomes a service road. From here on the walk is along a sealed road, past an old cemetery in the sand dunes, a few isolated houses, and through the golf course which spreads away on either side. Although a service road, it still makes for an interesting walk since once past the open spaces of the golf course, the bush takes over again. About 1.5 kilometres along the road a left fork leads to the club house. Ignore this and keep walking and about half a kilometre further on a sign on the left points down a track leading back to Congwong Beach. Follow this and return to the start of the walk on the beach, or continue along the service road and turn left to join Anzac Parade not far from the bus terminal.

Start

Eastern end of Prince Charles Parade, Kurnell. Take the train from the city to Cronulla, then the 67 bus to Kurnell.

Finish

Cronulla shopping centre. Catch the train back to the city.

Length/Time

Short walk along Yena/Muru tracks: 4 km/1 hour.
Medium walk returning to Kurnell from Potter Point: 10 km/2 hours.
Full walk terminating at Cronulla: 12.5 km/3 hours

Wheelchairs

Access to the Captain Cook Landing Place and Cape Solander Drive. No access to bush tracks.

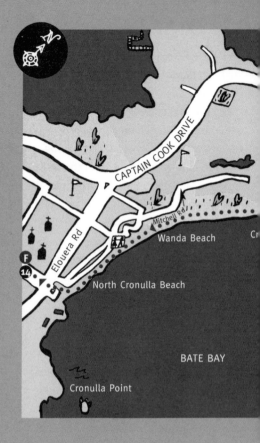

Walk key

1. Captain Cooks Landing Place Park |
2. Botany Bay National Park | 3. Cook's Well |
4. Obelisk | 5. Forby Sutherland's grave |
6. Discovery Centre | 7. Banks–Solander Track |
8. Tabbigai Gap | 9. Blue Hole Gorge |
10. Cape Baily Lighthouse | 11. Potter Point |
12. Boat Harbour | 13. Cronulla Beach |
14. Cronulla

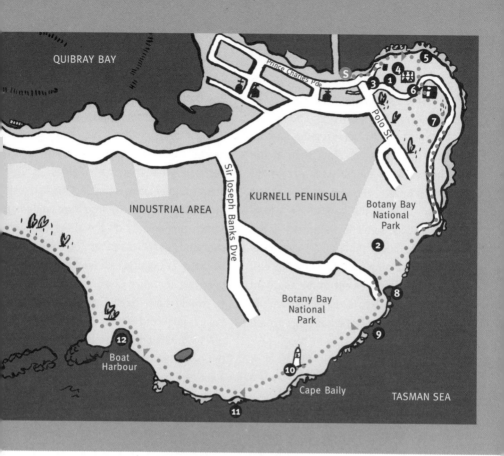

Walk No. 21

The Cape Baily Track
The foundation stone of a new world

The spot in Botany Bay where Lieutenant James Cook first put foot on Australian soil must surely rate as the most historically significant place on the continent. Many will argue – and among those doubtless would be Captain Phillip with his First Fleet of convicts – that Cook could have chosen a better spot. But for better or for worse, this was where Cook landed and history cannot be changed. This walk explores the area where Cook fulfilled his charter to discover the Great Southern Continent, and in so doing laid the foundation stone of a new world.

Catch the train from the city to Cronulla and board a 67 bus (Kurnell Bus Service) to Kurnell. Ask the bus driver to stop at the end of Prince Charles Parade, just past the oil jetty, rather than at the entrance to the national park. Access for vehicles is located 100 metres or so to the right, but entering the park along a foreshore walkway from the waterfront is the best way to begin the walk. The area is known as **Captain Cooks Landing Place |1|** and is the commencement of the southern section of **Botany Bay National Park |2|**; the northern section, at La Perouse, is covered in walk 20.

Captain Cooks Landing Place

Once through the foreshore entrance a constructed footpath known as the Monument Track leads along the beach to the actual spot where Cook landed. The park is well preserved with tall native trees, mostly Moreton Bay figs which provide good shade from the summer sun; undulating grassy slopes make it ideal for family picnics. This was once the favoured area of the Gweagal Aborigines who lived in the idyllic surroundings with a plentiful supply of food in the sandy bay or the bush-covered sand hills behind. Small wonder that they were not pleased at having their peaceful life disturbed by the arrival of whites.

Walk along the Monument Track and on the right beneath a tubular frame is the first feature of historic importance on this site – **Cook's Well |3|** – indicating the site where

Cook's men dug into the sand in an effort to find fresh water for their ship. A small tablet indicates the spot where the well was thought to have been dug, and another nearby commemorates the first conflict between whites and Aborigines. A few metres further along is the pockmarked rock on which Cook is thought to have landed; it stands prominently off the shore between two sandy beaches and may be surrounded by water at high tide. Indeed it must have been low tide when Cook landed, otherwise he would have been carried ashore and there is no record of that!

A mounted plaque on this rock records the event and the fact that a midshipman, Isaac Smith, is believed to be the first of *HMS Endeavour*'s crew and therefore the first Englishman to step ashore in Australia on 29 April 1770. He was also Captain Cook's nephew. Immediately adjacent on the shore is a sandstone **obelisk |4|** also commemorating the landing; this was erected in 1870, one hundred years after Cook made that significant step from his boat. A nearby tablet provides a little more information about the first meeting between Aborigines and the white sailors.

Continue along Monument Track, which is lined with Norfolk Island pines on the shoreline and figs and paperbarks on the inshore side, past a memorial to Sir Joseph Banks, the botanist who accompanied Cook on the barque *Endeavour*. Apart from spending a sizeable fortune to finance expeditions to his newly adopted country, Banks took an active part in the development of the colony, providing a much needed voice in Britain for the often forgotten people of the settlement in Australia. Small wonder he has become known as the 'Father of Australia'. The prolific native banksia shrub, many of which are to be found in this park, perpetuates his name and provides a fitting tribute to his work as Australia's first botanist.

A little further along the track is Cook's stream where water casks for his ship were filled, the well in the beach proving inadequate. Cross over this stream and on a small rise two monuments provide a diversion from the path. The first is what might be termed an elaborate headstone. It marks **Forby Sutherland's grave |5|**. Sutherland, a seaman on Cook's ship, died here in 1770 and he was the first European buried in Australia. The Shire of Sutherland, in which this area is located, is popularly thought to be named after him. There is however, no evidence to sustain this, although nearby Cape Sutherland was certainly named to perpetuate his memory. The second monument honours the Swedish botanist Daniel Solander, who also accompanied Cook on the *Endeavour* as assistant to Sir Joseph Banks. His name, like that of Sutherland, is also perpetuated in a nearby headland – Cape Solander – at the entrance to Botany Bay. Just offshore is a concrete pile which indicates the anchorage position of *HMS Endeavour*.

The Monument Track at this point curves back in from the shoreline past a timber cottage which was erected in 1902 as a

Opening Times

Discovery Centre: Mon–Fri 11am–3pm, Sat and Sun 10am–4.30pm.
Botany Bay National Park: Daily 7am–7.30pm.

Refreshments

Stores are located along Prince Charles Parade at Kurnell, and there is a kiosk near the Discovery Centre in Captain Cooks Landing Place Park. Water bubblers can be found in the national park. There are shops, cafes, restaurants and hotels in Cronulla. Water bubblers can be found in beachfront parks.

caretaker's cottage for the park. It replaces an earlier stone cottage built in the 1820s called Alpha Farm. Follow the track as it winds through the trees of the park towards a group of modern buildings known as the **Discovery Centre |6|**. This is a good point from which to begin the main part of the walk since it has toilets, a nearby kiosk and an education and information centre providing material on the background history of the region and the natural history of the park. The displays of paintings, artefacts and photographs provide an interesting and educational collection relating to the events that took place on this spot some 230 years ago.

Rugged cliffs of the coastline

Botany Bay National Park

Take the path directly away from the entrance to the Discovery Centre to a road from which there is a choice of three trails to follow. They all arrive at the same destination and the choice between them relates to the route they follow. The road sweeps around to the left and follows the coast, providing superb views across the entrance to Botany Bay and Cape Banks. The left of two bush trails is known as the Muru Track while the right hand path is called the Banks–Solander Track. Both offer a delightful stroll through the dry woodland typical of the vegetation in this sandy environment.

Probably the best choice is the **Banks–Solander Track |7|**, also called the Yena Track, which is clearly marked on the opposite side of the road, slightly to the right of the path

from the Discovery Centre. Follow the track into the bush which at this stage is dominated with native trees such as angophoras, scribbly gums and red bloodwoods. Cheese tree, blueberry ash, small wattles and coast banksia are prominent in the shrubby undergrowth with the yellow pea flower, found almost solely in this area of Sydney, providing a colourful contrast. Blue flax lily and other wildflowers will be seen flowering in season among the brush underfoot or on either side of the boardwalks provided in places to cross swampy areas.

After about five minutes' walk, a well-marked diversion indicates a detour along the Banks–Solander Track, which runs through an area with an interesting range of tree and plant species, many of which are labelled. A few small swampy areas – typical of the patchy swamps to be found in a number of places across the dunes – have a variety of vegetation, mostly in the form of swamp banksia, sedges, prickly tea tree and lemon scented bottlebrush, to name but a few. This is a delightful digression for lovers of native bush and the information boards provided help identify some of the lesser known species. Birds, particularly honeyeaters, flitter through the scrub, while the odd wattle bird can be identified by its raucous squawk. You will most likely also hear the mournful call of the crow, while rosellas and kookaburras add to the colour and noise of the bush.

The track rejoins the main path – which is the Yena Track now – near a splendid cabbage tree, one of the most useful of native plants for the early inhabitants. Both Aborigines and white settlers boiled and ate the buds of this plant and used its leaves to make baskets and bags. Another plant that proliferates here is the so-called native sarsaparilla, which is not really a true sarsaparilla but rather a native pea flower, hardenbergia. Its leaves were boiled by the early settlers to make a tea which prevented scurvy, while the Aborigines used it to poison fish in local streams. Continue along the now fairly wide track through a magnificent forest of large trees, mostly angophoras and scribbly gums whose contrasting colours give the bush the appearance of a giant painting.

Shortly afterwards there is a distinct change in the bush environment as the salt-laden air of the sea breeze makes itself felt and the track moves out towards the cliff tops. Now the trees are distinctly smaller and the coastal species become more predominant, in particular banksia, coastal wattle, tea tree and grevillea. The track widens and rejoins the road almost directly opposite a service road that loops down to a picnic area on the cliff tops, with superb views out to sea and across to the coastline north of the entrance to Botany Bay. For those seeking only a short walk, this is a good point to turn back, either by following the road back around the coast or by taking the Muru Track back through the bush. Either involves turning left along the road; the Muru Track turns off after about 100 metres.

To continue with the longer walk, turn right at the junction of the Yena Track and the main road and keep walking until you reach the car park just beyond Cape Solander, about two kilometres from the Discovery Centre. Now the views to the south open up and the formidable cliffs, still being carved by the sea from the sandstone table on which Sydney is built, provide dramatic examples of nature at work along the coastline. The road ends here and the walk continues into the shrub-covered coastal region, first along the cliff tops and then through the sand dunes. The going can get heavy at times and this part of the walk is recommended only for walkers who are fairly fit.

The track from the car park is to the left across the flat rock platform of the cliff top;

it is quite easy to see. Walk along this flat strata area, heeding the warning of the growling seas beneath the cliffs and taking care not to get too close to the edge. Children must be watched very closely along this stretch. The surrounding scrub is knee-high coastal heath, and patches of sand among the inshore vegetation indicate the presence of extensive sand dunes. Small birds swish in and out of the shrubs, catching insects without hesitating in their rapid flight, and an occasional lizard will scurry across the rocky path. Otherwise wildlife is not a very dominant feature of this part of the walk. The topography is impressive. At intervals along the coast, a sword-like slash cuts into the cliffs from seawards, creating a deep culvert into which the seas incessantly surge with each angry wave.

Tabbigai Gap |8| is the first of these and the track has to head inland to get around the end of it. The natural scenery here is spoiled somewhat by a service road and a discharge pipe from the oil refinery at Kurnell, but once across the other side, it resumes as a nature trail. Once again coastal scrub and sand, together with the ubiquitous rock platforms, create an environment so typical of the eastern Sydney coastline. Just to the south of Tabbigai Gap are the remains of a few fishing shacks, perilously clinging to the cliffs but now abandoned as the area has been reclaimed as part of the national park. Inland, the sand dunes become steeper and higher and in the far distance the white dome of the top of Cape Baily Lighthouse appears,

incongruously sticking up among the scrub. The trail starts to get more difficult to follow here, especially as it moves inland to get around the next cleft in the cliffs – **Blue Hole Gorge |9|**.

Take care along this section because the track is not very well marked and it is extremely easy to get lost among the dunes and the scrub. Look for signs of previous walkers, for the ocean winds, blowing the sand across the dunes, can quickly cover the path and make the track hard to spot. An incongruous feature among the sand dunes along this part of the track is the presence of freshwater swamps, one of which is quite large in area. Follow the path round the edge of these 'hanging' swamps – and watch your step or you are likely to get wet feet as pools of water are concealed beneath the sedges and marshy growth. These swamps provide an ideal habitat for frogs, birds and insects, and swallows can be seen swooping across the surface constantly. There is a wide variety of swamp plants here including yellow marsh flower, woolly frogmouth and round-headed bristle rush, not to mention the sedges.

After Blue Hole Gorge pick up the track, which is now wider and easier to follow as it moves in through the dune scrub towards **Cape Baily Lighthouse |10|**. This beacon has for decades provided guidance for ships making their way up and down the coast or heading into Botany Bay; its light can be seen almost 20 kilometres out to sea. Keep walking past the lighthouse, through the dunes which now form a uniform environment with patches of sand interspersed between quite thick stands of tea tree and coast wattle. Eventually the dunes fall away and are replaced by a large open sandy area, one which gives a very clear indication of the extent to which people can make a mess of their habitat. The dunes are pushed back to allow access for pipes which seemingly carry both refinery discharge and sewage effluent to be pumped into the sea at nearby **Potter Point |11|**.

Hurry across this area and pick up the track on the other side which winds along the foreshore around a large dune known as Botany Cone. The national park ends near here and beyond it the dunes form a recreational park for four-wheel drive vehicles. A rough service trail runs down to Potter Point and if the walk is getting too much, you can return to Kurnell by this road which cuts back through the oil refinery to the main road. However, this is not the most attractive of walks, and is not much shorter than the full walk to Cronulla. Continue along the coast the short distance to the pretty little inlet of **Boat Harbour |12|** and then walk the length of **Cronulla Beach |13|** to the town centre.

Walking along a beach can be very tiring, but if you keep close to the water's edge the wet sand is firmer and makes it much easier. At all events it is a much more pleasant way to end the journey than by walking back through the refinery area. Part of this long beach, known as Wanda Beach, was the site of the tragic discovery in the 1960s of the bodies of two young girls. Found murdered in the sand dunes, their killer has never been apprehended. Once back at **Cronulla |14|**, walk up Kingsway from Dunningham Park, just past the North Cronulla Surf Life Saving Club, turn left into the Mall and enjoy a well-earned rest and perhaps a meal before catching the train back to the city from the railway station in the next street, relaxed and fulfilled after your long walk.

Walk key

1. Goddards Wharf |
2. Governor Phillip Park |
3. Barrenjoey Boatshed |
4. Barrenjoey Head |
5. Pittwater | 6. Barrenjoey
Lighthouse | 7. Grave of
George Mulhall | 8. Palm
Beach

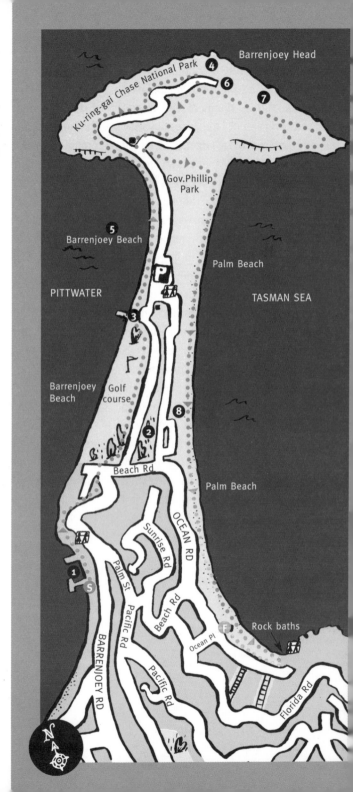

Palm Beach to Barrenjoey Head

Shipwrecks and smugglers

Start

Goddards Wharf, Palm Beach. Catch the 190 bus from Town Hall or Wynyard or the L90 bus from Central or Town Hall.

Finish

Ocean Road shops, Palm Beach. Catch L90 or 190 bus to city.

Length/Time

3.5 km/1.5 hours

Wheelchairs

Access to Governor Phillip Park and Ocean World, Palm Beach. No access to Barrenjoey Head.

The 115 metre high promontory of Barrenjoey Head makes a perfect windbreak for sailors sheltering from the prevailing north-east winds. By the same token it offers the perfect spot in which to land illicit cargoes on dark nights. In the early 1800s this isolated place was well removed from civilisation and customs officers, making it a popular spot with smugglers. Walk along the beach where smuggled barrels of spirits were landed and climb the headland which provided a perfect lookout for customs men and eventually brought the operation to an end.

There is a little of a lot in this walk. No major feature, perhaps, but a lot of interesting facets of the coastal scene, including delightful beach walks, interesting flora and fauna, a touch of history and superb views. Add to that a few interesting homes belonging to the rich and famous, and you have quite a mix.

From the city, take the L90 bus to Palm Beach and alight at **Goddards Wharf |1|**, which is on the Pittwater side of the peninsula. This is the focal point of many water activities on the Hawkesbury River estuary; ferry and tour trips to dozens of places across Pittwater, Broken Bay and along the Hawkesbury River start from this jetty. The lazy old wooden ferry boats that usually run these trips are from another era – a time when life moved at a more leisurely pace – so if you have time to fit one of these waterborne tours into your walk it will be well worth while. The ferries chug across to the beaches of Kur-ing-gai Chase National Park, on the other side of Pittwater, and around West Head, as well as along the Hawkesbury to some interesting riverside hamlets. Information about these ferry tours can be obtained at Goddards Wharf. There are also shops, cafes and restaurants here; this is a good place to stock up with drinks and snacks for the walk.

Governor Phillip Park

Now a word of warning. The walk from Goddards Wharf to **Governor Phillip Park |2|**, the first part of the Barrenjoey excursion, is along the main road which winds around Palm Beach headland. This is a busy road and the footpath is not kerbed but merely marked with a white line, so be very careful when walking along this stretch as the traffic can be hazardous. Indeed, it might be wise to jump back on the bus for the five-minute ride from Goddards Wharf and get off at the entrance to the park.

From this point the high bluff of **Barrenjoey Head |4|** is visible in the distance across the long sand spit which divides it from Palm Beach. Walk along the road through Governor Phillip Park, keeping the golf course on the left and the grassy recreation area on the right. Alternatively, you can walk along either of the beaches – the still water beach of Pittwater to the left or the ocean surf beach on the right. By way of variety, why not walk along the harbour beach on the outward journey and return along the ocean beach. Walking along a soft sand beach can be very tiring however, so bear this in mind when planning the route; the hard sand of the still water beach makes for easier walking.

About halfway along the road the golf course ends in a car park and the beach is obstructed by the **Barrenjoey Boatshed |3|** and jetty (you can walk around it). Float planes operate from this spot, running a scheduled service from Sydney Harbour or taking joy flights along the coastline and the northern beaches – an interesting activity for another day. Indeed, an easy way to reach this walk is to take a float plane from Rose Bay and land at this point, thus avoiding the long bus trip from the city and enjoying a scenic coastal flight at the same time. There is a kiosk at the boat-sheds and toilets in the nearby park – last comfort stop before the climb!

The sand dunes from this point to the foot of Barrenjoey have been stabilised and revegetated, mostly with coastal wattle, since big waves have been known to crash over the spit in storm conditions. The spit itself is a quite amazing landform. At one time, the high, rock and bush-covered outcrop of Barrenjoey Head was an island, separated from the mainland in much the same way that adjacent Lion Island is. The phenomenon known as longshore drift, in which offshore currents carry sand sediments along the coastal beaches, gradually built a sandbar across the stretch of water joining the island to the mainland, forming a neck of sand dunes which today supports the Governor Phillip Park, the golf course and a large recreational area. Seeds blown by the wind from other coastal areas, carried by birds or floated on the tide germinated, took root and covered the sand spit with vegetation, creating an isthmus where once there was an island.

Walk along the western foreshore of **Pittwater |5|** which at all but very high tide provides easy, firm sand walking as far as the rocky promontory. Tucked into the corner under the high headland is a neat little cove, frequently used as an anchoring spot by yachts as it offers perfect shelter from the prevailing north-easterly winds. This is where the smugglers operated in

Opening Times
Pittwatwer/Hawkesbury ferry tours: Ask at Goddards Wharf.

Refreshments
Restaurants, cafes and shops are on Barrenjoey Road, the Pittwater side of Palm Beach, and on Ocean Road, Palm Beach. There is a kiosk at Barrenjoey Boathouse. Water bubblers can be found in Governor Phillip Park and Ocean Road Reserve.

the early to mid-1800s, sneaking round the corner of the bluff at night and dropping anchor in the sandy cove in its lee. The beach made a good landing spot for illicit cargoes, and access to the city, albeit long and arduous in those days, was not a problem when the stakes were so high. A customs house was established here in 1843 to prevent this trade but was closed in 1900. In the corner of the cove is an old cottage, not related to the customs presence, and a corrugated iron boatshed. Just behind the boatshed a National Parks and Wildlife Service sign indicates the track to the top of Barrenjoey Head. Bear right from the beach past the boatshed and follow the rutted old vehicle track which once serviced the lighthouse at the top and which is gradually being restored in places although vehicle access is not permitted.

Barrenjoey Lighthouse

Barrenjoey Head

The track veers round to the left and starts to get steep. In places the surface consists of laid stone slabs, but much of it is over bare rock and in places the going can get fairly rough. Where there are no rocks or stones it can get muddy, especially after rain, and some of the rock surfaces can become slippery, so a little care is needed here. Close to the start of the upward climb stone steps lead off into the bush on the right. Supposedly constructed by smugglers but more likely the path of the early lighthouse keepers before the service road was opened, this is the alternative route to the top. Which path you take will depend

on whether you like to climb steep hills. The service road, which was first built in 1880 to haul building materials to the top for the construction of the lighthouse, offers a rough but reasonable gradient whereas the steps make for a steeper although probably quicker climb through the bush. The best solution might be to take one up and the other down; both have their merits and both run through pleasant bush scenery. In this book we shall cover both by taking the vehicle track up and the path to come back down.

The vehicle track winds upwards through fascinating coastal bush, where in places the trees almost meet overhead. Tall shrubs and small trees such as old man banksia, she oaks and coastal tea tree dominate the larger growth, while native shrubs such as melaleuca, grevillea and bottlebrush are very much in evidence at a lower level. The undergrowth is heavily infested with introduced weeds in places but the parks people are working on an eradication program, as you can see in places along the walk. In the undergrowth wildflowers appear from time to time; with the fringed lily and flannel flowers providing contrasting colours to the grevillea and bottlebrush blossoms.

As the track winds higher the views through the trees and from the occasional rock outcrop become more and more spectacular. Towards Palm Beach the green of the regenerated dunes is quite spectacular and contrasts strikingly with the gold of the sand and the blue water on either side. The full length of Pittwater begins to reveal itself as you gain elevation; a magnificent inlet that in summer is covered with the white confetti of sailboats and fringed by the olive green hillsides of the Kur-ing-gai Chase National Park which forms almost the entire western shoreline.

It is interesting to compare the two shorelines from this elevation. On the slopes of the eastern one, suburban development has covered the hillsides with a matrix of houses, while the timbered western slopes remain much as they were when the smugglers first sneaked around Barrenjoey Head. The sheltered waters of Pittwater impressed Governor Phillip when he explored it in 1788. It is one of a number of enclosed waterways that run off Broken Bay, the extensive estuary of the Hawkesbury River, and Phillip saw it as a potential harbour. Although used to some extent commercially, its relatively shallow waters precluded it from challenging Port Jackson as the major site for the new settlement. The first settlers arrived on the shores in 1800 but development was slow and it was not until 1880 that a regular coach service from Manly was established.

Onwards and upwards; there is nowhere else to go as the track, getting rougher in a few spots, grinds towards the top. An occasional track will lead off into the bush on either side, but these merely provide access to a rocky outcrop or clearing used as a lookout or sightseeing spot. Now glimpses of the stone tower of **Barrenjoey Lighthouse |6|** and its accompanying keepers' cottages start to appear through the bush, reassuring those who are finding the going a little heavy that the summit is not far away. The track levels off abruptly and the bush opens out onto a flat, cleared space with the stately sandstone lighthouse in the middle. None of the keepers' cottages are occupied, nor is the lighthouse, but there are plenty of paths to walk around and take in the magnificent ocean, coastal and estuary views on all sides. A cairn, reputedly built with stones from the first lighthouse, is located near the present lighthouse and carries a plaque indicating the direction of the main coastal features.

To the north, across the wide entrance to Broken Bay, the coastline of Bouddi National Park sweeps from Box Head northwards as far as Third Point and the treacherous reefs that lie along that coast can be seen as surf breaks on them. Many a fine ship has been lost on these reefs, including the steamer *SS Maitland*, after whom the popular Maitland Bay was named. To the west of Box Head is Lion Island, the sphinx-like sentinel standing at the mouth of the Hawkesbury River and a significant nature reserve. The Hawkesbury River itself winds inland past West Head and Lion Island on its long journey to the foothills of the Blue Mountains, joining the Nepean River to almost cut off the city of Sydney. If the headwaters of the Nepean at Cataract penetrated the eastern escarpment just a few kilometres more to reach the ocean near Wollongong, Sydney would be an island!

The vegetation at the top of Barrenjoey Head is quite different to that encountered on the way up. The constant battering from spray-loaded ocean winds has reduced plant life to only the hardiest species. Stunted casuarina, prickly moses, coastal tea tree and grevillea are predominant although surprisingly under the shelter of these thick shrubs are some quite superb wildflowers, notably a fine specimen of flannel flower. Fauna does not appear to be as prolific as in some other bushy coastal walks although lizards will be found wherever there is a sunny rock to lie on, and the smell of a fox is not uncommon – perhaps one of the reasons the wildlife is sparse.

Rosellas and honeyeaters will be seen in the bushier parts, although again birds do not seem as prolific here as in some other coastal bush areas.

Walk past the cairn and down a few stone steps which lead into the scrub. This track leads to the eastern side of the headland and is well worth following although it can be somewhat overgrown. Just below the lighthouse an iron railing surrounds the **bush grave of George Mulhall |7|**, one of the early lighthouse keepers; a surprising find in the middle of thick scrub. Follow the track all the way and eventually it will come to a cairn marking the site of one of the lighthouses known as Stewart Towers, two wooden structures erected in 1868 as the result of some tragic shipwrecks in previous years. This was in fact the second light to be established on Barrenjoey, the first having been built around 1855.

The present lighthouse, which is a quite magnificent sandstone structure standing 19.5 metres above the peak of the headland and 113 metres above the sea, was designed by the Colonial Architect James Barnet and completed in 1881. It has a notable gallery around the lantern cantilevered on stone brackets and with a gunmetal balustrade. Its light flashes in groups of four every 20 seconds, and is visible 35 kilometres out to sea. Adjacent to the lighthouse are the head keeper's house and attendants' building, both constructed of rough dressed stone. The entire group of buildings is now preserved as part of Australia's heritage and listed on the State Heritage

Register. They are not open to the public. The lighthouses were built at a time when Pittwater was a busy harbour, and while the trend today is away from commercial shipping and towards leisure boating activities, the need for guidance past the treacherous coastal reefs has not diminished. Even with today's modern navigation equipment, the welcoming flash of Barrenjoey light at night is a great comfort to an offshore mariner, for although there are no longer any lighthouse keepers, the light is still maintained and functions automatically.

Having climbed the vehicle track on the way up, it is worth taking the alternative path down. Walk round the southern face of the lighthouse and a track will be seen leading down steps beneath the keeper's cottage and into the bush below. While quite steep in places, on the downhill run it is quite manageable for the average walker and apart from a few overhanging branches, is readily accessible right the way to the bottom where it rejoins the track and leads out onto the beach. Walk back along the beach and through Governor Phillip Park to join the main road at the foot of the Palm Beach bluff. Alternatively, as mentioned earlier, a route through the regenerated dunes or along the ocean beach provides a little variety on the way back to the road.

The ocean side of the sandy peninsula that joins Barrenjoey Head to the mainland is typical of many similar coastal features along the eastern side of the continent. The high sand dunes, built by many centuries of pounding surf, create a magnificent ocean beach facing the Tasman Sea; the envy of many overseas tourists who visit this most northern of the Sydney beaches. It has been used as the location for a number of film and television productions, notably the soap programme 'Home and Away', which is screened in numerous overseas countries. Like most of the northern beaches, it is relatively unspoiled and only the residential buildings at the southern end impair what is otherwise a pristine, natural beach. A stroll along the fine white sand of Palm Beach is a great way to round out a walk to Barrenjoey Head.

Palm Beach

From the entrance to Governor Phillip Park, turn left at Beach Road, which rounds the corner to become Ocean Road, and follow it into the centre of **Palm Beach |8|**, originally known as Cabbage Tree Harbour because of the proliferation of cabbage tree palms behind the beach. Continue along the beach past the small shopping centre where on the right are some classic reminders of the elegance of the 1920s and 1930s in a group of magnificent old homes and beautifully laid out grounds. This is the Palm Beach of an era now gone. The modern homes, while still synonymous with wealth and opulence, somehow lack the dignity, the grandeur and the charm of their predecessors. The road ends at the corner of the beach, so walk back to the shops where a well-earned coffee or meal can be obtained. From here too the bus returns to the city.

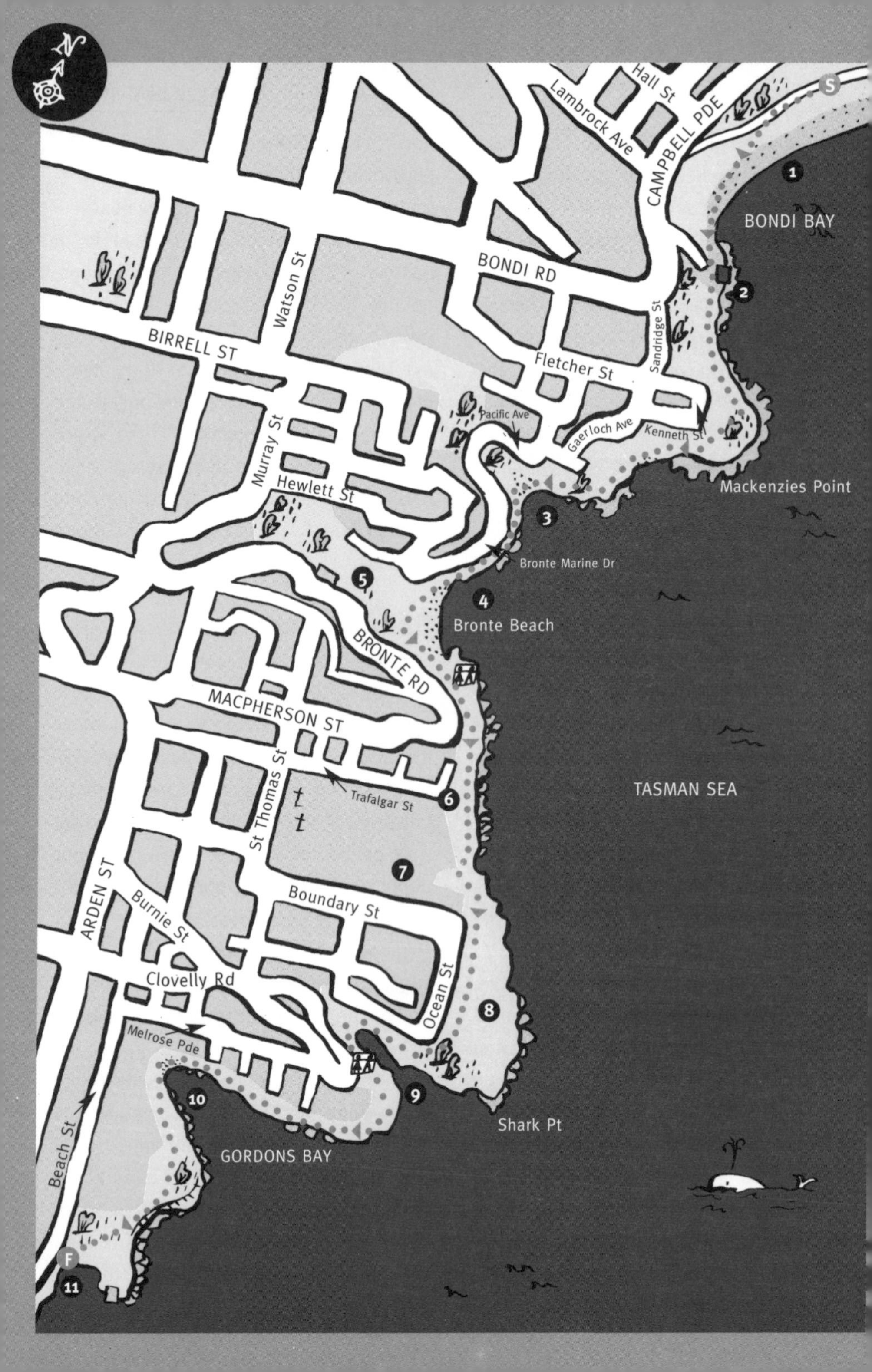

Hall St
Lambrock Ave
CAMPBELL PDE
BONDI BAY
BONDI RD
Watson St
BIRRELL ST
Sandridge St
Fletcher St
Pacific Ave
Gaerloch Ave
Kenneth St
Murray St
Hewlett St
Mackenzies Point
Bronte Marine Dr
Bronte Beach
BRONTE RD
MACPHERSON ST
St Thomas St
Trafalgar St
TASMAN SEA
ARDEN ST
Burnie St
Boundary St
Ocean St
Clovelly Rd
Melrose Pde
Beach St
GORDONS BAY
Shark Pt
S
F
1
2
3
4
5
6
7
8
9
10
11

Bondi to Coogee
A walk along the ocean cliff tops

Start

Campbell Parade, Bondi Beach.
Take a 380, 382 or L82 bus
from Circular Quay.

Finish

Coogee Beach. From Arden
Street take a 372, 374
or X74 bus back to the city.

Length/time

4.5 km/1.5 hours

Wheelchairs

Limited access only to parts
of the Bondi to Coogee walk
(see text). Easy access for
wheelchairs for the full length
of the Coogee south walk.

walk key

1. Bondi Beach | 2. Bondi Icebergs
Club | 3. Tamarama Bay | 4. Bronte
Beach | 5. Bronte House | 6. Calga
Reserve | 7. Waverley Cemetery |
8. Burrows Park | 9. Clovelly Bay |
10. Gordons Bay | 11. Coogee Bay

The massive sandstone cliffs that hold back the Pacific Ocean along Sydney's coastline have been dramatically carved into rugged sheer walls, sometimes a hundred metres high, by the constant assault of the sea. When nature shows its angry face, a walk along these cliffs can be exhilarating as giant waves pound the rocks, sending spray high up the cliff face. At other times it offers the placid, colourful, benign scene favoured by calendar and postcard photographers. Whatever nature's mood, this walk always ensures a fascinating and exciting adventure, well within the limits of the average walker. Because the walk itself is not suitable for wheelchairs, a short stretch at the end has been added to enable disabled people to also enjoy the beauty of the cliff tops.

Rugged cliffs that front a notoriously wild ocean might seem a most unlikely place to find an interesting walk. Yet this walk offers a fascinating combination of sea and land-scapes along well-made paths that wind up and down the cliffs and poke into placid little bays. Indeed, it is hard to imagine a walk with more delightful surprises than the cliff walk from Bondi Beach south to Coogee Beach, since around every corner something new and interesting appears. It begins at what is undoubtedly Australia's most famous beach – **Bondi Beach |1|**.

Only eight kilometres from the centre of Sydney this well known beach is within easy reach of many residential districts and as a result is well patronised all year round. The name is taken from the Aboriginal term 'boondi' – the noise of tumbling waves – and indeed a more appropriate description or a better example of onomatopoeia would be hard to find; round both head-lands and onto the wide sandy beach the tumbling waves keep up a constant boom-ing, day and night. The suburb behind the beach is mainly residential but during the summer it becomes swamped with visi-tors and the relatively narrow streets are choked with traffic. Before white settlers appeared on these shores a major Aborigi-nal work area was concentrated behind the beach, and an archaeological dig in the early years of this century uncovered an astonishing collection of tools, weapons, knives and other artefacts which the Cadi-gal people had used and discarded over probably thousands of years.

Campbell Parade is the main street along the beach front and this is alive with street cafes, pubs, tourist shops and all the trim-mings that go with a holiday resort. The park which fronts onto the beach has wide grassed areas, skateboard ramps and a pavilion renowned for its art shows and other cultural displays. The beach itself is known across the world for a variety of sports; most recently it has become the major venue for beach volleyball events including those of the 2000 Olympic Games. But the sport that is synonymous with Bondi Beach is surfing, and any day, summer or winter, there will be dozens of athletic young blonde-headed surfers out in the water challenging nature and defy-ing gravity as they race down the face of Bondi's famous waves. Yet another feature that is rapidly gaining interest across the world is the annual kite flying festival which is held on the beach front with competitions between international teams flying kites in an astonishing range of shapes and sizes. The quite remarkable skills of the kite fliers utilising the sea breeze to put their fragile craft through their manoeuvres, create a breathtaking spectacle of colour and excitement.

The walk starts at the southern end of the beach. Cross the park or walk along Campbell Parade then bear left into Notts Avenue behind the **Bondi Icebergs Club |2|**. This well known institution is home to those brave souls who swim in the rock baths throughout the year, defying even the coldest winter snap to plough up and down the length of the cold seawater pool. To prepare for the winter chill, ice blocks are thrown into the water as part of an initiation ceremony! Hunters Park runs along the right of the path and on the left, seemingly plunging straight over the cliff edge, are steps leading down to the water's edge. Follow these down the cliff face to the first of many surprises on this walk – an unusual little cove eroded into the cliff face, with a spectacular conical rock formation in the centre. Totally hidden from the top of the cliff and indeed visible only from seaward, this little cove is an unexpected delight. The surf can come tumbling in but the footpath is well constructed and other than in exceptional sea conditions should ensure a dry passage.

Steps climb up the cliff face on the opposite side making the walking a little heavy going but quite within the scope of those of average fitness. Ignore steps leading off to the right as these only provide access to streets above. Continue along the well constructed path around Mackenzie's Point where there are some interesting rock shelters and – surprise number two – spectacular views of the coastal cliffs stretching away to the south. This is a good spot for panoramic photographs, with Bondi Beach in one direction, the cliffs in another and the blue ocean all around. The path winds round the point and past the whitewashed walls of the Tamarama Surf Lifesaving Club to surprise number three – the delightful little **Tamarama Bay |3|**.

Refreshments

Cafes, restaurants, bars, hotels and kiosks can be found along Bondi Beach and Coogee Beach. There are kiosks at Tamarama, Bronte and Clovelly, and water bubblers in Bondi Park, Tamarama Park, Bronte Park, Burrows Park, Clovelly Bay Park and Dunningham Reserve (Coogee).

Tamarama Beach itself is just another pretty little beach like so many along this coastline, but behind it is Tamarama Gully; a deep green culvert that runs well back from the beach to a waterfall near the built up suburban area. Together with Tamarama Park, the grassy area near the beach, this creates a delightful recreational area with big trees and grassy slopes giving almost a rural ambience to the hinterland behind the beach. And recreation is synonymous with this gully, for at the turn of the century this was the location of one of Sydney's major amusement parks. For a decade before and after 1900 the green hollow was filled with every kind of entertainment from carousels and coconut shies to scenic railways and ferris wheels. It began with an aquarium, ironically called the Bondi Aquarium as in those days the tram had not reached Bondi. Then around 1906, what was effectively Sydney's first Luna Park – called Wonderland City – was established behind the beach front at Tamarama. However, the artificial entertainment soon lost its appeal and the neat little cove with its beach and green hollow returned to its natural state and has remained that way to this day.

Bronte

Walk across the promenade at the beach or detour up into the gully, then return to the southern side of the beach to continue the walk, which climbs a few steps to join Bronte Marine Drive. Keep to the road as it rounds the headland to the next indented bay (Nelson Bay) and **Bronte Beach |4|**. Although larger than Tamarama, this beach is smaller than either Bondi or Coogee, but far prettier, mainly because of its setting. The beach is backed by an extensive park, once part of the Bronte Estate, and is dotted with a variety of mature trees including Norfolk Island pines and Canary Island palms, together with a wide range of native trees and bushes including angophoras, flame trees, figs, banksias and wattle.

Bronte House |5| is a two-storey stone bungalow with a hipped roof and lean-to verandahs located on the southern side of Bronte Park, well in from the beach. A long service wing extends southwards to what was once two tower rooms but which has been altered since the house was first built in 1846. Originally owned by Robert Lowe, the house features a well developed garden. The original estate extended down to the foreshores incorporating what is now Bronte Park and it was during that time that many of the fine trees which now offer shade to families on summer picnics were planted. This pleasant setting is probably as good a place as any to take a break, either in the park or on the beach front. There are picnic facilities scattered around, shops and cafes in nearby Bronte Road, as well as a kiosk near the Surf Lifesaving Club.

Resuming the walk, cross the beach front, climb some steps and head up the steep gradient to join the road at the cliff top. This road can be dangerous since it goes through a narrow cutting and has no footpath, but it has been made a one-way street, so traffic should not be too much of a problem. At the top the road swings around to the right, but cross instead into the cliff top park known as **Calga Reserve |6|**. Continue across this open space to the next surprise – **Waverley Cemetery |7|** – although it may not really be such a surprise since this unusual cemetery is visible from a number of points along the walk prior to reaching it. A relic of the days when this part of the coast was well removed from the city, Waverley Cemetery is unique in that it sprawls across the top of the cliffs which form the coastline and can be seen from many miles out to sea. Indeed, it is so conspicuous from seaward that it is included on naval charts as a navigation mark for passing vessels.

From Calga Reserve, walk into the cemetery along the bottom service road. If you are interested in Australian history, a wander through the headstones will reveal some well known names – Henry Lawson, Thomas Kendall and Lawrence Hargrave are just three Australian notables who are buried here. And apart from the famous, many of the headstones reveal interesting and often tragic events that claimed the lives of those early Australians who now spend eternity on this peaceful headland close to the sea. Follow the service road around the lower end of the cemetery as it leads out through the south-east corner to the Clovelly Bowling Club. Continue past this and turn hard left beside the second bowling green.

A large open grassy space known as **Burrows Park |8|** covers the headland here

A rock sculpture carved by the sea

and you can either walk out around this and enjoy the coastal views, or simply walk down beside Ocean Street to where the next surprise awaits – **Clovelly Bay |9|**. This narrow but deep cleft in the coastline has been enhanced on both sides with concrete platforms at sea level that run along much of its length back to a small sandy beach at its head. The effect is that of a very long swimming pool – perhaps the largest swimming pool in the world – with a shallow reef at the seaward end to almost close it off from the ocean. Take the footpath down from the road and follow it along the side of the inlet through a mixture of exotic and native shrubs, mostly coast rosemary and wattle. Continue through this neatly landscaped area

The wheelchair walk

Such a magnificent walk should not be denied those with disabilities, but unfortunately the track between Bondi and Coogee has few spots where wheelchairs can be used. However, a forward-thinking Randwick Council extended the walk for around 1.5 km southwards from Coogee Beach, in such a way that it provides easy access for people with limited ability and particularly for wheelchairs. There are no steps and only modest gradients, yet this exciting cliff top walk is the equal of any available to the physically fit.

The walk begins at the southern end of Coogee Beach beside the Coogee Surf Lifesaving Club where the path leads into Grant Park. On the left, opposite a children's playground, is a sign indicating steps down to the Ladies' and Children's baths. These baths were constructed in 1866 when mixed bathing was not permitted and the pool on the north side of the beach was restricted to men. To this day, men are forbidden to enter this pool as a result of a legal challenge in 1996 which made an exception to the Anti-discrimination Act, enabling the baths to keep their women-only status. This was to cater for the local Muslim women who are not permitted to bathe in the presence of men.

A little further on the path another set of steps leads off to the left, this time to Wylie's Baths; historic baths now classified by the National Trust. Grant Reserve contains a variety of interesting trees and shrubs, mostly native, but with young Norfolk Island pines climbing up to the sky between them. The footpath, still quite level, but now a little rough, skirts Neptune Road to an even wider open space called Trenerry Reserve. At the far end of this reserve, the exciting part of the walk begins, for a boardwalk, specially constructed to provide easy wheelchair access, leads off across the cliff top.

At the start of this boardwalk, the grey sandstone cliff edge plunges sheer into the ocean on the left. On days when the swell is up this can be an awesome sight as huge waves roll in and explode with a thunderclap roar into a fury of foam, often spattering the top of the cliffs with spray and spume. In total contrast, on the right are the remnants of an age-old cliff top swamp where researchers from the University of New South Wales have discovered in the peat evidence of plant and animal life that existed 1000 years ago. Today the small swamp is home to a number of frogs and birds, notably the white-faced heron. A regular visitor in summer is the tiny Golden-headed Cisticola, only 10cm long and rarely seen elsewhere in Sydney. The boardwalk climbs an easy gradient past an information board describing an old mansion, 'Battysberg', built on the cliffs in the 1880s for a local wealthy merchant.

The old house has gone but steps and retainer walls of the original estate are still clearly visible. The outlook from this building must have been without peer, its 180 degree panorama of ocean horizon a changing picture with every mood of the wind, weather and sea. This is the end of the boardwalk, as a ramp and steps lead up to the suburban streets and away from the cliff edge.

It is time to turn around and head back along the boardwalk, enjoying the delights facing to the north now. An interesting feature just out past the bay is the rocky outcrop of Wedding Cake Island, well known to offshore yachtsmen and fishermen. If the swell is running it will be a spectacular mass of white foam and spray.

Walk back to the surf club to rejoin Carr Street at the southern end of Coogee Beach. Look across the beach and visualise the scene in the 1920s, when Coogee was a fashionable beachside resort, boasting a pier with a theatre and ballroom as well as the various pier amusements so beloved of that era. Bear right into Arden Street where you can relax over a cup of coffee at one of the many street cafes, or visit the famous Coogee Bay Hotel.

and past a kiosk overlooking the beach until you reach the beach itself and its small but pleasant little park.

Continue across the beach and along the southern side of Clovelly Bay. This is a favourite place for training divers. The path climbs up behind the surf club, across a large carpark and leads to **Gordons Bay** |10|. This deep inlet has an underwater nature trail of interest to divers. Small boats make a colourful picture all nestled together on the steep slope at the head of this quite delightful little bay.

Coral trees create a shady cover for the path as it climbs out of Gordons Bay and after a short walk up Major Street, joins the footpath across Dunningham Park, on the northern headland of **Coogee Bay** |11|. Take the steps leading down onto the beach or the footpath across to Coogee Beach Plaza where there are picnic tables, toilets, street cafes and all the facilities usually associated with a popular holiday spot. The walk terminates here and a number of buses on Arden Street allow for the return journey to the city.

Bibliography

Messent, D. *The Rocks*. David Messant Photography, Sydney, 1996.

Spindler, G. *Uncovering Sydney*. Kangaroo Press, Sydney, 1991.

Stephensen, P. & Kennedy, B. *The History of Sydney Harbour*. Reed, Melbourne, 1980.

Sydney's Best Bushland Walks – Fairley. Envirobook, Sydney, 1997.

The Australian Encyclopedia (3rd edition). The Grolier Society of Australia, 1979.

The Heritage of Australia, Australian Heritage Commission, Macmillan, Sydney, 1981.

Toghill, J. *Sydney Harbour*. Reed, Melbourne, 1991.

Index

Aborigines 4
  Birchgrove 126
  Bondi 186
  Clifton Gardens 63
  Clontarf 94
  Fort Denison 50
  Grotto Point 97
  Hunters Hill 150
  Kurnell 170
  Little Sirius Cove 58
  Manly 72
  Milk Beach 88
  Royal National Park 160
  Watsons Bay 66
Admiralty House,
  Kirribilli 29, 32, 50
Adolphus Street, Balmain 129
Albert, Frank 114
Alexandra Street,
  Hunters Hill 154

Alfred, Prince, Duke of
  Edinburgh 95
Alfred Street, Parramatta 146
Alfred Street, Woolwich 151, 152
Alice Street, Parramatta 145
All Saints Anglican Church,
  Hunters Hill 148, 154
Allee 155
Ambrose Street, Hunters Hill 154
Andrew (Boy) Charlton
  Swimming Pool 9, 13
ANZAC Bridge 31, 101, 102–4
Anzac Memorial 46
Archibald Fountain 46
Arden Street, Coogee 191
Argyle Cut 18, 24–5, 29, 30
Argyle Place 23–4, 26
Argyle Stairs 25
Argyle Stores 18, 26
  opening times 21

Argyle Street, Millers Point 25–7, 30
Art Gallery of NSW 39, 45
  opening times 41
Ashton Park 56, 62
Atherden Street, The Rocks 26
Athol Bay 56, 61
Australian Museum 39, 45–6
  opening times 41
Avenue, The, Hunters Hill 155

Bakehouse Place 18, 27
Balmain 5, 127–9
Balmain, William 124
Balmain Colliery site 123, 125
Balmain Fire Station 129
Balmain Town Hall 123, 129
Balmain Watch House 123, 127
  opening times 125
Balmoral Naval Hospital
  78, 80, 83

Bank Street, Pyrmont 103
Banks, Sir Joseph 170–1
Banks-Solander Track 168, 172–3
Bare Island Fort 162, 165
  opening times 165
Barn, The 48, 55
Barnet, James 42, 45, 69, 182
Barrenjoey Boatshed 176, 178
Barrenjoey Head 176, 178, 180–3
Barrenjoey Lighthouse
  176, 181–3
Bass, George 158
Bath house, Parramatta 138, 144
Batman, John 144
Battysberg 191
Bayview Hill Road, Rose Bay 86
Beach Road, Palm Beach 183
Beare Park 114
Beatty Street,
  Balgowlah Heights 99
Bell, John 54
Bennelong 11, 126
Bennelong Point 11
Bennelong Pond,
  Bicentennial Park 131, 137
Bent Street, Sydney 43
Bicentennial Park 130–7
  opening times 133
Billabong, Bicentennial Park
  131, 133
Billyard Avenue,
  Elizabeth Bay 113–14
Birchgrove 124–6
Birchgrove House 126
Birchgrove Park 126
Birchgrove Road, Balmain 125
birds
  Bicentennial Park 134–7
  Botany Bay National Park 173
  Cape Banks 167
  Dobroyd Head 99
  Little Sirius Point 59
  Middle Head 80, 83
  Rose Bay 89
  South Head 67
  Sydney Harbour National
    Park 61
Blacket, Edmund 46, 128
Blackwattle Bay 101, 102

Blackwattle Bay Studios 101, 107
  opening times 103
Blaxland, John 144
Bligh House 23
Bloxsome, Oswald 54
Blue, Billy 34, 35
Blue Fish Point 76
Blue Hole Gorge 168, 174
Blues Point 29, 35
Blues Point Road,
  McMahons Point 35
BMA House 43
Boat Harbour, Cronulla 168, 175
Boer War Memorial 144
Bondi Beach 185, 186
Bondi Icebergs Club 185, 186
Boomerah 109, 111–12
Boomerang 109, 114
Botanic Gardens
  see Royal Botanic Gardens
Botany Bay National Park 162,
  165–7, 168, 170, 172–5
  opening times 171
Bouddi National Park 182
Boundary Road,
  Paddington 119
Box Head 182
Boyd, Ben 26
Bradfield Park 29, 33
Bradley, William 61
Bradleys Head 56, 61–2
Bridge Road, Ultimo 102, 107
Bridge Street, Sydney 41
Bridgeclimb 36–7
Brisbane, Governor 143–4
Brislington 138, 142
  opening times 141
Broken Bay 181
Bronte Beach 185, 188
Bronte House 185, 188
Bronte Marine Drive,
  Bronte 188
Broomoo House 127
Brougham Street,
  Woolloomooloo 14
Broughton Street,
  Kirribilli 33
Brown Street, Paddington 119
Bundeena 156, 158–9

Bunker, Captain 25
Bunker Hill 18, 25
Burrows Park 185, 189
buses
  Balmain 124
  Birchgrove 124
  Coogee 191
  Hunters Hill 150
  Kurnell 170
  La Perouse 164
  Manly 72
  Middle Head 80
  Mosman Junction 63
  Paddington 118
  Palm Beach 178
  Rose Bay 86
  Spit, The 94
  Taronga Zoo 60
  Watsons Bay 66
  Woolloomooloo 110, 115
  Woolwich 155
bush see flora
Butlers Stairs 9, 14, 115
Byrock 112

Cable Station, La Perouse
  162, 164
  opening times 165
Cadman's Cottage 18, 20
Cahermore 128
Calga Reserve 185, 189
Camp Cove 64, 66
Campbell, Robert 5, 21
Campbell Avenue,
  Paddington 120
Campbell Street, Balmain 127
Campbells Cove 18, 21–2
Campbells Parade, Bondi 186
Campbells Wharf 21
Cape Baily Lighthouse 168, 174
Cape Banks 162, 166–7
Cape Solander 171
Cape Sutherland 171
Captain Cook's Landing
  Place Park 168, 170
Carmelita 112
Caroline Street, Balmain 127
Carr Street, Coogee 191
Carrara 88

Castle Rock *93*, 95–6
Cathedral Street,
  Woolloomooloo 14
Catherine Adamson (ship) 67
Cavill, John 128
Challis Avenue, Potts Point
  109, 112–13
Charles Street, Balmain 129
Chief Secretary's Building
  39, 42
Chowder Bay *56*, 63
Chowder Bay Army Base *78*, 80
Chowder Head *56*, 63
Christison Park 69
Church Street, Parramatta 142
Circular Quay 10, 20
Clarke, John 151
Clarkes Point Reserve 151
Cliff Street,
  Watsons Bay 66, 68
Cliffe, Captain 63
Clifton Gardens *56*, 62–3
Clontarf Cottage,
  Balmain *123*, 129
Clontarf Reserve *93*, 94–5
Clovelly Bay *185*, 189
Clyde Bank 23
Cobblers Beach *78*, 83
Cockatoo Island *123*, 124,
  148, 152
Colgate Avenue, Balmain 127
College Street, Manly 76
College Street, Sydney 45
Collins, David 72
Collins Beach *71*, 72
Congwong Bay Beach *162*, 164
Conservatorium of Music *9*, 17
Convent of the Immaculate
  Conception, Balmain 129
Coogee Bay *185*, 191
Coogee Beach 190–1
Coogee Beach
  wheelchair walk 190–1
Cook, Captain James
  3, 66, 164, 169, 170
Cook's Well *168*, 170
Coolong Road, Vaucluse 90
Cooper, Robert 118
Cooper Lane, Paddington 119

Cooper Street, Balmain 127–8
Cooper Street, Paddington 119
Corso, The, Manly 77
Cove Street, Birchgrove 125
Cove Street,Watsons Bay 66
Cowper Wharf Road,
  Woolloomooloo 13, 15, 110–11
Crater Cove *93*, 98
Cremorne Point 51–3
Crescent, The, Annandale 106
Crescent Street, Hunters Hill 153
Cronulla *168*, 175
Cronulla Beach *168*, 175
Cronulla Street, Cronulla 158
Cumberland Street,
  The Rocks 25, 30
Curlew Camp 59
Curraghbeena Point
  48, 53, *56*, 58
Customs House *39*, 40
  opening times 41
Cutler Footbridge
  116, 119–20

Dairy cottage,
  Parramatta *138*, 144
Darley Road, Manly 72, 76
Darling Street, Balmain 127–9
Darling Street, Rozelle 124
Darling Street Wharf,
  Balmain 129
Darlinghurst Road,
  Potts Point *109*, 115
Dawes, Lieutenant 22
Dawes Point 22–3, *29*, 31
Dawes Point Battery *18*, 22
Dawn Fraser Pool *123*, 125
  opening times 125
Deloitte, Q.L. 126
Deloitte Avenue 126
Department of Education
  building 41
Dillon Street, Paddington 119
Discovery Centre, Captain Cook's
  Landing Place *168*, 172
Dobroyd Head *93*, 96, 98
Dolphin Hotel, Balmain *123*, 128
Domain, The *9*, 12–13, *39*, 43
Dowling Street,

Woolloomooloo 14
Duke Street, Balmain 129
Dunbar (ship) 67, 68
Dunningham Park 191

Earth Exchange 26
East Esplanade, Manly 72
Edgecliff Road, Woolwich 151
Edward Street, Balmain 128
El Alamein fountain 115
Elizabeth Bay House *109*, 113
  opening times 111
Elizabeth Bay Road,
  Elizabeth Bay 114
Elizabeth Farm House *138*, 145
  opening times 141
Elkington Park 124–5
Embarkation Park *109*, 115
Engehurst *116*, 118
Eric Street, Bundeena 159
Esplanade, The, Manly 77
Ewenton Street, Balmain 129
Experimental Farm Cottage
  138, 145
  opening times 141

Fairfax Walk *71*, 75
Fairlight rock pool *93*, 99
Fairy Bower *71*, 76
Fairy Bower Road, Manly 76
Farm Cove *9*, 12
fauna, North Head 74
Federal Road, Glebe 106
ferries
  Blues Point 33
  Bundeena 158
  Cremorne/Mosman 50, 55
  Manly 72
  McMahons Point 35
  Parramatta 140
  Pittwater/Hawkesbury 178–9
  Taronga Zoo 60
  Woolwich 150
Ferry Road, Glebe 107
Ferry Street, Hunters Hill 154
Field Studies Centre,
  Bicentennial Park *131*, 135
Fig Tree Bridge 155
Figtree House *148*, 155

First Fleet Park *18*, 20, 30
Fisher Bay 94
Fitzroy Avenue, Balmain 125
Fitzroy Gardens *109*, 115
Flinders, Matthew 158
  statue *39*, 43
float planes
  Pittwater 178
  Rose Bay 86–7
flora
  Ashton Park 62
  Barrenjoey Head 181–2
  Bicentennial Park 136
  Botany Bay National Park 172–3
  Dobroyd Head 98
  Grotto Point 96
  Jibbon Beach 159
  Little Sirius Point 59
  Middle Head 80, 83
  North Head 74
  Rose Bay 86, 89
  South Head 67
  Sydney Harbour National
  Park 60
Forbes Street,
  Woolloomooloo *9*, 14–15
Forsyth Street, Glebe *101*, 107
Fort Street School 24
forts 6, 11
  Bare Island 165
  Bradleys Head 61
  Cape Banks 166
  Dawes Point 22, 24
  Fort Denison 24, 32, 50–1
  Fort Macquarie 11, 24
  Fort Phillip 24
  Middle Head 78–83
    guided tours 81
  North Fort *71*, 75
    opening times 73
  South Head 64–9
Forty Baskets *93*, 99
Franki Avenue, Woolwich 151
Frenchmans Bay *162*, 164
Futuna Street, Hunters Hill 153

Gale Street, Woolwich 151
Gap, The *64*, 68–9
Garden Island 111

Garden Island Dockyard
  9, 13, *109*, 111
  opening times 111
Gardner, William 128
Garibaldi 154
Garrick Avenue, Hunters Hill 153
Garrison Church,
  The Rocks *18*, 23
Gatehouse Art Gallery, Parramatta
  opening times 141
George Street, Parramatta
  142, 146, 147
George Street, Sydney
  22–3, 25–7, 46–7
Gilchrist Place, Balmain 129
Gipps, Governor 144
Gipps Street, Paddington 120
Gladstone 155
Gladstone Avenue,
  Hunters Hill 152
Gladstone Park, Balmain *123*, 129
Gladstone Street, Balmain 129
Glassop Street, Balmain 125
Glebe Island 104
Glebe Island terminal *101*, 104
Glebe Point Road, Glebe 106–7
Glebe Rowing Club *101*, 107
Glenmore Gin Distillery 118
Glenmore Road, Paddington
  116, 118–20
Glenview Street, Paddington 119
Globe Street, The Rocks 27
Gloucester Walkway 25
Goddards Wharf *176*, 178
Gordons Bay *185*, 191
Gourlay Avenue, Balgowlah 99
Government House *9*, 17
Governor Phillip Park
  176, 178, 183
Grant Park 190
Great North Walk 153
Greenway, Francis
  17, 44–5, 69, 143
Greenway Lane, The Rocks 27
Gregory Place, Parramatta 146
Greycliffe House *85*, 89
Grotto Point *93*, 95–7
Grove Street,
  Birchgrove 126

gun emplacements
  Bare Island 165
  Bradleys Head 61
  Cape Banks 166
  Dawes Point 22, 24
  Fort Denison 24, 32, 50–1
  Middle Head *78*, 78–83
  guided tours 81
  North Fort *71*, 75
    opening times 73
  South Head 64–9
Gunnamatta Bay *156*, 158

Hacking, Henry 158
Hallen, Edward 46
Hambledon cottage *138*, 146
  opening times 141
Harbour Bridge *see* Sydney
  Harbour Bridge
Hargrave, Lawrence 189
Harrington Street, The Rocks 26
Harris Street, Parramatta 145
Harrisford, Parramatta 147
Harry's Café de Wheels *109*, 110
  opening times 111
Hart Street, Balmain 129
Hassall Street, Parramatta 145
Hawkesbury River 182
Henry Head *162*, 166
Hermit Bay *85*, 87
Hermitage, The *85*, 87
Hermitage Walk 86–91
Hero of Waterloo Hotel *18*, 23
Hickson Road,
  Dawes Point 22, 26
Hills Stairs 14
History House *39*, 42–3
HMAS Kuttabul 112
HMAS Sydney 61
HMAS Watson 64, 66, 68
  naval chapel *64*, 68
HMS Endeavour 170, 171
HMS Sirius 40–1, 53, 54, 59,
  111, 132
Hodges, John 142–3
Homebush Bay 132
Hopetoun Avenue 91
Hopewell Street,
  Paddington 120

Hordern Stairs 14, 115
Hornby, Sir Phipps 67
Hornby Lighthouse 64, 67
Hosking, John 88
Hosking Street, Balmain 128
hospital site, original,
  The Rocks 18, 27
Houison Cottage,
  Parramatta 138, 145
Hughes Street, Potts Point 115
Hunter, Captain 132
Hunter, Governor 24, 143
Hunter Street, Parramatta 144
Hunters Hill 148, 148–50, 153–55
Hunters Hill Post Office 155
Hunters Hill Town Hall 155
Hyde Park 4, 39, 46
Hyde Park Barracks 39, 44–5
  opening times 41

Illoura Reserve, Balmain 123, 128
Iluka Street, Clifton Gardens 63
Intercontinental Hotel 42
International College of Tourism
  and Hotel Management 76
Ithaca Road, Elizabeth Bay 114

Jacob's Ladder 64, 69
James Craig (ship) 105
James Craig Road, Rozelle 105–6
Jane Street, Balmain 129
Jenner House 109, 112
Jessie Street Gardens 40
Jibbon Beach 156, 158, 159
Jibbon Bombora 156, 161
Johnson, Reverend Richard 104
Johnsons Bay 104
Johnston Street, Balmain 128
Jones Street, Pyrmont 103
Joubert, Didier 150, 155
Joubert, Joules 150, 154
Jubilee Park 106
Juniper Hall 116, 118
  opening times 119

Keba 125–6
Kellett Street, Potts Point 114–15
Kellys Bush 148, 151–2
Kendall, Thomas 189

Kendall Lane, The Rocks 27
King Avenue, Balgowlah 99
King George Street,
  McMahons Point 35
King Street, Concord West 133
Kings Cross 114–15
Kingsway, Cronulla 175
Kinsella, Judge 119
Kirribilli 32–3
Kirribilli House 32, 50
Kirribilli Point 29, 32, 50

L'Astrolabe (ship) 164, 165
La Boussole (ship) 165
La Pérouse, Comte de 163–4
La Pérouse monument 165
La Perouse Museum 164
Lady Bay 64, 66–7
Lady Hopetoun (ship) 105
Laings Point 66
Lake Belvedere,
  Bicentennial Park 131, 135
Lancer Barracks,
  Parramatta 138, 145
Lands Department building 41
Lane Cove River 153
Lauderdale Avenue, Fairlight 99
Lavender, George 34, 35
Lavender Bay 29, 34–5
Law Courts Building 45
Lawson, Henry 189
Leichhardt Bicentennial Park
  101, 106
Leigh Memorial Uniting
  Church 144
Lennox, David 142, 144, 146
Lennox Bridge,
  Parramatta 138, 142
Lewis, Mortimer 42
Light Rail Transport 102
Lincoln Crescent,
  Woolloomooloo 15
Linden House
  (Lancer Barracks) 145
  opening times 141
Lion Island 182
Little Congwong Beach 165
Little Manly Point 71, 72
Little Sirius Cove 56, 58

Little Sirius Point 56, 59
Liverpool Street,
  Paddington 119–20
lizards, blue-tongue 86
lizards, monitor 99
Loftus Street, Bundeena 159
Loftus Street, Sydney 40
London Hotel, Balmain 129
Longnose Point 123, 125–6
Lord Nelson Hotel 24
Louisa Road, Birchgrove 125–6
Lowe, Robert 188
Lower Fort Street,
  Dawes Point 22–3
Lucas, Penelope 146
Luna Park 29, 33–4

Macarthur, John 145–6
Mackenzie's Point 187
Macleay, Alexander 113
Macleay Street,
  Potts Point 112–13
Macquarie, Governor Lachlan
  4, 117, 143
Macquarie Lighthouse 64, 69
Macquarie Place, Sydney
  4, 39, 40
Macquarie Street, Parramatta 144
Macquarie Street, Sydney 42–5
Macquarie's Wall 16
Major Street, Coogee 191
mangroves 131–7
Manly 71, 72
Manly Art Gallery and Museum,
  opening times 95
Manly Beach 71, 72, 77
Manly Wharf 71, 72, 93, 99
Manning Street, Potts Point 113
Maritime junk yard 101, 106
Marsden, Samuel 142, 144
Marsden Street, Parramatta 142
Marshall Street, Manly 72
McElhone Stairs 9, 14, 115
McElhone Street,
  Woolloomooloo 14
McLeod Street, Mosman 58
Mercantile Hotel 25
Merchants House 18, 26
Merilbah 155

Metro Theatre 115
middens 94
Middle Head 78, 78–83
Middle Head defence battery 78, 82
military bases see forts
Military Road, Mosman 61
Milk Beach 85, 88
Mill Lane, The Rocks 27
Millenium Parklands 136
Millers Point 23–4
Milson, James 33, 50
Milson Road, Cremorne Point 51
Milsons Point 29, 33
Minmi (ship) 167
Mint Museum 39, 44
Mission Steps 27
Monument Track 170
Morella Road, Clifton Gardens 63
Mornington House 153
Mornington Reserve 148, 152–3
Mort, Thomas Sutcliffe 41, 126–7
Mort Bay 126–7
Mort Bay Park 127
Mort Dock 5, 123, 126
Mosman, Archibald 54
Mosman Bay 48, 52–5, 58
Mosman Rowing Club 48, 54
Mosman Wharf 58
Mount Street, Hunters Hill 155
Mrs Macquarie's Chair 9, 13
Mrs Macquarie's Point 9, 12
Mrs Macquarie's Road, Sydney 13, 15
Mulhall, George, grave of 176, 182
multiculturalism sculpture, Bicentennial Park 131, 135
Muru Track 172–3
Museum of Contemporary Art 18, 20
opening times 21
Museum of Sydney 39, 41–2
opening times 41

National Parks and Wildlife Service Information Centre 20
opening times 21

nautical mile measurement 62
naval establishments
Athol Bay 61
Garden Island Dockyard 13, 110–12
HMAS Kuttabul 112
HMAS Watson 64, 66
Neilsen Park 85, 89
Neptune Engineering Company site 29, 35
Neptune Street, Coogee 190
North Fort & Artillery Museum, opening times 73
North Harbour Park 93, 99
North Head 71, 74–6
North Sydney 29, 32, 33–4
North Sydney Olympic Pool 29, 34
opening times 31
Notts Avenue, Bondi 186
NSW State Archives see State Archives
Nurses' Walk 27

obelisk, Captain Cook's Landing Place 168, 170
Obelisk, Hyde Park 46
obelisk, Macquarie Place 4, 40
Obelisk Beach 78, 80–1
Observatory, Parramatta 138, 143
Observatory, Sydney see Sydney Observatory
Observatory Hill 24
Ocean Street, Clovelly 189
Oceanworld 93, 99
opening times 95
O'Connell Street, Parramatta 144
Old Commodore Hotel 35
Old Government House, Parramatta 138, 143
opening times 141
Old South Head Road, Watsons Bay 69
Old St Augustine's Church, Balmain 123, 129
Onions Point 150
Opera House see Sydney Opera House
Orient Hotel 27

Ormond Street, Paddington 118
Orwell Street, Potts Point 115
Our Lady of Lebanon church, Parramatta 145
Our Lady of the Sea, Watsons Bay 64, 69
Overseas Passenger Terminal 20–1, 30
Oxford Street, Paddington 118, 121

Pacific Street, Watsons Bay 66
Paddington 118–21
Paddington Reservoir 116, 121
Paddington Town Hall 116, 121
Paddington Village 116, 120
Palm Beach 176, 183
Park Street, Sydney 46–7
Parkhill Arch 71, 76
Parliament House, State 39, 44
opening times 41
Parramatta 3–4, 138–47
Parramatta Park 138, 143–4
gatehouse 143
Parramatta River 132, 138, 140–1, 146
Passy 148, 154
Passy Avenue, Hunters Hill 153
Peace Monument, Bicentennial Park 131, 135
Petrarch Avenue, Vaucluse 91
Phillip, Governor Arthur 3–4, 16, 20, 21, 40, 66, 72, 140, 145, 181
Pinchgut see forts, Fort Denison
Pittwater 176, 178–9
Playfair Street, The Rocks 26
Point Road, The, Woolwich 150
Pope Paul VI Reserve 101, 106
Port Hacking 156, 158
Port Hacking Point 156, 160
Potter Point 168, 175
Potts, Joseph 111
Potts Point 111–13
Powells Creek 133–7
Prince Charles Parade, Kurnell 170
Prince George Parade, Hunters Hill 152

Prospect Street, Paddington 120
Punch Street, Balmain 125
Purchase Street, Parramatta 146
Pyrmont Bridge 102
Pyrmont Bridge Road,
    Pyrmont 102

Quarantine Station 71, 73–4
    opening times 73
quarries
    Mosman Bay 54
    Windmill Hill 24
    Woolloomooloo 13–14
Queen Elizabeth II Gates 9, 12
Queen Victoria Building 39, 47
Queens Beach 85, 86
Queens Wharf 138, 146

Raglan Street, Mosman 58
Rangers, The 48, 54
Reef Beach 93, 99
Reiby, Mary 26, 155
Reiby Place 40
Reiby Street,
    Hunters Hill 155
Reid Park 48, 54
Reid Street, Woolloomooloo 14
Reinga 150
Reynold's Cottage 18, 26
River Street, Birchgrove 125
Rivercat ferries 140
Riverside Theatre,
    Parramatta 142
Rob Boy Hotel, Balmain 129
Robertson, James 52
Robertson, Sir John 52
Robertsons Point 48, 51–2
Rocks, The 5, 18–27, 29, 30
Rocks Markets, The 25
    opening times 21
Rocks Square, The 18, 26
Rocks Visitors Centre, The 20
    opening times 21
Rockwall 109, 113
Rockwall Crescent, Potts Point 113
Rose Bay 85, 86–7
Rose Hill 3, 140, 142–3
Rose Street, Birchgrove 126
Roslyn Gardens 109, 114

Roslyn Street, Potts Point 114–15
Rowntree, Captain 129
Royal Australasian College
    of Physicians 43
Royal Australian Artillery
    Museum 75
    opening times 73
Royal Australian Historical
    Society 43
Royal Botanic Gardens 9, 12,
    15–16, 39, 43
    opening times 11
Royal Hotel, Paddington 118
Royal National Park 156, 158–61
Rozelle Bay 101, 102
Ruse, James 145
Ruse Street, Parramatta 145

Sacred Heart Convent School,
    Rose Bay 85, 86
Sailors' Home 18, 20
Sandringham Memorial
    Gardens 46
Sandy Bay 94
Scottish Hospital 116, 119
Serpentine Street,
    Hunters Hill 153
Shadforth Street, Paddington 120
Shark Bay 85, 89
Shark Island 85, 86, 88
Shelly Beach 71, 76
shipwright's cottage,
    Balmain 123, 128
Short Street, Watsons Bay 66
Signal Station,
    Watsons Bay 64, 69, 117
Sirius Cove 54
Sirius Cove Reserve 58
Slighclene 112
Smith, Isaac 170
Smith Street, Parramatta 145
smugglers 179–80
Solander, Daniel 171
South Head 64, 64–9
spiders 135–6
Spit, The 94
Spit Bridge 94–5
SS Maitland (ship) 182
St Andrew's Cathedral 39, 47

St Ioannis Greek Orthodox
    church, Parramatta 145
St James Church, Sydney 45
St James Square 39, 45
St John Street, Balmain 127
St Johns Cathedral, Parramatta
    138, 144
    opening times 141
St John's Cemetery, Parramatta
    138, 144
St Luke's Hospital 114
St Mary's Cathedral,
    Sydney 39, 45
St Mary's Church,
    Balmain 123, 128
St Patrick's College, Manly 71, 76
St Paul's College, Manly 76
St Peter's Anglican Church,
    Watsons Bay 64, 69
St Peter's Catholic Church,
    Hunters Hill 153
Stack Street, Balmain 128
State Archives 27
    opening times 21
State Library 43–4
    opening times 41
Steel Point 85, 89
Street, Jessie 40
Strickland House 85, 88
Stuart Street, Manly 72
Suez Canal 26–7
Sutherland, Forby,
    grave 168, 171
Sydney, early history 3–6
Sydney Cove 5, 9, 10
Sydney Fish Markets 101, 102
    opening times 103
Sydney Grammar School 46
Sydney Harbour 6, 32, 75, 98
Sydney Harbour Bridge 28–37
    climbing the arch 36–7
    pylon 29, 31
    opening times 31
    walking across 31–2
Sydney Harbour National Park
    56, 60–2, 66, 67, 89, 96
Sydney Hospital 39, 44
Sydney Observatory 18, 24
    opening times 21

Sydney Opera House 9, 10–12
  opening times 11
Sydney Place 14
Sydney Town Hall 39, 46–7
Sydney's Heritage Fleet 101, 105
  opening times 103

Tabbigai Gap 168, 174
Tamarama Bay 185, 187–8
Tank Stream 20, 40, 41
Taronga Zoo 56, 58, 60
  opening times 59
Taylor Street, Glebe 107
Taylors Bay 56, 62
Tench, Captain Watkin 140
Thames Street, Balmain 127
Thames Street Wharf,
  Balmain 127
Tilbury Hotel 15
Tingara Beach 88
'The Toaster' 10
Tom Thumb (boat) 158
trains
  Concord West 133
  Cronulla 158, 170
Treasury Building and Premier's
  Office 42
Treillage, Bicentennial Park
  131, 134
Trenerry Reserve 190
Trouton Street, Balmain 127
Trumfield Lane, Mosman 58
Tusculum 109, 113
Twemlow, Charles 150–1

Union Street, Balmain 128
Upper Fort Street, Millers
  Point 24
Utzon, Joern 10–11
Valentia Street Wharf 148, 150

Vaucluse Bay 85, 90
Vaucluse House 85, 90–1
Vaucluse Point 85, 90
Verge, John 113
Vernon Street, Hunters Hill 152–3
Victoria Avenue,
  Concord West 133
Victoria Barracks 116, 121
  opening times 119
Victoria Road, Rozelle 124
Victoria Street,
  Potts Point 109, 115
Vincent Street, Balmain 129
Vivian Street, Manly 76

walks, length of 7
Wallace Lane, Balmain 129
Wallace Street, Balmain 129
Walsh Bay 35
Wanda Beach 175
Ward. Frederocl 125
Wardell, William Wilkinson 45
Watchtower, La Perouse 162, 164
Water Funland, Manly
  opening times 95
Water Street, Birchgrove 125
Waterview Street, Balmain 127
Watson Road, Millers Point 24
Watsons Bay 64, 66
Watt Park 29, 34
Wattle Street, Ultimo 102
Watts, John 145
Waverley Cemetery 185, 189
Waverley Hotel, Balmain 127
Wayside Chapel 115
Wedding Cake Island 191
Wells Street, Balmain 127
Wentworth, William Charles
  89, 90–1
Wentworth Park 102

Wentworth Road 90
West Circular Quay Road,
  The Rocks 20–1
West Head 182
whaling 54–5
Wharf Road,
  Birchgrove 126
wharves
  ferry 10
  finger 13, 35
White Horse Point 123, 124
Whiting Beach 59
wildflowers see flora
William Street, Balmain 128
Windmill Hill 24
Windmill Street,
  Millers Point 23
windmills 14, 23
Woodstock 151
wool stores 5, 10
Woollahra 118
Woolloomooloo 9, 13–15
Woolloomooloo Bay 110
Woolpack Hotel,
  Parramatta 142
Woolwich 148, 150–3
Woolwich Dock 148, 151
Woolwich Road, Hunters Hill 152
Workingmen's Institute,
  Balmain 129
Writers Walk 10
Wylde Street, Potts Point 111–12
Wylie's Baths 190

Yeend Street Wharf,
  Birchgrove 126
Yena Track 172–3
Young Street, Balmain 124

zoo see Taronga Zoo

Notes